A Guide to Speech Production and Perception

Mark Tatham and Katherine Morton

Edinburgh University Press

© Mark Tatham and Katherine Morton, 2011

Edinburgh University Press Ltd
22 George Square, Edinburgh

www.euppublishing.com

Typeset in Times New Roman
by Servis Filmsetting Ltd, Stockport, Cheshire, and
printed and bound in Great Britain by
CPI Antony Rowe, Chippenham and Eastbourne

A CIP record for this book is available from the British Library

ISBN 978 0 7486 3651 8 (hardback)
ISBN 978 0 7486 3652 5 (paperback)

The right of Mark Tatham and Katherine Morton
to be identified as author of this work
has been asserted in accordance with
the Copyright, Designs and Patents Act 1988.

Published with the support of the Edinburgh University
Scholarly Publishing Initiatives Fund.

Contents

Detailed Table of Contents

DETAILED TABLE OF CONTENTS

INTRODUCTION

There are changes taking place in how speech and language research and teaching are handled in our universities and other higher education institutions in the UK, the USA and mainland Europe. What seems to be happening is a drawing out of a differentiation along academic lines, recognising an 'arts' element in, say, phonetics for language study (in language departments), but in addition a renewed and considerable emphasis on psychology, cognitive processing and cognitive modelling (in psychology departments), a firm recognition of the formal need for this area in speech technology (in engineering and computer science departments), and in particular a more formal structure to the area in departments dealing with the rapidly expanding area of studies in speech and language disorders. What we believe this means is a movement forward from a somewhat vague notion of 'speech and language' towards a clear understanding of the interrelated subdivisions within the field, and their importance within specific disciplines for both research and teaching. We are already seeing the beginnings of some restructuring to take account of this shift in viewpoint.

The subject of speech production and perception is vast, and this book is not about *what* do to when studying the area, or indeed *how* to do it. Our objective is to explain to the reader how people working in the area *think* about speech. We aim to provide a guide to the complexities of the field for learners and researchers, showing how a modern, unified approach is productive in understanding not just the discipline itself but its potential for enlightened application in neighbouring areas.

This is a textbook, but it is not a page-by-page description of speech production and perception. It is a reference textbook – one where you consult here and there, not one where you start at the beginning and go on to the end; though you can do that if you want to without things going wrong. There are two major classes of student the book is aimed at: those who have a background in phonetics and/or linguistics and who are going on to intermediate or advanced study, and those who are relatively proficient in another discipline – psychology, neuroscience, clinical studies, speech technology, etc. – and who need to understand something of how those of us who work in speech studies *think*.

1

Although our presentation is linear, we do not expect the reader to proceed linearly. For this reason you will find places where we deliberately include reminders. Sometimes this is done simply because the reader cannot be expected to have read everything which comes before a particular topic, or because there is a need to repeat and *expand* something explained rather more simply earlier.

We begin with some basic phonetics, presented a little differently from what would be expected in a beginning textbook. The idea is to build up a clear understanding of what is called classical phonetics – a term used for over a hundred years to describe a coherent theory of phonetics conceived within the broader field of linguistics (Jones 1918). Classical phonetics is very special and a perfect example of an elegant descriptive theory. It deals with characterising speech mostly with an anatomical focus, but importantly as perceived by the phonetician, standing in for the ordinary speaker/listener. Thus, for example, the basic unit used in modelling speech is the perceived articulatory or acoustic segment – something which does not actually exist in the physical world. If the reader is already wondering how something articulatory could not exist, you'll find plenty of discussion on this point in the book. Phoneticians assembled a theory based on how they felt the world of speech was organised – not how it actually is organised in accurate anatomical detail.

But because classical phonetics as a theory is so coherent and so well understood by phoneticians working within linguistics, it forms the bedrock of contemporary departures from the original ideas. The study of speech production and perception *includes* phonetics, but it is vastly bigger and more complex. For example, we focus not on a straightforward characterisation of the world of speech, but on explaining why it is the way it is – an approach dating only from the 1960s when researchers began to realise that we could observe phenomena and speaker/listener behaviour which classical phonetics had not addressed.

The study of spoken language is an extremely exciting area. You would expect us to say that, of course. But it *really* is – and the main reason for this is that it is impossible to proceed very far without realising that speech has an actual and a formal place in linguistics as part of language which is handled entirely in the speaker's mind (like semantics and syntax), and at the same time has a place in the worlds of acoustics – the physics of sound – of neurology, of physiology and so on. Speech has a cognitive aspect, but also a physical aspect. A central task of any modern approach to speech is an attempt to reconcile these two aspects, though philosophers and students of scientific method will recognise the enormity of the task.

The study of speech production and perception in these terms has really been with us only since the 1960s, and so this is a science in its infancy, still full of questions and inconsistencies. This book is about an attempt to get the reader to understand the subject area as a nascent science, and to make you aware of the excitement generated by unravelling previous inconsistencies, misconceptions and presuppositions and turning these into some coherent whole. The idea is to have the field make sense as a theory; and to introduce some neighbouring disciplines which can profit from this more coherent approach.

HOW TO USE THIS BOOK

You will notice that besides plain narrative text there are four text elements used in the book, in addition to the normal table of contents, indices and so on:

1. boxes in the margins containing definitions;
2. marked areas of text containing explanations;
3. tutorials;
4. evaluations.

Definitions and explanations have their own quick-reference indices at the end of the book, while the more substantial tutorials and evaluations are listed with their appropriate chapters in the Detailed Table of Contents at the beginning of the book.

1. *Definitions* are intended to provide a clear characterisation of basic terms and concepts in use in this area of study. You will find from time to time that a definition is repeated elsewhere in the book. This may be because the new context calls for a slightly different or fuller definition of a term. Sometimes a definition box will be labelled 'reminder' – this means that the definition is being repeated, perhaps because we feel that a user who is not reading the book from cover to cover may not have come across the earlier version.

2. *Explanations* are usually much fuller than definitions: they are intended to explain a term or concept, and perhaps give some background to its use. We have made no absolute distinction between definitions and explanations, but the separation of brief and more lengthy characterisations will enable readers from different backgrounds to speed up their reading of the material.

3. *Tutorials* are much more lengthy than explanations. They take the reader through a mini introduction to a stand-alone subcomponent of the field. While the more advanced reader can skip tutorials,

intermediate users in the field of linguistics will find tutorials helpful in understanding the many facets of the subject. Readers from other disciplines will find the tutorials invaluable in understanding the background to the running narrative text.

4. *Evaluations* are all about appreciating that this subject area – like most others – is not a cut and dried or fossilised discipline. On the contrary, it continues to evolve in ever more interesting ways. The very dynamism of the subject means that there are many areas of unresolved questions, leading inevitably to competing theories. Evaluations are intended to rehearse for you the various arguments put forward to support this or that theory. We explain their backgrounds where necessary, indicating the questions which have given rise to alternatives as they highlight unresolved issues. We say what aspects of the discipline this or that theory is good at explaining – and equally show where such theories fail to account for observations. These theories co-exist, meaning that there is often no 'winner', leading us, as writers and teachers, to try to be as fair and neutral as possible in our explanations. We do try, however, to give you the tools and arguments to come to your own conclusions.

Let us see how these various elements work by taking a look at Chapter 2, 'Studying Speaking'. As its name suggests, the chapter is about how we go about examining speech, unravelling speech segments from the continuous waveform, and how we classify and label these sounds or articulations.

The running text is straightforward enough – and can be read straight through without reference to other text elements. This would be a suitable approach for revision of earlier work encountered by an intermediate student, or a researcher in another field needing to brush up on speech in general. Straight away we get to talk about the physical continuousness of speech and how we segment the signals to examine the discrete sound elements we feel to be there. Definitions remind us what a continuous event is, and exactly what we mean by the idea of labelling sounds.

Events in speech are continuous, but the various properties of the signal are not synchronised – a definition box reminds us what synchronisation is. A graphical representation of these properties which is used in modern approaches is called a gestural score: we find a definition and a diagram illustrating the relationship between a sound wave and its associated articulation, viewed in terms of the time-governed movement of the articulators involved.

After more running text we come across an explanation of segmentation. We've been talking about segments and how the sound wave or dynamic articulation might be divided up to match our perception of segments, but here is an explanation of the actual problems of doing this. The explanation is not a definition, but an account of the problems and why they are important.

It turns out that the labels we've learned about are assigned (time for another definition) to areas of the signal, and that these labels are really abstractions rather than physical objects – 'abstraction' forms the basis of another definition, as does the notion 'physical world'.

And so the narrative continues. You see the basic idea: the narrative of Chapter 2 is for everyone – the beginner from some other discipline, the linguist who wants to brush up on basic concepts, the practitioner who needs to put concepts into a general perspective.

Eventually we come to a set of five tutorials (the number varies from chapter to chapter). These explain much of the material in theme-organised detail. So what is this Target Theory we've been discussing really all about? What are the details of classification of consonants and vowels, and what are these classes in depth? What does the almost philosophical term *abstraction* mean to us in our studies of speech production? Why is it that sometimes we think of two sounds as different in English, when in another language they are felt to be the same – for example, [l] and [r] in Japanese?

The chapter concludes with an Evaluation – a detailed explanation of competing ways of examining the phenomenon of aspiration, a feature of speech which subtly contributes to the perception of differing sounds, playing an important role in such differing languages as English, Portuguese, Hindi, etc. By the end of reading the evaluation you will be in a position to see why there are competing models and what their various merits are.

So, by means of the running narrative text, concise and clear definitions, longer explanations of what's going on, very detailed tutorials and finally head-to-head evaluation of alternative ways of looking at some aspects of what the chapter has been dealing with, students and researchers alike are beginning (this is only Chapter 2) to understand why those of us who work in speech think the way we do, what motivates us and what our research and teaching goals are.

Finally, when you get to the end of the chapter – revise the whole thing by reading quickly through the narrative text again, perhaps cross-checking a few of the definitions by using the Definition Index towards the end of the book.

CHAPTER 1 – WHAT IS SPEAKING?

INTRODUCTION

Spoken language is an on-going event. In this chapter we discuss the vocal tract structures and their movement – it is these which enable the physical production of speech. We introduce the concept of physical variability, since speech is by no means constant – there is considerable variation even when the *same* speaker repeats what they and listeners feel to be the *same* utterance. We also describe the relationship between the movements of the vocal tract and some of the acoustic features of the resulting sound wave.

AN EVENT IN TIME

Speaking is an event which occurs when we communicate verbally. The event *spans* time, and involves the use of the vocal tract to make appropriate sounds for communicating the speaker's thoughts to listeners. To make communication work, what speech is and the way in which it is used have to be understood by both speaker and listener. We often speak of the speaker/listener, since in most circumstances speakers are also listeners, and listeners are also speakers.

VOCAL TRACT STRUCTURES INCLUDE TWO BASIC SYSTEMS

UPPER AIRWAY SYSTEM, LOWER AIRWAY SYSTEM

The airway system above the vocal cords (the oral and nasal cavities, and the pharynx) is usually referred to as the upper airway system, contrasting with the lower airway system below the vocal cords (the trachea, bronchial tubes and lungs).

The respiratory system, involving the vocal tract (above the larynx – the UPPER AIRWAY SYSTEM) and the bronchial and lung systems (below the larynx – the LOWER AIRWAY SYSTEM), is the basis for all speaking. The laryngeal system enables airflow to be modified to produce various *source* sounds.

The respiratory system

The respiratory system is used primarily for breathing, and consists of the upper airway system with inputs for air through the nose and mouth, and the pharyngeal tube leading to the larynx. When inhaling, air flows from the larynx to the trachea and bronchial tubes, which convey it deep into the lungs where oxygen is exchanged into the blood for transporting to wherever it is needed in the body. When exhaling, air direction is reversed, taking carbon dioxide exchanged from the blood up and out through the nose and mouth. The direction and amount of flow of the air in either direction is controlled by a complex system of muscles which either expand (for flow in) or compress (for flow out) the lungs.

The laryngeal system

The laryngeal structure in the neck consists of a valve arrangement involving the vocal cords (sometimes called vocal folds), membrane-like structures spreading across the airway in the larynx. A complex system of tilting cartilages to which the vocal cords are attached enables continuously variable tension of the cords and valve control over the airflow. The primary function of this valve appears to be to prevent solid objects like food entering the trachea and then the lungs, but the control of the vocal cords extends considerably beyond this basic function, enabling closure, a range of partial closures and a range of types of edge vibration of the vocal cords to be incorporated into speech. The airflow is said to be *modulated* by the vibrating cords. Vocal cord control enables languages to use sounds based on vocal cord vibration, and also to introduce more subtle effects of changes to the VOICE QUALITY to convey mood and emotional feelings on the part of the speaker. An example of this would be the voice quality associated with anger, involving a protracted tensing of the laryngeal musculature.

Within the vocal tract two types of articulator are used in speech production – *fixed* and *movable*.

Fixed articulators

The fixed articulators provide a means of locating an articulation in a particular region of the vocal tract on a repeatable basis. This contrasts with movable articulators which move, relocate or change their shapes, under changing dynamic conditions as utterances unfold in time.

Teeth

In some languages (French, for example) the upper teeth are the PLACE OF ARTICULATION for the sounds [t], [d], [s], [z], though these sounds have an alveolar place of articulation in English. Contact is between the front of the tongue – for some speakers just the tip, for others the tip and blade – and the rear surface of the upper teeth, or the tip of the tongue with the rear surface of the lower teeth and the blade against the upper teeth. The tongue tip against the upper teeth, but allowing air to escape around the blade, can be involved in the production of the dental fricatives [θ] and [ð] in English.

VOICE QUALITY

Voice quality refers to variations in the physical and perceived type of voicing. Examples are *breathy voices* in which the sound of air leaking through part of the vocal cord valve is heard in addition to the usual vibration effect on the sound; *creak*, in which the vocal cord vibration becomes irregular in some speakers, particularly at very low vibration rates; etc.

PLACE OF ARTICULATION

In classical phonetics (defined in the Introduction), place refers to some fixed point in the vocal tract used as a reference for *where* the key parts of articulation lie. Place of articulation is usually linked to MANNER OF ARTICULATION. For example, an articulation can be said to be dental (involves the teeth) or velar (involves the velum), etc.

MANNER OF ARTICULATION

In classical phonetics, manner refers to how the articulators produce the sound or modify the airflow – e.g. *plosive, continuant* or *fricative*. For example, an articulation, using both place and manner categorisation, could be an alveolar plosive (a plosive at the alveolar ridge like [t, d] in English), or a bilabial fricative (a fricative involving both lips like the variants [φ, β] in Spanish, as in *los viejos* and *gran vía* respectively), etc.

Alveolar ridge

In English the place of articulation for consonantal sounds such as [t], [d], [s], [z] – as well as the approximant [ɹ], the lateral approximant [l], and the nasal stop [n] – is the alveolar ridge, the foremost part of the palate just behind the upper teeth. Some languages use the upper teeth as the place of articulation for the stops, rather than the alveolar ridge. Occasionally, even when the usual place is the alveolar ridge, languages like English use a dental stop when COARTICULATION forces the tongue forward. This occurs, for example, when the following sound is an interdental fricative ([θ] and [ð] in English, as in the word *eighth*).

Palate

The palate extends from the upper teeth at the front of the ORAL CAVITY to the soft palate and uvula at the back. The hard central section is referred to as the *hard palate*, or just the *palate*. Since it does not move, the palate is a useful reference point for place of articulation within the oral cavity – thus we speak of alveolar plosives [t] and [d] in English, for example, or velar plosives [k] and [g]. Some languages have sounds associated also with the central palate; for example, the palatal nasal [ɲ] in French, or the [−voice] palatal fricative [ç] in Welsh and German.

Movable articulators

The movable articulators in conjunction with the fixed articulators create places of constriction or narrowing within the vocal tract.

Jaw

Strictly, the upper jaw bone, which houses the teeth and supports the palate and velum, is a fixed articulator, but it works in conjunction with the lower jaw bone. The lower jaw is attached on each side of the upper jaw in a hinge-like way. The fixed palate and the movable velum are structures located within the upper jaw system; the lower teeth and tongue are located within the lower jaw system. The lips belong to both the upper and lower jaw systems.

Lips

The lips count as a place of articulation and are involved in *labial* sounds. *Bi*labial sounds involve both lips, and include the plosives [p] and [b] in English or [β] (the voiced bilabial fricative in Spanish *via* in some accents). Sometimes another articulator is involved, hence: labio-dental sounds (lips and teeth) and labialised sounds (sounds primarily located elsewhere, but involving a special configuration of the lips; examples include labialised velars like [kʷ, gʷ] involving lip rounding). The resonance of the oral cavity is affected by the shape of the lips. This is usually referred to in terms of (viewed from the front) lip rounding or lip spreading – with any

---

COARTICULATION

Coarticulation is the blending together or overlap of adjacent segments when they are spoken. Phonology (explained fully in Chapter 6) tends to keep segments distinct, but when we come to speak they blur into one another to produce a near-continuous sound wave. A major contributor to coarticulation is the inertia in the mechanical system of the vocal tract and organs of speech. And since inertia is time dependent, the degree of overlap of segments appears to be usually greatest when the speech is being delivered fast (see the TUTORIAL – Coarticulation Theory in Chapter 3).

ORAL CAVITY

The oral cavity is the section of the vocal tract extending back from the lips to (and usually including) the pharynx above the vocal cords in the larynx. The term contrasts with the nasal cavity: the section of the vocal tract extending back from the nasal opening to the velum/pharynx valve.

shape within the range of extreme rounded and protruded (as in French [y]] to extreme spread (as in French [i]). These extremes of lip rounding/ spreading do not occur in English, where we find less rounded (e.g. [u]) and less spread (e.g. [i] or [ɪ]) vowels.

Tongue

The tongue is a major articulator in all languages. The surface skin tissue conceals a complex of MUSCLES which are capable of fine control to achieve a very large range of movement and shapes in three dimensions. The tongue can protrude forward, curl laterally and vertically, bunch at its centre or back, move its tip relatively independently from its body, and so on. In fact all these shapes and movements are carefully organised and coordinated to enable speakers to produce a wide variety of sounds.

EFFERENT NERVE

If nerves convey signals from the central nervous system (the brain) to the periphery they are called *efferent* nerves. *Afferent* nerves take signals from the periphery to the central nervous system. The main efferent nerves are the relatively large *alpha* type.

MUSCLES AND MUSCLE GROUPINGS

Muscles are usually arranged in groups; this enables coordinated contractions to achieve particular configurations or shapes of the vocal tract – for example, the shape of the tongue during a vowel sound. The control of these groups has two levels: an overall control signal issued from the brain's motor cortex and arriving at the group mainly via an EFFERENT NERVE, and local stabilising or fine tuning signals between muscle members of the group (see Chapter 4 for TUTORIALS on how the musculature works)

Tongue movement modifies the oral cavity's acoustic resonance properties by changing its shape and volume; this is an essential feature of vowels and similar sounds (e.g. liquids). In the static characterisation of vowel sounds used in classical phonetics we use a basic two-dimensional matrix to indicate TONGUE POSITION. The dimensions are, vertically, tongue height in the oral cavity and, horizontally, tongue forward/backward position.

For descriptive purposes phoneticians recognise several important areas of the tongue's upper surface when characterising place of articulation: the back, front and blade are the key areas. The extreme front of the blade is called the tip. These areas cannot be given fixed boundaries because their exact size will vary from person to person, with variation in their use even within the same person's speech. Although objectively vague, defining these areas has proved useful in differentiating where and how the tongue is involved in producing particular sounds. Thus we speak of the front of the tongue being raised in the production of vowels like [i] and [ɛ] or the back being lowered in the production of vowels like [ɒ] and [ɑ]. The blade (with the tip) locates towards the front palate to form the constriction for [s] or the stop for [t], etc. We can say that these terms are neutral to variability – useful when linking phonetic and phonological descriptions, since phonology (see Hayes 2008 for an introduction to contemporary phonology) does not recognise such VARIABILITY.

TONGUE POSITION

Tongue position refers to the position of the tongue in the oral cavity in classical phonetics using the two dimensions of a vowel chart (see Figure 1.1 below). In fact, indicating position using a dot on the matrix is an abstraction: in the physical world the tongue displaces a large volume of the cavity which could never be characterised by a single point. This is of no importance in classical phonetics theory once we realise that this description of a vowel refers to its general position relative to other vowels in a two-dimensional, abstract, cognitive space needed for referencing vowels in phonology (where minor physical differences can have no significance so long as they do not change the categorisation of the sound).

VARIABILITY

Variability is about how speech objects (at either the cognitive or physical level) vary in their behaviour or rendering. So, for example, we may speak of an underlying phonemic object which exhibits variability or allophonic behaviour on the surface, or a segment in the planned utterance which varies phonetically due to coarticulation.

Modern phonetics and speech production theory model the introduction of variability as a tiered process. Phonemes (corresponding to the deepest cognitive objects in speech) are systematically varied in phonological processing to derive extrinsic allophones used in representations at the output level of phonology (the speech plan). Within phonetics, the planned extrinsic allophonic objects are varied systematically by physical processes originating in the mechanics of the vocal tract or in the aerodynamics of the production process.

	Cognitive domain			Physical domain		
		SPEECH PLAN (cognitive)	SPEECH PLAN (physical)			
Phonemes	→Phonological processes	→Extrinsic allophones	→Target sounds	→Phonetic coarticulation processes	→Articulation	
	Introduces cognitive/voluntary variability			Introduces physical/involuntary variability		

There is also additional variation at the phonetic level due to the fact that the production processes are not perfect; that is, a certain amount of random or spurious behaviour is intrinsic to the aerodynamic, mechanical and acoustic processes. Because it is abstract, there are no such unintended random effects at the cognitive, phonological level. Hence:

Variability	Source
Phonological	Voluntary (e.g. the alternation of clear or palatalised /l/ /lʲ/ and dark or velarised /l/ /lˠ/ in English) – often language-specific
Phonetic	Determined by coarticulation (e.g. the nasalisation of vowels between nasal consonants in English - /mæn/ → [mæ̃n]) – basically language-universal
Physical	Random – unsystematically occurring in all speech sounds

- Note: Sometimes what appears to be random may serve some purpose we have not yet noticed or described. For example, some variability is thought to be associated with emotive content in speaking but as yet this has not been fully modelled. Some researchers are currently attempting to draw up databases of detail variants in the acoustic signal. We look at this in Chapter 8, where we consider *detail classifiers*.

Manner of articulation is also often determined by the tongue's position and shape. So we have degrees of constriction (for example, for fricatives like [s] or [ʃ], or for plosives like [t] or [g]), and also some more dynamic or time-constrained manners like trills, taps and flaps. There are also one or two other manner effects – for example, retroflex consonants involving a curling upwards of the tongue tip like the retroflex nasal [ɳ] in Swedish.

Velum

The velum is the back, movable section of the palate, also known as the soft palate, terminating with the uvula. This area of the palate serves as the place of articulation for such sounds as the English velar stops [k] and [g]. The velum, together with the uvula, acts as a valve to control airflow from the pharynx into the nasal cavity. Closed, the valve directs all of the airflow into the oral cavity to form oral vowels and consonants; open, airflow is directed through the nose for nasal vowels and consonants. Although in phonology and phonetics we speak of oral sounds and nasal or nasalised sounds, in reality the operation of the velum does not produce a binary oral vs. nasal airflow. Often the valve only partially directs the flow of air into the oral or nasal cavities.

Phonologically, many sounds are wholly oral, though none is wholly nasal: sounds like the bilabial stop /m/ and the alveolar or dental /n/ involve rendering with airflow into the oral cavity, as do the nasal vowels in languages like French (*bon* /bõ/), Portuguese or Polish, or the nasalised oral vowels of English in words like *man* [mæ̃n] and *moon* [mũn] (phonologically without nasality: /mæn/ and /mun/ respectively).

- Notice that we have used square brackets for *nasalisation*, since it is a phonetic phenomenon of vowels in certain contexts in English. Since *nasality* is a phonological phenomenon in French, we have used / brackets. Nasality is phonological; nasalisation is phonetic.

THE ACOUSTIC SIGNAL

The acoustic wave produced during speaking forms the *carrier* for transmitting spoken information between speaker and listener. We speak of the information being *modulated* onto the carrier. The ACOUSTIC SIGNAL (Johnson 2003) is intended to be heard, and then understood. These are two separate processes, with hearing being essentially physical and passive in nature (see Chapter 7), while understanding involves active cognitive interpretation of the signal (TUTORIAL – THE ACOUSTIC SIGNAL).

Speech acoustics arc determined by the way the structures of the vocal tract are configured to affect the AERODYNAMICS of the vocal tract system as a whole. Air is flowing to or from the lungs through this system from or to the outside world, and in its most basic form an alternating in/out flow constitutes vital *breathing*. This flow is said to be *modulated* for the purposes of producing speech sounds. Most of the sounds in the world's languages are modulations of outward flowing air, *egressive* sounds, but a number are modulations of inward flowing air, *ingressive* sounds. There are one or two rarer types of sound, such as the clicks of Zulu, which involve neither full ingressive nor egressive flow but rely on sucking air into an area (strictly, volume) between two places of constriction.

Function and acoustics

Laryngeal action

Laryngeal action involves introducing MODULATION to an egressive airstream using the vocal cords found in the larynx. These vibrate,

---

ACOUSTIC SIGNAL
The acoustic signal is produced using the aerodynamic properties of the vocal tract. It is the acoustic signal which is detected and heard by the listener prior to cognitively based perception. The commonest ways of imaging the signal for speech investigations involve two-dimensional (amplitude vs. time) *waveforms* and three-dimensional (frequency vs. amplitude vs. time) *spectrograms*.

AERODYNAMICS
Aerodynamics is a general term for an area of study within physics dealing with the movement of gases, their flow and pressure in various environments. In speech we are interested in airflow through the vocal tract in both *ingressive* and *egressive* directions (into and out of the lungs), and in the pressure of the air in the vocal tract and oesophagus below the larynx. It is important to emphasise the dynamic nature of the behaviour of air in speech production – the air is rarely static, undergoing almost continuous flow and pressure changes as speech unfolds.

MODULATION
Modulation is the overlaying of relatively rapid changes on an otherwise smooth or slow-changing system. In the case of vocal cord modulation, it is the breaking of the smooth flow of air out of the lungs into a pulsed flow into the pharynx and thence into the oral and nasal cavities.

FORMANT

A formant is a grouping or band of frequencies in the spectrum, determined by the current resonant properties of the oral or nasal cavities as the air flowing through them is set into resonance. The range or width of the band is the formant's bandwidth. Because of its relatively irregular shape the oral cavity normally produces at least six formants for any one uninterrupted or unconstricted sound (like a vowel), of which the lower three or four trigger the perception of a *particular* vowel in the listener. Vowels are differentiated by the *relative* placing of these formants within the spectrum.

FREQUENCY

Frequency is the measured rate of vibration of some component of the acoustic signal. So, for example, we speak of fundamental frequency, or f0, of the speech wave, or of the centre frequency of formants. Pitch, especially when dealing with f0, is the *perception* of fundamental frequency: it is relative and abstract. The correlation between frequency and pitch is not linear or one-to-one. Notice that the symbol for fundamental frequency, f0, has a lower case 'f'; the upper case 'F' is reserved for *formant*.

RESONANCE

In speech the air in the oral and nasal cavities can be set into resonance – that is, start vibrating – when a source of energy *excites* it. For example, the energy source can be the pulsed flow of air from the larynx when the vocal cords are vibrating, or the turbulent airflow created when air is forced through a narrow gap, as in the production of fricatives. The centre frequency of a resonance band of frequencies is determined by the size and shape of the resonator.

chopping the airflow and interrupting its smooth passage through the larynx during around half or more of the sounds in most languages. This action develops a complex signal which enters the oral cavity, where the resonance potential develops a set of FORMANTS in the spectrum of the sound. Changing rates of vibration of the vocal cords are perceived by the listener as changes of intonation as the speech unfolds in time – that is, as changes in the direction of pitch movement: up or down over time. We speak of the fundamental frequency – an objective term – of vocal cord vibration. The corresponding word for perceived fundamental FREQUENCY is *pitch* – a subjective term.

Velar movement

Velar movement involves raising or lowering the velum, found towards the back of the palate where it changes from relatively hard tissue to movable soft tissue. Raising the velum prevents air from flowing into the nasal cavity and out through the nose, introducing a valve blocking the flow of air and thus the sound from potential RESONANCE in the nasal cavity, leaving only oral cavity resonance. Lowering the velum allows the air into the nasal cavity, activates the potential nasal resonance and generates a nasal formant structure which gets added to any formants derived by resonances in the oral cavity. Some sounds, like [m] (stopped at the lips) and [n] (stopped at the alveolar ridge) in English, allow the air to exit only through the nose via the velar valve and nasal cavity – these are called nasal sounds or, for short, *nasals*.

Other sounds, like all the vowels in English under normal circumstances, allow air to exit only through the mouth via the oral cavity by using the velar valve to block nasal airflow – these are called oral sounds. In some cases air exits through both the oral and nasal cavities; this happens with the nasal vowels of French and Portuguese, among other languages. Although English has no nasal vowels, its oral vowels are sometimes nasalised when coarticulated with adjacent nasal consonants. So, for example, the [æ] in *man* and the [u] in *moon* are always nasalised to a certain extent as the velar valve, open for the initial [m . . .] and then open again for the final [. . . n] fails to close fully for the inter-nasal vowel. The faster the speech delivery the less likely it is the valve will close fully, and the more likely that some nasal quality is added to the otherwise oral vowel. Phonologically the vowel remains oral, and English phonology does not permit nasal vowels, except in a few loan words: for example, *sangfroid* [sɑ̃ŋfrwɑ], *vin ordinaire* [vɛ̃nɔrdinɛr].

Tongue movement

Tongue movement is very carefully controlled in speech and is involved in most sounds. The tongue is anchored at its root, but is progressively free to move towards its blade and tip, with the body of the tongue still able to move around in the centre area of the oral cavity. The tongue's shape is very complex, but phoneticians have decided that a TWO-DIMENSIONAL DESCRIPTIVE MODEL is adequate for distinguishing most of the sounds that the tongue is involved in. The two dimensions are forward/backward and up/down, and the tongue's position is mapped onto this space. In reality, of course, the tongue's positions are not really just a set of small points in the oral cavity, so the mapping is an abstraction with only approximate correlates in the physical world. It so happens that there is a strong correlation between this abstract map of tongue positions and the way listeners think of the *distances* between the sounds they hear. The two-dimensional map is especially helpful with vowel sounds. Although we now have the instrumental means to provide accurate mapping of the entire tongue as it moves around the oral cavity, the original two-dimensional chart, based on perception of vowel sounds, is still invaluable to phoneticians (Figure 1.1).

Tongue movement also provides the means of introducing a CONSTRICTION (partial or complete) at locations along the cavity for the production of fricatives and stop consonants. In English the palatal stops are the alveolar pair (voiceless, voiced in the phonology) [t, d] and the velar pair [k, g]. The palatal fricatives are the alveolars [s, z], the palato-alveolars [ʃ, ʒ], and in loan words the voiceless velar fricative [χ] (Scottish *lo<u>ch</u>*) and the voiceless alveolar lateral fricative [ç] (Welsh *<u>Ll</u>andudno*).

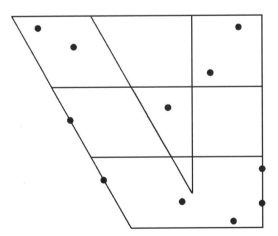

Figure 1.1 The classical phonetics vowel chart – a stylised two-dimensional representation of the area within the oral cavity. The left of the chart is towards the front of the mouth and the right towards the back. The dots on the chart represent vowel 'positions'. Starting on the top left and proceeding anti-clockwise, these are for English: [i], [ɪ], [ɛ], [æ], [ʌ], [ɑ], [ɒ], [ɔ], [ʊ] and [u], with [ə] in the centre.

TWO-DIMENSIONAL

A model is two-dimensional if it uses just two parameters or features of the data under scrutiny – in this case the front/back and up/down axes of a cross-section of the oral cavity. The cross-section is through the middle of the oral cavity, giving a graph rather like an X-ray picture, which is also two-dimensional. Contrast this with a three-dimensional description, which would take into account depth and changes from left to right in the oral cavity, resembling a magnetic resonance imaging (MRI) scan.

DESCRIPTIVE MODEL

A model of some observed data is said to be descriptive if it meets the criteria for descriptive adequacy – level 2 on the adequacy scale of observational–descriptive–explanatory. A descriptive model takes a set of observations and links them together, drawing out patterns in the data in such a way that the resultant description is meaningful (i.e. is about the entire set of data) and productive (i.e. can be used in the theory for such functions as predicting more data, establishing the range of data). Descriptive models are more useful than observational models, since these simply enumerate data rather than spotting patterns in it. Explanatory models go one stage further and focus on explaining why the observed data and patterns are the way they are.

CONSTRICTION

A constriction occurs in the oral cavity usually when a mobile articulator – lips, tongue, velum – comes close to (partial constriction) or touches (complete constriction) a fixed articulator – teeth, palate. Sometimes the two articulators are mobile, as in the case of the upper and lower lips becoming involved, for example, in [p] and [b] – the English bilabial stops or plosives.

ORAL CAVITY

The oral cavity is the three-dimensional space in the mouth, bounded in the front by the lower and upper teeth, at the top by the palate (subdivided into the alveolar ridge, the centre palate, the velum and the uvula), at the back by the top of the pharynx, and at the bottom by the tongue (subdivided into root, back, centre, front, blade and tip).

For some consonantal sounds – particularly the stop sounds [t/d], [k/g] in English – the front and back of the tongue move out of the freely occupied positional *space* within the ORAL CAVITY and touch its periphery or boundary. So for [t/d] contact is made with the alveolar ridge (the front of the palate just behind the upper teeth), and for [k/g] the back part of the palate. In other languages there are other places where the tongue can touch, but in all cases for stop consonants, or plosives, the seal or constriction formed is sufficient to stop airflow out of the mouth in egressive sounds. We will go into tongue movement and positioning in more detail when we deal with different types of sounds in Chapter 2.

Lip shape

Lip shape ranges from a maximally rounded tense appearance (found in French [y]), through a less rounded shape (found in English [u]), through a neutral (neither particularly rounded nor spread – found in English [ɒ] or [ɑ]), to a more spread shape (found in English [i$_{Eng}$]) or a very tense spread shape (found in French [i$_{Fr}$]). In addition, of course, the lips can be flattened and closed, to be held sufficiently tense to prevent air flowing out of the mouth. This is found in sounds like [p/b], bilabial plosives, and [m], the bilabial nasal. Labio-dental fricatives like [f/v] involve the lower lip in contact with the upper teeth. Bilabial fricatives are found in some languages ([β] in Spanish) and, unlike plosives, do not involve complete stopping off of the airflow.

There are other anatomical structures which are important in speaking, but these are the main ones for the moment. We are illustrating the way in which phoneticians and others go about dealing with the data of speech.

SUMMARY

So far we have seen that it is useful to identify various key anatomical structures used in the production of speech to contribute to the way in which the aerodynamic system produces the acoustic signal. We can see that these structures can be manipulated (by the underlying musculature) to produce a huge variety of shapes of the vocal tract to modulate or change the egressive and sometimes ingressive airstreams. We have also seen that in certain sounds, notably those we classify as vowels, the structure of the larynx – in particular the vibrating vocal cords – is used to produce a source sound which undergoes changes due to resonance as it passes through the upper vocal tract (TUTORIAL – THE ACOUSTIC SIGNAL). Tongue movement is carefully controlled to change the size and shape of the oral cavity; this influences the way potential resonances change the source sound to produce different vowel sounds which the listener can identify.

Speakers, of course, need to know (usually not consciously) what structures are used to produce speech sounds and how to control them to make the appropriate sound on demand. In their turn listeners need to know which sounds match up with which linguistic units – abstract sounds – to identify words and larger syntactic units from the speaker's sound wave. It is in this sense that we say that there is *shared knowledge* between speaker and listener, and in normal circumstances all speakers are themselves listeners and all listeners are speakers. This concept of shared knowledge is very important in linguistics and psychology. If there were no shared knowledge, perception as we know it would not be possible – sounds would come out differently every time they are used and listeners would not be able to sort them out (see Chapter 7).

In this chapter we have begun to introduce the notion that in an abstract way we can usefully label speech sounds for unique identification purposes. Thus, by focusing hard on what we hear it is quite easy to notice that individual instances of the sounds vary quite a lot, particularly from speaker to speaker. We can group such variations together under common labels. This labelling task captures an important property of human perception: the ability to recognise a kind of abstract *sameness* among sounds even when in a more objective sense they are *not* precisely the same. We speak of CATEGORISING sounds as part of the perceptual process, and later we shall learn how this is done (see Chapter 7). For the moment, let us just note that we must make a sharp distinction between a sound (a physical, measurable entity) and the label we put on that sound (a cognitive entity measurable only in how it relates to other such labels) (TUTORIAL – TWO BASIC CONCEPTS – FUNDAMENTAL FREQUENCY AND RESONANCE).

CATEGORISE

Sounds vary quite a lot, even when spoken by the same person. If we were to notice and take into account every detail of these variations, understanding speech would be very difficult because everything would tend to sound different. Instead we tend to ignore these details, putting sounds into a number of distinct categories; we categorise them in our minds despite all the minor physical differences. Categorisation is an important property of human perception and the way in which we deal with language in general. There are two main types of category: those which serve to distinguish between words (e.g. speech /spitʃ/ vs. speed /spid/ - different phonemes), and those which reveal a language's preferences (e.g. feel /fil̴/ vs. /l̥if̴/, in which the two /l/ extrinsic allophones are different, but do not distinguish between words.

THE ACOUSTIC SIGNAL

TUTORIAL

In acoustics the signal is usually characterised parametrically – that is, in terms of what is happening simultaneously to a number of key features. There are three main features or parameters for describing the waveform: time, frequency and amplitude.

TIME

This is the duration of a selected time period during the signal. For example, in calculating the fundamental frequency of a sustained vowel we may look to measuring the number of vocal cord vibrations in, say, 10 ms. The horizontal axes (the x-axes) of waveforms and spectrograms are based on unfolding time, running from left to right on the graphs. Time is usually measured in seconds (s) or milliseconds (1 ms = 0.001 s) in speech research; older, particularly US, publications also included centiseconds (1 cs = 0.01 s).

FREQUENCY

The number of oscillations or vibrations (measured in Hz, or Hertz) in the sound wave per unit time – usually 1 s. So we can speak of a pure sine wave of 100 Hz: one which has 100 vibrations per second. All speech has a complex waveform which can be thought of as made up of many simple or sine wave components; these components are all included in the graphical representations of the signal, including waveforms and spectrograms, though the way they are presented in the image differs between types of display (see Chapter 11).

AMPLITUDE

WAVEFORM

A waveform is a two-dimensional graphical representation of the speech sound wave. The graph unfolds in time (the x-axis), with instantaneous amplitude shown vertically (the y-axis). The origin, or zero, is usually placed centrally on the y-axis so that negative and positive amplitude can be shown, below and above 0, respectively. Figure 1.2 shows a typical speech waveform.

Amplitude is measured in dB or decibels, logarithmic units of the sound's intensity. In graphical form decibels are usually presented linearly in speech research. There is room for confusion here. Although the units of amplitude themselves are a *logarithmic* representation of the intensity of a sound, they are presented in visible form along the scale of a graph (say, the y-axis of a waveform) *linearly*. The space between each unit on the graph's axis is the same, though.

A tabular presentation of these three quantities or *parameters* is possible, but they are more commonly and more usefully presented graphically in speech studies as WAVEFORMS, SPECTRA and SPECTROGRAMS. In the table here we see time, quantised into 10-ms frames, unfolding as frequency increases along with amplitude. Notice that amplitude is indicated by measuring *down* from some hypothesised maximum of 0 dB; so *increasing* amplitude means the negative numbers seem paradoxically to go down.

SPECTRUM

A spectrum is a two-dimensional graphical representation of the speech sound wave at a *single moment in time* or sometimes averaged over a brief period of time. Usually the vertical y-axis represents amplitude and the horizontal x-axis represents frequency. A stylised spectrum for a single vowel rendering can be seen in Figure 1.3.

Time	Frequency in Hz	Amplitude in dB down from 0
1st 10 ms	100	−25
2nd 10 ms	102	−24
3rd 10 ms	104	−23
4th 10 ms	106	−22
. . .		
nth 10 ms	120	−15

Figure 1.2 Waveform of the utterance *The big black cat sat down.*

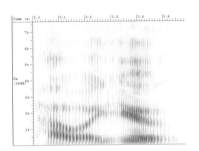

Figure 1.3 Spectrogram of the utterance *How are you?* The vertical axis represents frequency ranging from 0 Hz (at the bottom) to 8 kHz (at the top). Time runs from left to right.

1. In waveform IMAGING the signal is presented as a two-dimensional graph in which the horizontal axis (the *x*-axis) represents time and the vertical axis (the *y*-axis) represents amplitude (see the above definition). Hence waveforms involve the direct representation of two of the three acoustic parameters; frequency is 'concealed' in the representation, but can always be calculated if necessary. Thus the waveform graph shows how the amplitude of the signal changes over time.

2. In a spectrum an instantaneous image of the signal is shown; this is an image of the signal at a single moment in time. Technically the single moment means *no* time, but in practice the presentation is of a smear of a very brief moment of time, chosen in the analysis software. A spectrum is a two-dimensional graph in which usually the vertical axis represents amplitude and the horizontal axis represents frequency. Thus, for the chosen moment in time, the graph shows the amplitudes of the signal's component frequencies – remember the speech signal is a complex wave thought of as consisting of many simultaneous simple waves each of a particular frequency. The spectrum enables us to see the amplitude relationship between the component frequencies of the complex wave.

3. A spectrogram combines all three acoustic parameters of time, frequency and amplitude by introducing a third dimension to the graphical representation. As with a waveform, the horizontal *x*-axis represents time unfolding from left to right, but in spectrograms the vertical *y*-axis represents frequency, with the scale displayed vertically above an origin of 0 Hz. The third parameter, amplitude, is shown as the graph's *z*-axis standing out from the flat, two-dimensional surface and represented in the image as a colour scale or in shades of grey. Thus typically, a higher amplitude of any one frequency

SPECTROGRAM

A spectrogram is a three-dimensional graphical representation of the speech sound wave with time running from left to right (the *x*-axis) and frequency running vertically (the *y*-axis) above a zero origin. The third parameter of amplitude stands proud of the two-dimensional surface (the *z*-axis) by using colour or shades of grey. Figure 1.3 shows a typical speech spectrogram; details of what a spectrogram shows will be discussed later.

IMAGING

Imaging is the visual representation of an object or event which is not itself visible. For example, imaging an *acoustic* speech waveform involves *graphical* representations on two- or three-dimensional surfaces such as paper or a computer screen. Imaging here transforms the acoustic signal into a visual representation. Remember that what is on the computer screen is not the acoustic signal – it is a graphical representation of the signal. Imaging involves processing the signal for display, and during this processing, errors can and do occur. It is important to choose the parameters of the display very carefully to avoid spurious errors interfering with our interpretation of the image (see Chapters 10 and 11 to see how this works in practice).

17

will be shown as a brighter colour or a darker shade of grey. A spectrogram is often, in fact, an image presenting a large number of static spectra (sometimes called slices) horizontally – so closely that time seems to be continuous.

TUTORIAL

TWO BASIC CONCEPTS –
FUNDAMENTAL FREQUENCY AND RESONANCE

When describing or researching speech sounds we employ a number of concepts which are useful abstractions to help us understand what's going on in speech (Fant 1960, 1973). Here are two main concepts: fundamental frequency and resonance.

FUNDAMENTAL FREQUENCY

The fundamental frequency of a sound (the rendering of a vowel, for example) which has vocal cord vibration is taken as the lowest measurable frequency in the spectrum of the sound *as it unfolds in time*. In practice, this corresponds to the rate of vibration of the vocal cords. Fundamental frequency is a concept in *acoustics* and therefore in *acoustic phonetics*, but there is a corresponding abstract concept in *phonology*. In phonology we are often concerned with the way the fundamental frequency of a stretch of speech is perceived to change; thus we might perceive a rise in pitch towards the end of a sentence, signalling a question, or a fall in pitch towards the end, signalling a statement. The phenomenon of perceived changes in pitch is called *intonation*. Because intonation is a perceived concept and because it is *relative* in nature, it is completely abstract and cannot therefore be measured in a waveform or spectrogram. What we can do, however, is measure the physical acoustic signal which gave rise to a perceived intonation pattern. When we do this we are measuring a *physical correlate* of what is perceived – the physical correlate of a cognitive phenomenon. The correlates rarely match in a one-to-one, or linear, way. We cannot actually measure intonation, only measure its correlate of changing fundamental frequency.

This particular dichotomy runs right through speech studies and is one of the things which makes the study of speech so interesting: speech exists in an objective and measurable physical world, but at the same time it exists in a cognitive world of intention (on the part of the speaker) and perception (on the part of the listener). It is very important to keep the terminology associated with these two worlds separate and to remember that only one world – the physical world – is open to direct physical investigation or quantifiable measurement.

RESONANCE

In speech, resonance is the vibration of the air as it flows through areas of the vocal tract, such as the oral or nasal cavities. The potential for vibration or oscillation is due to the size and shape of the cavity through which the air is flowing as it passes on its way either into the lungs (for *ingressive* sounds) or out of the lungs (for *egressive* sounds). For resonance to take place, the resonant frequencies due to the cavity size are ideally present already in the vibrating air flowing through the system. In egressive sounds the vibration already present is caused by the vocal cords as the air flows through the larynx, passing from the trachea below to the pharynx above. The airflow here is modulated, or set into vibration, producing a complex sound which includes a whole spectrum of frequencies. The subsequent resonance in, for example, the oral or nasal cavities amplifies, relatively, the resonant frequency at the expense of the frequencies on either side of it in the spectrum. We say that particular frequencies, relative to each other, are *amplified* while others are *attenuated*. Not only is the *source* sound wave from the vocal cords complex in nature, the resonances themselves are also complex, having not just one *area of resonance* in the spectrum, but several. In the static vocal tract, we speak of this complex of resonances, and when these are dynamically in actual operation – that is, during a piece of real speech – we speak of *formants* being introduced into the final sound which will emerge from the mouth and/or nose. Thus the spectrum of the speech as heard by a listener will be a distortion of the sound produced at the vocal cords by its modification into a set of formants due to the resonance effects of the cavities through which the air-borne sound has passed. Figure 1.4 shows stylised versions of the spectrum of the periodic source sound, the oral cavity's resonant characteristic and the spectrum of the final signal as it emerges from the mouth. We speak of the laryngeal source sound as being *filtered* by the oral cavity's resonance characteristics.

Resonance is therefore a concept allied to the associated concept of formant. Resonances have the potential of producing formants when excited by an acoustic signal. Resonances and formants are given physical correlating measurements in terms of their centre frequencies, their relative amplitudes

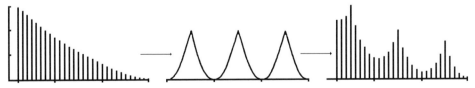

Figure 1.4 Filtering effects of the oral cavity's resonance properties. The vertical axis in the stylised diagrams represents amplitude, with 0 in the bottom left corner, and the horizontal axis represents frequency. To the left is the spectrum of the laryngeal source sound, in the centre the filter, and to the right the effect of the filter on the source. Notice the emergence of a formant structure (the peaks) in the signal.

and their bandwidths – how much of the spectrum each occupies. Frequency and amplitude are the physical quantities measured in the characterisation of resonances and formants. Remember: resonance is the *potential* for vibration or oscillation of the various cavities; formants are the *actual* results of bringing resonance into play in speaking. Formants are important because listeners use their grouping in patterns to determine which sounds are being heard (see Chapters 7 and 8).

FURTHER READING

Abercrombie, D. (1967), *Elements of General Phonetics*, Edinburgh: Edinburgh University Press.

Daniloff, R., G. Schuckers and L. Feth (1980), *The Physiology of Speech and Hearing: An Introduction*, Englewood Cliffs, NJ: Prentice Hall.

Fant, G. (1960), *Acoustic Theory of Speech Production*, The Hague: Mouton.

Fant, G. (1973), *Speech Sounds and Features*, Cambridge, MA: MIT Press.

Harrington, J. and S. Cassidy (1999), *Techniques in Speech Acoustics*, Dordrecht: Kluwer.

Johnson, K. (2003), *Acoustic and Auditory Phonetics*, Oxford: Blackwell.

King, D. W. and D. G. Drumright (2009), *Anatomy and Physiology for Speech, Language and Hearing*, 4th edn, Florence, KY: Delmar Cengage Learning.

Ladefoged, P. (2006), *A Course in Phonetics*, 5th edn, Boston, MA: Thompson, Wadsworth.

Lehiste, I. (1967), *Readings in Acoustics Phonetics*, Cambridge, MA: MIT Press.

Raphael, L. J., G. L. Borden and K. S. Harris (2007), *Speech Science Primer, Physiology, Acoustics, and Perception*, 5th edn, Baltimore: Lippincott Williams and Wilkins.

CHAPTER 2 – STUDYING SPEAKING

INTRODUCTION

Although we see that physically speech is mostly a continuous event in time, discontinuities and physical changes can regularly be seen on waveforms. Moreover, listeners report that they hear 'sequences of individual sounds'. We address the question (often vexed) of how the physical signal might be segmented. Following on from the earlier introduction to variability, we discuss some apparent invariances arising from the process of segmentation of the sound wave. Classes of segments are discussed: types of vowel and consonant, for example, and their defining characteristics.

SEGMENTATION OF CONTINUOUS EVENTS

Speech is an almost CONTINUOUS EVENT, despite the fact that we use separate or discrete LABELS when we identify sounds. The articulators rarely stop moving during a phrase or sentence, and only briefly on a non-diphthong long vowel or during the stop phase of a plosive consonant. Even in these cases there is some movement or tendency to move towards the next sound's position for the articulators. We speak of a *continuous trajectory* for the articulators, interrupted from time to time by pauses. The articulators do not always pause in a synchronous way; for example, during a voiced alveolar fricative [z] the tongue may pause for a few tens of milliseconds, but the vocal cords keep moving. In a word like *asp* /æsp/ the lips are on the move towards closure for the /p/ *before* the /s/, and keep moving while the tongue pauses a little for the fricative (Figure 2.1).

There is often independent behaviour between the articulators: they start moving, peak and stop moving ASYNCHRONOUSLY, because their roles *vary*

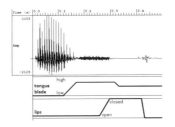

Figure 2.1 Waveform of *asp*, and stylised representations of lips and tongue blade movement. Notice how the tongue and lips move in anticipation of the timing of required acoustic effects.

CONTINUOUS EVENT

An event spanning a length of time during which there are no or few obvious physical boundaries. For example, in the sentence *How are you?* (Figure 1.2 above) it is hard to spot any clear boundaries in the acoustic waveform, despite the fact that we assign three separate words to the signal, and feel that there are around five or so separate sounds strung together.

LABEL

We assign the symbolic labels of the International Phonetic Alphabet (IPA) to stretches of acoustic signal or articulatory movement. Usually it is hard to discover boundaries in the signal between such labels, but fairly easy to identify *zones* or *areas* of the signal to which the various labels belong. Sometimes the zones may actually overlap, even though our symbol labels do not. By their nature, these symbols need to be written sequentially, and this also happens to correspond to a speaker/listener's *feeling* that sounds are sequenced in speech.

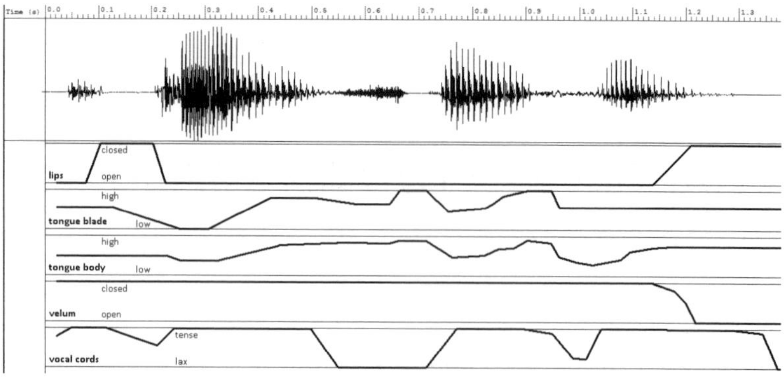

Figure 2.2 Waveform and several parameters, shown as articulatory phonology tracks, for the utterance *The boy stayed home*. From bottom to top, the parameters are: vocal cords, velum, tongue body, tongue blade and lips. Notice that events in the various parameters are not synchronised – it is rarely possible to locate them, say, by drawing vertical lines to represent segment boundaries. It is for this reason that trying to spot segments in the acoustic signal is rarely possible.

ARTICULATORY SCORE

An articulatory score is a graphical representation of unfolding articulation – called a score because of its resemblance to an orchestral score in music. Parallel tracks (like the staves in music), each representing a constriction point in the vocal tract, unfold in time from left to right. The tracks are stacked so that the behaviour of each can be compared with the others. This particular type of representation focuses on, and emphasises, the movement of the articulators, and contrasts sharply with traditional IPA notation (and many spelling systems), which emphasise the abstract sequencing of *whole segments*. Because the focus here is on how speech unfolds in time, the score is often called a *gestural* score (Browman and Goldstein 1986). Gestures are associated with how movement occurs in time (Saltzman and Munhall 1989).

ASYNCHRONOUSLY/ SYNCHRONOUSLY

Two events occur *synchronously* when they begin at the same time or in step, and *asynchronously* when they begin out of step with each other. When two sine waves begin simultaneously and both start with a positive-going waveform, or both with a negative-going waveform, they are also said to be *in phase*. Note also the phrases *in sync* and *not in sync* as shorthand versions of *synchronously* and *asynchronously* respectively.

in important ways from segment to segment during an utterance. What is clear from this observation is that as far as the articulators are concerned we do not start a segment, hold it and then stop, ready for the next one. The movements of articulators are usually continuous, slow down or speed up here and there, pause briefly from time to time – all asynchronously. The *apparent* synchronisation we feel is a property of how we *perceive* speech, rather than a property of how it actually *is*. The diagram in Figure 2.2, of an ARTICULATORY SCORE, illustrates the point.

We tend to think of segments as having articulatory or sound targets (TUTORIAL – TARGET THEORY), but the idea of a string of individually specified segments tends to blur as the string of planned segments is *rendered* – turned into actual articulations and sounds. Thus the boundaries for any particular *intended* sound tend to be lost in the continuous movement between articulations. Often, particularly when we speak quickly, there is not enough time to hit the target, let alone dwell on it.

In practice this blending together of sounds, and the almost continuous movement of the articulators, is of little consequence; the human perceptual system is well equipped to identify what the speaker's intended targets were. Of course, there are limits; the blurring could be so great in extremely rapid speech that even the most attentive listener would miss the intended message. Importantly, speakers are almost always sensitive to the listener's limits and avoid this situation; after all, speakers are also listeners and know about such problems because they experience them too.

Phoneticians need to identify the speaker's intended sequence of sounds or articulations in continuous speech. This is done by SEGMENTING the sound wave. Similarly, listeners can identify the intended sounds in the continuous signal; they too could be said to be segmenting the sound stream. It would seem an easy task for phoneticians to simply do what listeners do. The problem is that we are not exactly sure how listeners identify individual sounds, but what we do know is that part of the process involves knowing quite a lot about the sound system of the language being used. So how do we solve the problem of segmentation in practice?

SEGMENTATION

Although the term *segmentation* has usually been used for this process in modern phonetics, it presents a bit of a problem: segmenting implies literally chopping up the signal into isolable segments, each of which is a particular sound in the sound stream. If we try to do this by literally chopping up the signal using a waveform editing program, we run into serious difficulty because of the blending or blurring effect: identifying the beginnings and ends of sounds is often quite impossible with any degree of certainty. This has led some researchers to question whether in running speech it makes sense to speak of the beginning and end of a sound.
Here is the problem:

- speakers think of speech in terms of a sequence of sounds they intend to make;
- they work out articulatory or acoustic targets for these sounds;
- but in trying to produce the sequence of targets in a short space of time things go wrong: the intended sounds blend together;
- the blending occurs differently between the different articulators (or parameters) involved (see the articulatory score in Figure 2.2 above);
- the blending is so serious in most cases that identifying the beginning and end of sounds is usually impossible;
- but phoneticians and listeners need nevertheless to get at what underlies this continuous signal.

There is another way of looking at things. Instead of trying to cut the signal up into short stretches, the phonetician can identify general areas of the sound stream which are associated with the speaker's intention to produce a sequence of different sounds. These general areas can then be labelled with a symbolic representation (from the phonetician's set of symbols) *without* trying to identify precisely which parts of the signal are involved – we speak of the symbols being ASSIGNED to the signal. The symbols stand for an *association* between the speaker's intended sequence of sound and the sequence of areas of the signal. Thus a labelling or identifying process is achieved without trying to make artificial exact cuts in the signal.

Similarly, the task of the listener is to assign a symbolic representation or labels to a stretch of sound, rather than to identify short, precise stretches of sound. The *speaker's* thoughts are of a sequence of sounds, but this turns out to be unachievable at the speeds we use for speech – so a blur is produced. The phonetician or *listener* can label areas (blending, blurring or overlapping) of the signal to produce a sequence of symbols corresponding to the speaker's intended sequence of sounds.

The process of segmentation is thought of less literally these days; we usually no longer make the attempt to cut the signal in precise places, but rather try to use all available cues within the signal to produce a sequence of appropriate labels. The phonetician's task here is very similar to the listener's: label the sequence symbolically – discard the difficult and

ASSIGNMENT

Assignment is the process of association of an abstract, non-varying or robust symbol with a physical object – even one which has added or inherent variability. For example, two different versions of the same word (perhaps even spoken by different speakers) will be assigned the *same* IPA representation. Associating the same representation with different acoustic versions of the same word captures the speaker/listener's feelings that they *are* the same.

varying actual signal. This is drawn out in the articulatory score illustrated above in Figure 2.2. Here the focus is away from any vertical segmentation of the signal and towards the way in which the on-running parallel parameters or tracks contribute to the overall signal.

In more technical terms, we speak of applying an abstract labelling system to the physical signal. The fact that the labelling system is abstract is what enables us, as scientists, to move away from the variability of the actual signal. We move towards the sameness we need to draw out in order to make sense of the signal for the purpose of perception (as listeners), or explanation (as phoneticians) (TUTORIAL – SAMENESS AND VARIABILITY).

The speaker's decisions about how to speak a word or phrase are cognitive and therefore ABSTRACT; they are intended to match as precisely as possible the listener's perception of the signal. We assume that speakers want to be understood. Equally, therefore, the listener's perception and sequence of labels are themselves abstract.

The matching of events or objects in the PHYSICAL WORLD with our abstract human intentions or perceptions is an extremely difficult area of cognitive psychology. Something we do so easily in real life is proving very difficult to understand in our science.

THE ORGANISATION OF PERCEIVED EVENTS

SPEECH EVENTS are perceived by listeners in response to the acoustic waveform they hear. The perceived events are reported by the listener as a SYMBOLIC REPRESENTATION of the physical signal, and we speak of this symbolic representation as having been assigned to the signal. The symbolic representation is not itself *in* the signal; to repeat: it is assigned to it by the listener.

What the listener perceives relates only to a considerable simplification of the physical signal, and lacks the variation and blurring associated with the COARTICULATORY DIFFICULTIES (see Chapter 3) of the mechanics of articulation or the details of acoustics. What variations *can* be perceived are allocated a symbolic representation by the listener largely because that is what the speaker intended should be done.

COARTICULATORY DIFFICULTY

Speakers seem to plan their utterances as a string of segments. In attempting to render the plan as actual articulations, there appears to be a blurring of segments due to the mechanical and aerodynamic properties of the vocal tract. This coarticulation, as it is known, is generally not noticed by listeners. However, sometimes it can be controlled, and on these occasions listeners do pick up on the changes, especially if they are used to linguistic effect. This is discussed under 'Coarticulation' in Chapter 3, and later under 'Cognitive Phonetics' in Chapter 4.

ABSTRACT

In phonetics/phonology an object or event is said to be abstract if it exists in the mind and derives from a cognitive process in the speaker/listener. Abstract phonological objects in a speaker's plan have to be subsequently rendered in the physical phonetic world.

PHYSICAL WORLD

The physical world is the world outside the human mind, contrasting with the abstract world which exists only in the mind. The physical world is open to objective measurement – such as the measurement of the properties of the sound wave.

SPEECH EVENT

Speech event is a term often used ambiguously to mean an actual physical event such as an articulation or acoustic signal, or to mean the speaker's intention of that event or the listener's perception of the event. It is sensible to clarify the term whenever it is used.

SYMBOLIC REPRESENTATION

A symbolic representation is an abstract representation of some phenomenon (object or process) which may itself be physical or cognitive. In speech production and perception studies, for example, a sequence of symbols like the IPA can be used to *transcribe* a cognitive representation of the speech sound wave. It is usually assumed that the corresponding cognitive representation takes the form of symbols in the speaker's or listener's mind. In classical phonetics the IPA can transcribe the phonetician's more objective, trained view of the acoustic signal.

So, for example, speakers of English readily perceive the difference between a physical, clear or palatalised $[l_j]$ and a dark or velarised $[l_\gamma]$. The clear $[l_j]$ usually precedes a stressed vowel, as in *leaf* $['l_jif]$, whereas the dark $[l_\gamma]$ occurs at the end of a syllable or preceding a consonant, as in *feel* $['fil_\gamma]$; if these are reversed the change is immediately recognised by the listener as wrong, or not conforming to the expectation for English. The two variants of the underlying phonemic /l/ which is used to contrast *leaf* /lif/ with *beef* /bif/ and equally to contrast *feel* /fil/ with *feet* /fit/ are there because this is part of the speaker's UTTERANCE PLAN. Here the same symbol is used in both *leaf* and *feel* – because it is the *same* underlying phoneme; the difference arises only when the plan is put together later.

	Speaker		Acoustic signal	Listener		
Original words	Phonemic, word-distinguishing representation	Derived utterance plan	Phonetic transcription of the physical signal	Assigned utterance plan	Assigned phonemic representation	Decoded words
leaf →	/lif/ →	$/l_jif/$ →	$[l_jif]$ →	$/l_jif/$ →	/lif/ →	leaf
feel →	/fil/ →	$/fil_\gamma/$ →	$[fil_\gamma]$ →	$/fil_\gamma/$ →	/fil/ →	feel

Note the use of different brackets in the table here. The forward slash is used to bracket abstract cognitive (or phonological) representations in the minds of speakers and listeners; that is, the representations distinguishing words and utterance plans. Square brackets surround abstract transcriptions of the physical waveform; they are abstract because they are still symbolic representations rather than the waveform itself.

These perceived events do not exist in an isolated form; they are *always* associated with each other in systematic ways. Phoneticians exploit these feelings of association to classify and organise sounds in ways which make them easier to understand from the points of view of both production and perception. That is why the phonemic symbol /l/ is visually associated with the utterance plan symbols $/l_j/$ and $/l_\gamma/$ and the symbols of the phonetic transcription $[l_j]$ and $[l_\gamma]$. The use of 'l' throughout shows we are dealing with a representational family or grouping, while the subscript diacritics '$_j$' and '$_\gamma$' and the brackets '/' and '[ ]' indicate the systematic way in which variant members of the family or group are associated.

THE AIRSTREAM MECHANISM

Most speech sounds are made using a PULMONIC EGRESSIVE AIRSTREAM. In some languages, a pulmonic INGRESSIVE movement of the air is used in addition for some sounds, and in a few, air trapped in the vocal tract is released under pressure to create a very brief egressive flow, or sucked

---

UTTERANCE PLAN

The utterance plan is the abstract plan generated by the speaker specifying how they would like the utterance to sound. In practice the resulting acoustic signal never quite matches the plan because of mechanical, acoustic and other artefacts introduced in the production process (see COARTICULATORY DIFFICULTY above, and 'Coarticulation' in Chapter 3).

in to create a brief ingressive flow. These are not used in our example languages, but do occur in some African and other languages.

> **PULMONIC EGRESSIVE/INGRESSIVE AIRSTREAM**
>
> An airstream originating in the lungs (hence 'pulmonic') and flowing outward, through the larynx towards the oral and/or nasal cavities and thence into the outside world, is termed a pulmonic egressive airstream. This contrasts with an *ingressive* airstream, which is sucked into the lungs from the outside, through either the mouth or nose or both.

MODIFYING THE AIRSTREAM

SUPRAGLOTTAL CAVITIES
The cavities of the vocal tract above the glottis in the larynx area are called supraglottal cavities.

PHONOLOGICAL OPPOSITION
The term *phonological opposition* usually refers to the use of contrasting sounds to differentiate words.

Speech sounds are produced by systematically modifying the airstream, which is usually egressive. As air moves from the lungs, the first area where modification can take place is the larynx, containing the vocal cords. The vocal cords are either held apart, allowing relatively free airflow into the SUPRAGLOTTAL CAVITIES, or they come together under tension, creating the conditions giving rise to glottal vibration or SPONTANEOUS VOICING. This is what allows the PHONOLOGICAL OPPOSITION of voiceless and voiced sounds. There are two main possibilities: sounds are produced with or without vocal cord vibration.

> **SPONTANEOUS VOICING**
>
> Spontaneous voicing in the phonetics literature refers to vibration of the vocal cords, which takes place automatically when they are held with fairly constant tension and air pressures below and above are in a careful balance – higher below the glottis and lower above. There are three terms in the equation: T (vocal cord tension), $P_{subglottal}$ and $P_{supraglottal}$ (air pressure below and above the vocal cords, respectively) where $P_{subglottal} > P_{supraglottal}$. If these three quantities are not in the correct balance, spontaneous voicing will fail.
>
> - IMPORTANT: Note the confusing use of the term *voicing* here. We prefer to use *voice* and *voicing* for phonology and *vocal cord vibration* for a correlating effect in phonetic

CONSTRICTION
A constriction in the oral cavities requires a narrowing of the air passage by moving articulators closer together; for example, moving the tongue (a *mobile* articulator) closer to the palate (a *fixed* articulator), or the lower and upper lips together (both mobile articulators).

There are various areas in the vocal tract where we can further modify how *freely* the air flows. This is done by introducing CONSTRICTIONS. The airstream can be comparatively free (we call this *free airflow*) or interrupted to some degree (we call this *stopped* or *partially stopped airflow*). Vowels have comparatively free airflow, though there is a small constraint on airflow when the tongue is high in the mouth, as in [i] or [u]. Among consonants, stops have completely interrupted airflow, whereas fricatives have partially interrupted airflow. With fricatives the degree of interruption varies with the narrowness of the constriction; thus in English [s] interrupts the airflow more than [ʃ] because the latter has a wider gap for the air to flow through. In general, the narrower the constriction, the higher the spectral frequency band of the fricative, and the higher its relative amplitude (TUTORIAL – THE ACOUSTIC SIGNAL, Chapter 1).

Vocal cord vibration is caused by setting the vocal cords under a near-constant tension to the point where they block the airflow, which in turn then forces its way between them (because the subglottal air pressure rises), whereupon they come back together again (because the air pressure between them drops and the subglottal air pressure falls) to interrupt the flow again in a cyclical fashion. Were it not for the subglottal air pressure, the tense vocal cords would stop the airflow completely, as in the glottal stop [ʔ] (e.g. in Cockney *paper* [peiʔə]). The vocal cords sometimes only partially stop the airflow, as in the voiceless glottal fricative [h] or in whispered speech. The larynx is therefore a special constriction point in the vocal tract – special, because the vocal cords can be manipulated in a number of different ways to produce linguistically contrastive effects.

ARTICULATORY CLASSES – CLASSIFIED BY TYPE OF CONSTRICTION

In this chapter, we are using classical phonetics as the basis for describing how sounds are made in terms of what we do with the vocal tract to produce them. Classical phonetics did not attempt to get behind the articulation and say something about the mechanisms involved in initiating or controlling how it takes place; we do this in Chapters 3 and 4. Bear in mind in this section that classical phonetics is a STATIC MODEL focused on individual *linguistically relevant* (rather than random) articulations or sound segments; it is essentially a surface description rather than an explanation of what is happening below the surface to produce the segments (Cruttenden 2008).

In classical phonetics the segment is either some abstract *target* the speaker is aiming at to execute or render the planned utterance, or an idealised actual sound which has not been modified by any coarticulatory factors associated with the running context – this is why we call it a *static* model.

The initial level of classification of consonants rests on how constrictions modify the airstream. Three main types are recognised: fricatives, stops or plosives, and a further, less common, type: affricates (TUTORIAL – CLASSES OF CONSONANT IN ENGLISH).

ADDING RESONANCE

Independently of what happens in the larynx in terms of vocal cord vibration, during a sound the cavities of the vocal tract add RESONANCE to the SOUND PRODUCING SYSTEM. Resonance can be thought of as a filtering process, adjusting the glottal sound as it moves through the vocal tract as MODULATED AIRFLOW.

- The TUTORIAL – TWO BASIC CONCEPTS – FUNDAMENTAL FREQUENCY AND RESONANCE, Chapter 1, is concerned

STATIC MODEL

In speech, a model is static when it considers segments more or less in isolation without paying much attention to how and why segments behave differently in dynamic running speech.

SOUND PRODUCING SYSTEM

The overall system comprising the lungs, the supraglottal cavities (including the oral and nasal cavities) and the articulators which border the cavities – lips, teeth, palate, velum, uvula, tongue, pharynx – all of which can be manipulated to produce sounds sufficiently distinct to be usable on a consistent basis in language.

REMINDER: RESONANCE

The vibratory response of an acoustic system, like the vocal tract, to input energy – say, airflow from the lungs. Resonance of a body, or the air contained in it, is characterised by a formal statement of its characteristics in terms of resonant frequencies and their amplitudes.

mainly with what resonance actually is. This section is about how it is produced and its *linguistic function*.

The complex shape of the vocal tract, especially when the constrictions referred to earlier occur, contributes to a complex resonance pattern imposed on the glottal sound, This is largely what contributes to the overall characteristics of the sound coming out of the mouth and/or nose. Even when the vocal cords are not vibrating – as in voiceless sounds and whispered speech – the low-amplitude frication of the air passing between the slightly tensed vocal cords and the length of the vocal tract excites the resonance. Many parts of the vocal tract are mobile, enabling us to alter the size and shape of the vocal tract as the air passes through, thus changing the audible resonances. These changes give rise to many of the differences between speech sounds.

MODULATED AIRFLOW

As the vocal cords open and close they change the otherwise laminar or smooth flow of air through the glottis into one which is pulsed in a way reflecting the characteristics of the vibrating vocal cords and the rate of their vibration. In normal speech the airflow is chopped into bursts occurring within the approximate range of 80 to 350 bursts per second: 80–350 Hz. The acoustic characteristics of the changing modulated signal are given as its spectrum: its frequency and amplitude characteristics over time.

So we now have two mechanisms which can be used to differentiate speech sounds:

1. the presence or absence of vocal cord vibration;

2. manipulable resonance filtering effects modifying the glottal source sound;

and in addition the sound is further modified by the radiation characteristics of the lips:

3. radiation at the lips – differentiates between, for example, [i] (spread and tensed lips) and [y] (tightly rounded lips) in French; there is no other difference between these two sounds, which share the same tongue position.

Aerodynamic object	Vocal tract	Acoustic effect	Linguistic category
Pulmonic egressive airstream			
↓	→ Larynx	+/− Vocal cord vibration	Vowels, voiced/voiceless consonants
↓	→ Vocal tract	Resonance	Vowels, sonorant consonants
↓	→ Lips/nose	Radiation	
Final speech sound			

By combining the presence or absence of vocal cord vibration with many different resonance possibilities in the vocal tract, sounds can be systematically produced for use in creating a phonological inventory of sounds in a particular language. Different languages will use different sets of sounds, sometimes overlapping considerably, and sometimes hardly at all (TUTORIAL – VOWELS AND VOWEL-LIKE SOUNDS IN ENGLISH). German, Dutch and English use many of the same sounds, but differ more from languages like French and Portuguese.

LABELLING SOUNDS/ARTICULATIONS AND CLASSES

Phoneticians need to identify and label the sounds they perceive as making up the speech of a language. They do this with a SYMBOLIC REPRESENTATION consisting of a set of main symbols to identify not just the sounds but also the ARTICULATION or GESTURE associated with the sound. Thus the symbol [i] stands for both an articulation with the tongue high in the front of the mouth, the vocal cords vibrating and the nasal cavity blocked off, *and* the sound we hear associated with the articulation. In practice this ambiguity in the meaning of the symbol is usually not a problem.

Bear in mind, however, that the exact positioning of the articulators, and therefore the precise nature of the associated sound, can and does vary enormously, not just from speaker to speaker but within a single speaker's repetition of the sound. The linear context of a sound – which sounds occur before and after – also causes significant variation in the articulation. We also note that the underlying structure of, say, a syllable can contextually influence the articulation of one of its component sounds.

We can understand this better by realising that the *symbol* is really associated not with the actual sound or articulation but with the *category* a speaker or listener assigns them. So, for example, if a speaker *intends* to produce a particular sound the label is associated with the intention, even if the actual articulation and sound produced are not exactly as intended. Similarly, if a listener perceives a particular sound – even if it differs in detail from some norm (say, the sound produced in isolation, if that is possible) – they will assign the symbol to that sound. Importantly, if the speaker repeats the sound or the listener hears the repetition they will be assigned the SAME symbol, even if they differ from some earlier version.

In both the production and perception of speech the idea of SAMENESS plays a very important role. For the moment we should just note that human beings focus on the similarities between varying sounds rather than on their differences. If the reverse were true every single sound would be felt to be different, whether this was the intention or not – every single utterance of a simple word like *dog* would be felt to be a different word.

SYMBOLIC REPRESENTATION

A symbolic representation stands for some phenomenon (object or process) which may be physical or cognitive. In speech production and perception studies a sequence of symbols, like the IPA, is used to *transcribe* a cognitive representation of the speech sound wave.

ARTICULATION

An articulation (see also GESTURE) is a deliberate setting up of the vocal tract to produce a particular sound.

GESTURE

The production of a speech sound, focusing particularly on dynamic aspects of the articulation, is called a gesture. It is often represented in terms of the features of the articulation or its vocal tract parameters (see 'Articulatory Phonology' in Chapter 3). In theories of speech production where the syllable is the basic unit, the gesture is associated with that unit, rather than with individual sounds which might, in other theories, make up the syllable.

SAME, SAMENESS

Two speech sounds or articulations, when measured physically, are the same if their measurements are identical. But cognitively, when intended by the speaker or perceived by the listener they are the same if they are assigned to the same category, even if they differ physically.

By focusing on the similarities of these different utterances the listener can identify or label every occurrence as the same word, *dog*.

The symbol (like those in the IPA) therefore represents some ideal, rather than some actual sound. In this sense we say that the symbol is an abstraction, an idealised version of what actually happens. So, for example, the word *cat* will always have the same basic phonemic representation, /kæt/, in a language even if any one pronunciation differs slightly from others. It is not until the variation is deliberately produced by the speaker that we say the pronunciation is different. Thus, some speakers will pronounce cat as /kæt/, whereas others will say /kæt˺/ (/t˺/ is an *intended* unreleased /t/) – deliberately changing the way /t/ is pronounced according to their accent; both speakers are pronouncing the same word, /kæt/, though. We shall see later that there are different levels of abstraction and different levels of physical rendering (TUTORIAL – ABSTRACTION).

> **IPA**
>
> The *International Phonetic Association* was founded in the late nineteenth century in Paris by the phonetician Paul Passy and continues to this day. One major achievement of the Association was to develop the *International Phonetic Alphabet* (also called, confusingly, *IPA*) with the object of enabling an unambiguous symbolic representation of the sounds of the world's languages. In fact, the symbol usage is not unambiguous, and often it is necessary to add extra information. So, for example, [t] indicates an alveolar [t] of the kind we would usually come across in English, and at the same times indicates a dental [t] such as we would find in French. In this book we disambiguate wherever possible, thus for example: [t_Eng] vs. [t_Fr] or [t] vs. [t̪] respectively.
>
> The symbols used here are taken from the IPA. Historically, other symbol systems have been used for representing speech and there are contemporary variations.

In classical phonetics speech sounds were seen to be divisible into two major subsets – the consonants and vowels. Vowels were usually defined as those sounds with a comparatively free-flowing airstream, whereas consonants have an impeded or partially impeded airstream. These days we would be more likely to define segments less physically and more according to their phonological function: vowels in phonology are those segments which occupy the NUCLEUS part of a syllable, and consonants are those which lead up to the nucleus – the syllable's onset – or those which lead away from the nucleus – the syllable's coda.

> **SYLLABLE NUCLEUS**
>
> The nucleus (or peak) of a syllable is its pivotal or central segment – usually a vowel, as in /dɔk/ *dock*.

In the physically based classical approach, once identified, each subset – vowel or consonant – could be characterised within the framework of a system of classification showing how the sounds relate to each other mostly on an articulatory basis, though sometimes acoustic relationships are invoked. So, for example, [i] is a high front vowel whereas [ɑ] is a low back vowel (an articulatory relationship), but [ɑ] is an oral vowel whereas [ɑ̃] has a nasal quality or nasal formant; this last comparison invokes how the sound is made in articulatory terms, how it sounds subjectively and how it is structured acoustically. Classifications in more modern approaches tend to be less confusing.

PLACE AND MANNER OF ARTICULATION

Consonants

Consonants are initially classified two-dimensionally, or using two parameters: PLACE and MANNER OF ARTICULATION.

Thus, [b] is a bilabial (place) stop or plosive (manner); [f] is a labio-dental (place) fricative (manner). In a graphical representation of this classification, a matrix is set up with the rows corresponding to the different manners of articulation and the columns corresponding to the different place of articulation. In each cell of the matrix is entered a symbol indicating the sound produced at this intersection of the two parameters. This reveals, however, that for each cell there are often two possibilities. Thus there are two bilabial plosives in English: [p] and [b]. They are distinguished by whether or not there is potentially accompanying vocal cord vibration. In classical phonetics potential vocal cord vibration is called VOICING, and this therefore constitutes a third parameter for the classification of consonants – place, manner, voicing. There are other, more subtle parameters, such as 'rounded lips' on some consonants, syllabic (for /l̩/, /r̩/, /m̩/, /n̩/ etc.).

	Bilabial		Labio-dental		Dental		Alveolar		Post-alveolar		Velar		Glottal	
Plosive	p	b					t	d			k	g		
Nasal		m						n				ŋ		
Flap							ɾ							
Fricative			f	v	θ	ð	s	z	ʃ	ʒ			h	
Approximant									ɹ					
Lateral approximant							l							

The matrix here illustrates a consonant chart based on the current IPA standard. Only the consonants for southern British English have been included. Even on a very full chart not all cells would be filled with a symbol. The theory of phonetics needs to explain why there are blanks in the chart:

- Are some of the potential articulations *impossible*, e.g. voiced glottal fricatives, because it would not be possible to produce both vibration *and* frication at the vocal cords? Voicing needs some tension in the vocal cords to bring them together for vibration, whereas frication needs them held somewhat apart but with *more* tension.

- Are some sounds *simply not used* in the language, but could be (e.g. voiceless bilabial or alveolar nasals are not allowed in English)?

PLACE OF ARTICULATION

The place of articulation for a speech sound is an indication of where in the vocal tract a constriction of some kind is made, usually by bringing a movable articulator against (for plosives) or near to (for fricatives) a fixed articulator.

MANNER OF ARTICULATION

This refers to how narrow or tight the constriction is: stops or plosives involve complete constriction (e.g. [p] or [g]), fricatives often a near-complete constriction (e.g. [θ] or [ð]), affricates start with a complete constriction relaxing into a period of nearly complete constriction (e.g. [t͡s] or [d͡ʒ]), and liquids (e.g. [l] or [r]) leave a much greater gap between the two articulators – tongue upper surface and palate.

REMINDER: VOICING

In classical phonetics voicing refers to a segment's potential to have vocal cord vibration as its main source of sound. In practice the vocal cord vibration is often incomplete or sometimes missing altogether – though because of its phonological function the segment is still referred to as *voiced* to contrast it with corresponding voiceless segments. Try not to confuse voicing (strictly these days a phonological feature) and vocal cord vibration (a phonetic feature); voicing and vocal cord vibration may or may not correlate fully.

- Would some sounds be *too close* in articulatory or perceptual terms to be readily distinguished in any *one* language (e.g. dental and alveolar plosives are mutually exclusive on this basis – French uses dental ones, English uses alveolar ones)?

Vowels

Vowels are classified according to the position in the oral cavity, on a cross-sectional plane, of what was originally thought of as the highest part of the tongue. This was later modified to the most significant part of the tongue to contribute to its overall SHAPE – and both were later shown to be much too simple because in reality the entire tongue surface participates in setting up the shape of the oral cavity, not just a single point. Thus a two-dimensional graph or chart can be set up with rows representing a high–low dimension and columns representing a forward–backward dimension. Points are marked on this graph showing the relevant tongue 'position' corresponding to a particular vowel.

Thus [i] is shown high and forward on the graph, and is classified as a high front vowel; and [u] might be shown as a high back vowel, high and at the back of the graph (see Figure 1.1 above). Two other dimensions which cannot be shown on a two-dimensional projection are necessary to classify vowels exhaustively: LIP ROUNDING and NASALITY. Lip rounding is necessary but not phonologically significant in English, though it is, for example, in French, German, etc. Nasality is not significant in English, but it is distinctive in French, Portuguese, Polish, etc. An often neglected fifth dimension or parameter is *tone* as found in Mandarin Chinese, though this is not usually shown on vowel charts.

REMINDER: LIP ROUNDING

Although part of the specification of sounds like [u], lip rounding is non-distinctive in English. In some languages, however, lip rounding is used phonologically to distinguish words; for example, French *dit* [di]$_{Fr}$, as in *il a dit . . . (he said . . .)*, and *dû* [dy]$_{Fr}$, as in *il a dû (he had to . . .)*. Here the two words *dit* and *dû* are distinguished solely on whether there is lip rounding on the syllable's vowel nucleus.

REMINDER: NASALITY

Nasality occurs when the velar valve – the mobile back of the palate – is open to allow the flow of air into the nasal cavity, where it resonates, introducing a nasal formant into the resulting sound. Some languages use this effect for phonological contrast (e.g. French contrasts *beau* /bo/$_{Fr}$ and *bon* /bõ/$_{Fr}$). In English, nasalisation occurs when air leaks into the nasal cavity during a vowel, commonly when it is sandwiched between two nasal consonants (e.g. *man* [mãn]$_{Eng}$ or *moon* [mũn]$_{Eng}$).

ACOUSTIC ANALYSIS

This refers to the acoustic analysis of the signal corresponding to the pronunciation of a planned sound. We speak of the analysis of the sound as rendered phonetically. The signal, like all acoustic signals, is analysed in terms of its frequency (its spectral content), its amplitude and its duration (time) (TUTORIAL – ABSTRACTION) for the way in which these correspond to their more abstract correlates of pitch, loudness and length.

TONGUE SHAPE

The idea of tongue height as a rather vague single point on the tongue turned out to be false: it is in fact the entire shape of the tongue and how it plays a role in altering the size and shape or the oral cavity which is responsible for the differing sounds vowels. However, there does turn out to be a real use for the vowel chart in providing a *perceptual space map*. Listeners can and do make comments about how sounds relate to one another using spatial (rather than acoustic) terms. In fact listeners can be coaxed into drawing such maps on paper by asking them how far or close particular vowel sounds are to a fixed vowel, such as [ə], roughly in the centre of the two-dimensional chart of the oral cavity. These drawings turn out to be remarkably similar to the classical phonetics vowel charts. Perhaps unsurprisingly it is also possible to plot classificatory graphs based on ACOUSTIC ANALYSIS of vowel sounds – and these too turn out to be remarkably similar to the vowel charts and to vowel perceptual space maps (Ladefoged 2003).

	Front	Central	Back
Close	i		u
	ɪ	ʊ	
Mid		ə	
Open-mid	ɛ	ɜ	ɔ
	æ	ʌ	
Open		ɑ	ɒ

The matrix here is an adaptation of the standard IPA vowel chart, showing the main vowels of southern British English. The chart is two-dimensional and was originally intended as an abstract representation of a cross-section (front to back) though the oral cavity in the area of possible tongue positioning.

TARGET THEORY

TUTORIAL

In Target Theory (MacNeilage and DeClerk 1969) the target is the physical specification of a planned phonological unit (an extrinsic allophone in phonology). This specification exists for the purposes of showing how an abstract phonological unit might be physically rendered. The output of the cognitive phonology is a plan. This abstract plan is reinterpreted or rewritten as a specification consisting of a string of physical targets (specified PARAMETRICALLY) each corresponding to a phonological unit. The plan/target boundary was the subject of intense interest in the 1960s and 1970s, because it addressed the problem of interfacing abstract and physical objects. In linguistics terms the output level of phonology comprises the plan for rendering, and the input level of phonetics comprises the target string to begin the rendering process.

Abstract   *Physical*

Phonemic   PHONOLOGY → Utterance   Target   PHONETICS →   Acoustic
string →   plan   string →   output

It is always recognised that the interface between abstract and physical is a theoretically problematical area, and the philosophical problems associated with bringing them together are generally acknowledged (Lashley 1951; MacNeilage 1970). Linking cognitive phonology and physical phonetics in this way is, however, a satisfactory interim way of proceeding. It would be hard to see how, in speech studies, we can avoid trying to understand how abstract and physical phenomena correlate, even if to do so places us in a philosophically difficult area.

PARAMETRICALLY
A parametric specification is one in which the various features in the specification are represented separately so that their individual contributions to the entire event or object can be assessed.

SAMENESS AND VARIABILITY

TUTORIAL

Pronounce a single vowel, say /æ/; now pronounce it again. The two sounds are in fact *different* even though you intended to pronounce the *same* vowel. The feeling of sameness is so strong that often it is difficult to convince someone that the waveforms are not identical. In fact, every waveform is different from every other: the number of possible waveforms is pretty much infinite. This fact needs to be captured and accounted for in our theory. We *feel* the sounds are the same, but in fact they are different. This is where the phonetician's abstract labelling system comes in useful: we use the same label for sounds which sound the same or which function similarly in the language. There are two types of variant sounds:

- those which seem the same;
- those which function identically in the language, even if they do not sound exactly the same.

If it seems hard or impossible to make the sounds different, then we tend to use the same transcription for all variants. If the differences are large or interesting or seem to be made deliberately, we can note them in what phoneticians call *narrow transcription*. For this we use a different symbol or sometimes diacritics to mark the differences.

Take the /t/ in the word *later* pronounced in three different accents:

1. standard southern /leitə/;
2. cockney /leiʔə/;
3. US /leiɾɚ/ or /leiɾəɹ/.

- Note that in US English the final /r/ is deleted, as in most accents of English, but only after changing the quality of the preceding vowel. In the case of /ə/ this can be marked either by changing the symbol itself to /ɚ/ or by appending a /ɹ/ - though this should not be thought of as a separate sound in the actual pronunciation; the symbol /. . . r . . ./ is the voiced alveolar flap commonly used in US English in this context.

Educated speakers in the south of England use the usual released /t/ in this position; Cockney speakers regularly substitute a glottal stop here; and American speakers usually use a voiced version of the /t/. These variants are optional, and because of this have to be specified in the speaker's plan for the pronunciation of the word. The plan is transcribed using the / bracketing. In *all three* accents here the representation of the word prior to adding these variants has to be /leiter/, for two reasons:

- to identify this as the *same* morpheme or word in all dialects – i.e. we must have the same representation no matter what the dialect or accent, because we are representing the morpheme in *English*, not in any particular *accent* of English;
- to distinguish it from other words like *laser* /leizer/ – i.e. the representation must be unique to the particular morpheme *later*, and /t/ is used to distinguish it from others.

CLASSES OF CONSONANT IN ENGLISH

TUTORIAL

FRICATIVES

Fricatives are what we call *single-phase consonants*. This means that throughout their duration the articulations, and hence the sounds, are intended to be held constant, with relatively unvarying characteristics. All fricatives involve an APERIODIC SOURCE, producing a hiss-like sound. Many come in pairs, with the alternate having a second simultaneous periodic source in the form of vocal cord vibration. Thus, phonologically we have a voiced/voiceless opposition, and phonetically a vocal cord vibration presence/absence contrast. Remember that vocal cord vibration is the articulatory or acoustic correlate of phonological voicing – it is important to keep the terms separate: *vocal cord vibration* in phonetics, *voicing* in phonology. We sometimes refer to phonologically voiced sounds as [+voice] and voiceless sounds as [–voice] – here the square brackets enclose a *feature* (TUTORIAL – DISTINCTIVE FEATURE THEORY, Chapter 4).

English has the following pairs of fricatives (traditionally listed from the lips inwards, voiceless first in each pair): [f, v], [θ, ð], [s, z], [ʃ, ʒ]. In addition there is [h] – this is a fricative (some would call it a voiceless approximant) where there is a single aperiodic source produced at the vocal cords, which therefore cannot also be involved in producing a periodic source since the two are mutually exclusive. Occasionally, BREATHY VOICE is an exception.

Here is a chart of the fricatives of English, showing, by using + and/or –, the speaker's *intended* presence or absence of periodic and aperiodic sources and the approximate location of the point of constriction being used to generate the frication.

	Lips		Teeth		Alveolar ridge		Front of palate		Vocal cords
	f	v	θ	ð	s	z	ʃ	ʒ	h
Aperiodic frication	+	+	+	+	+	+	+	+	+
Periodic vocal cord vibration	–	+	–	+	–	+	–	+	–

In terms of the place of articulation of these fricatives, we see that we can involve the lips, the tongue tip and tongue blade as mobile articulators, and the upper teeth and the area of the palate immediately behind the teeth, the alveolar ridge, as fixed articulators. With most sounds the articulation involves both a mobile and a fixed articulator. We note some exceptions to this below, but for the moment the fricatives of English are classified as in the chart below.

PERIODIC/APERIODIC SOURCE

In periodic sources the sound is coming in more or less regularly timed pulses – vocal cord vibration is an example, as are trilled [r] sounds in Spanish, etc., and the bilabial trills [ʙ] found in a few languages. Aperiodic sources produce a more random, non-pulsed sound referred to as *frication* (*not* 'friction', which is a force generated when two surfaces rub together laterally, usually producing heat, and has little or nothing to do with speech). The aperiodic source in fricatives is produced by forcing air through a narrow constriction or gap; the actual width of the gap has an effect on the sound.

BREATHY VOICE

As a general rule, at any one place of articulation there is usually only one type of source at a time which is usable linguistically, though occasionally some languages break this rule. Hindi, for example, has a four-way plosive contrast: /p, pʰ, b, bɦ/, in which /bɦ/ is rendered with breathy voice produced by vibrating the vocal cords along only part of their length while allowing the escaping air through the resultant gap to generate frication. The effect is also used stylistically by some speakers, even in English.

35

	f	v	θ	ð	s	z	ʃ	ʒ	h
Lower lip	+	+	−	−	−	−	−	−	−
Upper teeth	+	+	+	+	−	−	−	−	−
Lower teeth	−	−	+	+	−	−	−	−	−
Alveolar ridge	−	−	−	−	+	+	+	+	−
Tongue tip	−	−	+	+	+	+	−	−	−
Tongue blade	−	−	−	−	−	−	+	+	−
Vocal cords	−	+	−	+	−	+	−	+	+

VARIABILITY IN THE PHYSICAL WORLD

In the measurable, *physical* world of actual articulations the picture is much less clear. There is no rigid separation, for example, between the tongue tip and the tongue blade, or between the involvement of the upper teeth and that of the alveolar ridge in an articulation. People all vary slightly as to how they form their own articulations for the sounds in a language, and, perhaps even more importantly, each individual speaker will make sounds slightly differently on each occasion the sound is made. What the classical phoneticians did was to recognise this variability (we discuss sources of variability in Chapter 3) and *remove* it from their charts because it was seen to be irrelevant to the language. After all, if one speaker has a tongue which is slightly longer than another's, or big teeth (or even a missing tooth), then their speech is going to sound slightly different – but this does not make any difference to the language unless the differences are really large. So rather than have some enormous (it would actually be infinite) table showing all possible variations or differences, we cut them all out in favour of a much simpler categorisation based on whether a feature is *linguistically relevant*. Differentiating between what is linguistically relevant and what is not is extremely important.

Notice that we are introducing a form of table different from the usual charts of classical phonetics. We have deliberately chosen this representation to emphasis its *binary* nature. In each of the cells of the matrix we have entered either a + or a −, so that we can indicate unambiguously the presence or absence of the feature in question. This binary representation has been used in phonological theory, where it is called *distinctive feature* notation (see the TUTORIAL – DISTINCTIVE FEATURE THEORY, Chapter 4). The classical phonetics charts do not bring this out very well, but it is clearly implicit, and points unequivocally to the *abstract* nature of the charts. This is why we say that these tables are an *abstract description* of what is actually going on physically. They are not an exact representation reflecting every detail of the physical facts, but a simplified or unvarying representation focusing on *linguistic content*. Technically the systematic omitting of detail and VARIABILITY in this way is called *data reduction*.

When we come to discuss perception in detail (Chapter 7) we shall find an even more important reason for focusing on this abstract representation. Speakers and listeners are *unaware* of most physical details and variations. The representations in the minds of language users (as opposed to phoneticians who are trained to spot details) are much like the tables above in terms of their simplicity and abstraction. We refer to the speakers' and listeners' feelings about speech as *cognitive representations*, and these commonly involve abstract utterance plans and proposed *targets* for a speech sound (TUTORIAL – TARGET THEORY). Cognitive representations of speech sounds are often dealt with in phonological theory rather than phonetic theory, but here we try to take both into account. The reason for this is that the logical conclusion arising from the abstract nature of the classical phonetics charts is that they are *de facto* cognitive representations rather than physical representations. This distinction was not made originally; phoneticians believed that their feelings and intuitions about speech sounds were much more objective than they really are.

STOPS OR PLOSIVES

Much of what we have said about fricatives carries over to stops in terms of classifiers like place of articulation, constriction and periodic vs. aperiodic sources.

Stops are modelled in classical phonetics as *three-phase consonants*; that is, during the course of their durations their basic characteristics change twice. The three phases are: stop, release and aspiration.

The stop phase

During this period, the airflow is stopped off by a total closure of the vocal tract. The concept of place of articulation is prominent here: we categorise stops according to place of articulation, just as we did earlier with fricatives. Stops also come in phonologically voiced/voiceless pairs like fricatives. During the stop phase there is little or no sound in the voiceless version, and an attenuated, or weakened, vocal cord vibration sound penetrating the wall of the neck and the cheeks in the voiced version.

The observations we made about abstraction in fricatives also apply to stops. The voiceless/voiced distinction is binary, abstract and cognitive in origin. In the physical world of phonetics the distinction between presence and absence of vocal cord vibration is not so clear as with the correlate in phonology. Because, to work at all, vocal cord vibration requires a supraglottal air pressure lower than the subglottal air pressure, it is clear that if the airflow is impeded above the vocal cords, then sooner or later the supraglottal air pressure will begin to approach and eventually equal the subglottal air pressure.

This means that vocal cord vibration will falter and eventually fail altogether – even during a stop which is labelled phonologically as [+voice]. By definition all stops involve complete constriction at some point in the vocal tract, and so the airflow must stop sooner or later. In some languages – French is a good example – the vocal cord vibration is stronger and continues longer than it does in English. Here the speaker takes steps to minimise the effects of the stop on the balance of air pressures above and below the vocal cords. This can be done by relaxing the cheek-wall musculature and by lowering the larynx – both ensuring that the oral cavity is enlarged, thereby prolonging the flow of air through the larynx.

The release phase

For both voiceless and voiced stops the second phase is their *release*. The constriction preventing the airflow is released as the articulators are pulled apart actively at a carefully determined moment in time.

- Note that an earlier model of stop production proposed that the articulators were *forced* apart by the ever-increasing air pressure during the stop phase; this

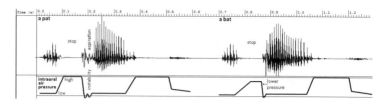

Figure 2.3 Waveform and intraoral air pressure for the two utterances a *pat* and a *bat*. Notice the instability in the intraoral air pressure following the release of [p], and how the effect is less following [b]. The instability prevents early vocal cord vibration in *pat*, whereas in bat the vocal cord vibration starts up just a few milliseconds after the release.

is false. Interestingly, we time the release of a stop identically whether we are speaking normally or for whisper, quiet speech, shouting, etc. This means that the time of the release does *not* correlate with the airflow through the system or the air pressure built up behind the stop, since each of these different ways of speaking requires a different pattern of airflow through the larynx.

When the stop is released the built-up air pressure behind it drops rapidly, disturbing the stability of the entire system, particularly in the region of the vocal cords. Typically the air pressure behind the constriction reaches a higher level during the phonologically voiceless stops than during those which are phonologically voiced. The reason for this is that during the rendering the of voiced ones the vocal cords do vibrate until the supraglottal air pressure gets too high; during the period of weak vibration there is *impedance* to the flow of air into the supraglottal cavity, so less chance for the air pressure to build up as high as it does when the speaker is rendering a voiceless stop. With voiceless stops there is no vocal cord impedance to the airflow, so it builds up above the larynx faster and to a greater degree.

For these reasons the release phase of a voiced stop is a little shorter and accompanied by a lower amplitude of frication than that of a voiceless stop. A shorter release time with a smaller sub-/supraglottal pressure difference means that with voiced stops a stable aerodynamic system is achieved earlier. This impacts on the third phase (Figure 2.3).

The aspiration phase

The third of the three phases modelled by classical phonetics is the *aspiration phase*, which in English occurs only after phonologically voiceless stops. In effect the voiced stops are two-phase since they lack aspiration. The aspiration phase of voiceless stops is characterised as a period of frication with no vocal cord vibration (see **EVALUATION – MODELLING ASPIRATION – THE CLASSICAL PHONETICS AND COARTICULATION SOLUTIONS**). The audible frication is due to the escaping air following the release. These observations in classical phonetics result in the abstract (or phonological) classification of stops in English shown below.

Articulators	p	b	t	d	k	g	ʔ
Lips	+	+	–	–	–	–	–
Tongue/alveolar ridge	–	–	+	+	–	–	–
Tongue/velum	–	–	–	–	+	+	–
Voice	–	+	–	+	–	+	–
Stopped vocal cords	–	–	–	–	–	–	+
Aspiration	+	–	+	–	+	–	–

For the pair [p, b] the construction for the stop is made by bringing the lips together; for [t, d] it is made by bringing the tip or blade of the tongue against the alveolar ridge (occasionally the back of the upper teeth); and for [k, g] by bringing the back of the tongue against the velar area of the palate. For [ʔ] the stop is made by bringing the vocal cords together – hence the physical impossibility of simultaneous vocal cord vibration: there can be no voiced glottal stop in a language. In all cases the stop is made with a degree of force sufficient to prevent the resulting build-up of air pressure from breaking through. Notice the alternation between vibrating vocal cords and aspiration – for classical phonetics these were mutually exclusive in this set of stops: if there is vocal cord vibration there is no aspiration (see **EVALUATION – MODELLING ASPIRATION – THE CLASSICAL PHONETICS AND COARTICULATION THEORY SOLUTIONS**).

AFFRICATES

In classical phonetics, affricates are modelled as a unified sequence of stop and fricative; the IPA transcription reflects this. In English there is one phonologically voiceless/voiced pair of affricates: [tʃ] and [dʒ]. These are single consonants in terms of how they behave linguistically in the phonology, rather like diphthongs in the vowel set (TUTORIAL – VOWELS AND VOWEL-LIKE SOUNDS IN ENGLISH). Sometimes is it useful to think of affricates as *slow-release* plosives. We find this in some accents of English; hence the frequent pronunciation in the Cockney accent of *a cup of tea* as /ə kʌʔ ə tsi/. We use / brackets because this *is planned*.

REMINDER: VOICE

In the table we have used the term *voice* because that is the term used in classical phonetics. There is no argument with this, since the term is abstract and phonological. When considering, though, the physical correlates of phonological voicing it is usually the case that in English vocal cord vibration fails during voiced stops for the reason mentioned above. In some languages (our archetypical example is French) the vocal cord vibration does *not* fail because speakers go to special lengths to keep the vocal cords vibrating.

VOWELS AND VOWEL-LIKE SOUNDS IN ENGLISH

TUTORIAL

MAKING VOWELS

There are a number of features associated with the normal production of all vowels (Ladefoged 2003) in English:

- The vocal cords are vibrating, producing a pulsed airflow to drive the sound. This sometimes fails in unstressed vowels in rapid speech: *education* [ɛdʒɪkeiʃn̩].
- The velum is raised, preventing airflow into the nasal cavity. This sometimes fails between nasal consonants: *man* [mæ̃n].
- Constrictions within the vocal tract are kept wide to prevent closure or the creation of frication. There is sometimes frication with very high vowels, e.g. French *oui!* has almost a very close, often *voiceless*, palatal fricative to replace the [i] – see below.
- The vocal cord source sound produces resonance within the oral cavity to produce the sounds characteristic of the various vowels – e.g. the differing formant patterning associated with different vowels.

With vowels, we are dealing primarily with sound originating at the vibrating vocal cords but which is *modified* by resonance in the vocal tract above the vocal cords. The final sound quality we hear is directly dependent on the size and shape of the oral cavity in which the sound is resonating. We have *direct control* over the size and shape by means of moving the tongue around into well-defined *areas* in the oral cavity – this way we are able consistently to produce the expected differences between the various vowels. In classical phonetics these areas are called tongue *positions*.

So, vowel sounds are made by:

- producing a pulsed, voiced source sound at the vocal cords;
- allowing that sound to resonate in a controlled way in the oral cavity before it passes out of the mouth.

Normally in English, the velum is raised against gravity to keep the velar port closed; this ensures that air does not flow into the nasal cavity and that nasal cavity resonance is kept to an absolute minimum. There are no deliberate nasal vowels in English, though occasionally vowels do become nasalised; that is, air leaks through the velar port.

CLASSIFYING VOWELS

As with consonants, to make sense of the patterning of vowel sounds to distinguish words they need to be systematically classified in a way which indicates how they relate to one another. The relationship is provided by stating how the tongue is moved to different positions in the oral cavity to produce the various resonance effects associated with the different vowels.

The trickiest area for not going too close to the palate is in the extreme front of the oral cavity near the teeth (this is because the jaw, hinged at the back, is most mobile in this area). We do well in English here because we have no vowel sound which is extremely close to the teeth or alveolar ridge. The closest is [i] (as in *beat* [bit]), which is just far enough away to avoid frication. But in French the sound [i]$_{Fr}$ is a little closer to the teeth. An enthusiastic pronunciation of *oui!* [wi]$_{Fr}$ will sometimes produce audible frication, a characteristic of this vowel in some speakers of French.

In classifying our vowel sounds a chart with two axes is used (see Figure 1.1 above). Phoneticians mark out in a stylised way the physical area within which the tongue can move – sometimes called the *vowel trapezoid* or *vowel rectangle*. Whatever terminology is used – whether it is geometrically correct or not – this rigid figure with its squared-off stylisation serves us well in enabling us to talk about *vowel positions* and compare among them. Do note, however, that this stylisation is part of what we call a *process of abstraction*, inasmuch as it does depart from the reality of the actual tongue articulation involved in vowel production. We have already observed that phoneticians regularly make this kind of abstraction, and that it often corresponds more to how sounds are *perceived* than to how they are produced.

DIPHTHONGS

Diphthongs are long vowel articulations during which the tongue moves – shifting its position from one vowel sound to another during its duration. You can hear diphthongs in words like: [ai], *mine* [main], *save* [seiv], *ear* [iə], *moat* [moʊt]. In transcribing these sounds we use a pair of vowel symbols, the first indicating where the sound begins and the second where it ends. You should note, though, that the transcription of diphthongs is much more impressionistic than the transcription of non-diphthongs – the symbols indicate much more where we perceptually feel the sound to start and end. For this reason there is often disagreement and inconsistency when it comes to transcription. In English the greatest effort is put into the initial part of the diphthong, with the sound slightly tailing off as the segment proceeds. In different languages the timing of the transition between the two positions differs, and some languages may well appear to emphasise the second position.

RESONANT VOWEL-LIKE CONSONANTS

English has a number of consonants which have vowel-like features from the point of view of how they are physically made. We call them consonants because in the language they function in the same way as the other consonants – like plosives and fricatives. For the moment, let us just take three possibilities – all voiced approximants, although an earlier term was frictionless continuants.

1. the central approximant [ɹ] in words like *red* [ɹɛd] and *array* [əɹei];
2. the lateral approximant [l] in words like *leaf* [l̪if] and *full* [fʊl̪ˠ];
3. the semi-vowel approximants [w] and [j] in words like *will* [wɪl̪ˠ] and *you* [ju].

Approximants are made using a partial constriction or narrowing of the vocal tract. In [ɹ] the front of the tongue is raised a little to form the narrowing, though there are many variants of this particular sound in the various accents of English. In [l] the tip or blade of the tongue is raised to touch the alveolar ridge or upper teeth, but rather than this forming a complete stop, air is allowed to escape round the sides of the tongue. For [w] there is lip rounding and raising of the tongue towards the back of the palate, and for [j] the front of the tongue is raised towards the centre or front part of the palate. In all approximants there is a relatively free flow of air – not as much as with vowels, but more than with fricatives.

Approximants are transient in nature, in the sense that the mobile articulator does not stop moving at normal rates of utterance: the tongue, for example, moves towards the palate and then away in one continuous gesture. This is reflected in the acoustic signal, where no steady-state configuration is seen on a spectrogram, for example.

NASAL SOUNDS

The backmost part of the velum is muscular and flexible. The musculature can be used to raise the velum against gravity to come into contact with the back wall of the vocal tract (the upper pharyngeal area). Indeed in all languages most sounds are made with this *velar port* closed in this way, preventing air from flowing into the nasal cavity and thence out through the nose. Sounds made like this are called *oral sounds*.

The port, however, can be left open to enable the production of *nasal sounds*.

- Notice carefully the phraseology: the velar port has to be deliberately or *actively* closed to produce oral sounds, but is left open to produce nasal sounds *passively*. Some textbooks imply that the situation is the other way round, confusingly introducing the wrong idea that the closed port is the more 'natural'. It is certainly the case that nasal sounds occur less frequently, but they do require less effort in the sense that the velum does not have to be actively raised against gravity when the speaker is standing or sitting upright.

Although in English all nasal *consonants* are driven by the pulsed airflow of vocal cord vibration (that is, they are *voiced* in the terminology of classical phonetics or phonology), there are several cognate pairs possible among the consonants, depending on whether the velar port is open or closed.

- The bilabial stop [m] for example is the nasal counterpart of the bilabial plosive [b].
- The alveolar stop [n] is the nasal counterpart of the alveolar plosive [d].
- The velar stop [ŋ] is the nasal counterpart of the velar plosive [g].

In these examples the constriction is identical for the nasal and non-nasal sounds, as is the vocal cord vibration; the only difference is whether or not the velar port has been allowed to open to produce the nasal sounds.

Note that in English there are no nasal vowels. In some circumstances, though, oral vowels can have a certain degree of NASALITY – which is not the same as being NASAL. Two examples of this are the words man /mæn/ (pronounced: [mæ̃n]) and moon /mun/ (pronounced: [mũn]). In both these words the vowel section tends to have a lowered velum because the nasal consonants on either side require it to be lowered. Speakers living in some areas of New York City regularly emphasise vowel nasalisation in these environments, though it occurs to some degree in all accents of English.

> **NASAL, NASALITY**
> A sound is a nasal if it requires the velum to be lowered to produce nasal resonance when it is made *and* the resultant sound is linguistically distinctive. A sound is nasalised if for some reason nasality occurs, but the nasality itself is not linguistically distinctive.

ABSTRACTION

TUTORIAL

It is useful in theory building to make a distinction between abstraction and non-abstraction. An object which is *abstract* means that it is not *physically* identifiable except by correlation or representation. Thus in phonetic and phonological theory physical phonetic objects are usually related to abstract phonological objects. If we listen to the acoustic signal produced when someone says the word *cat* we *hear* a virtually continuous physical signal. We may, if we are native speakers of English, assign to this signal an abstract symbolic representation consisting of the sequence of three phonological objects /k/, /æ/, /t/. These objects are not physical; they are abstract labels assigned to a physical signal which in itself may or may not be objectively divisible into three stretches of speech.

There are two difficult points here.

1. Phonology in linguistics is abstract. Ambiguously, we also refer to phonological processes occurring within the speaker/listener. These are cognitive processes which are open to experimental investigation. Some researchers do not think of these processes as abstract in the same way that theories or models are abstract. However, we have tended to think of cognitive processes as abstract because they are not physically measurable. In this book we are trying to contrast the physical and non-physical processes involved in speaking and perceiving, and have emphasised the fact that the methodology of investigating physical events or facts differs from how we investigate non-physical events.

2. Generalisations are abstract at a level beyond their component factors. So for example, we may say that in English final phonological /d/ tends to lose much of its vocal cord vibration when rendered or realised as phonetic [d]. We can also observe that final /b/ does the same. Both these statements are abstract observations based on physical facts. We may then make the predictive generalisation:

> *All phonological [+voice] plosives in English lose much of their vocal cord vibration when phonetically rendered.*

This generalisation is more abstract than the statements which led to it. We can go one stage further and make a higher-level and yet more abstract *predictive* generalisation:

> *All [+voice]* consonants *in English lose much of their vocal cord vibration.*

In other words, there are *degrees* of abstraction. Generalisations are based on observation, but acquire predictive power concerning observations *not yet made.* This enables us to formulate hypotheses to be used as the basis of investigative experimental work (see Chapters 10 and 11).

In speech acoustics one of the main features or parameters of the signal is its duration or timing, which is expressed usually in milliseconds (ms). No such time is carried over to the abstract phonological representation assigned to the signal. Thus, whereas the acoustic signal of the word *cat* may have an overall physical duration of a certain number of ms, and there may be a part of the signal with periodic sound (perhaps corresponding to the sound assigned the label /æ/) with a duration of some other number of ms, the symbolic representation itself cannot indicate this. The most that can be said is that we *feel* certain sounds to have greater *length* (an abstract term corresponding to the physical *duration*) than others.

Some typical physical and abstract correlations are shown in the table below.

Measurable physical phenomenon	Abstract correlation	Descriptive level
Waveform 1	Cognitive intention – /æ/	Phonology
Waveform 2	Phonetic representation – [s]	Phonetics
Duration	Length	Phonology/prosody
Relative timing within an utterance	Rhythm and stress	Phonology/prosody
Frequency	Pitch	Phonology/prosody
Relative frequency within an utterance	Intonation, tone and stress	Phonology/prosody
Amplitude	Loudness	Phonology/prosody
Relative amplitude within an utterance	Stress	Phonology/prosody

Abstractions or abstract *representations* are useful if we want to ignore the variability which is always present in the physical signal. Thus, say the word *cat* several times, and each time it will be slightly different, but because a listener assigns the *same* abstract representation to the signal we say that the words are the same (see *sameness* defined above). The procedure in linguistics (specifically for our purposes, phonology and phonetics) is similar to that performed by a lay speaker/listener. We *think* of speech in terms of an abstract symbolic representation rather than directly in terms of its actual sound wave. The model is deliberately arranged like this to enable us to capture this property of observed speaker/listener behaviour – wherever possible, speech researchers adhere to this principle.

To push the idea to its extreme limits: technically no two sounds produced by a human being can ever be objectively and physically identical, and thus no two words could ever be classed as the same on only this basis. Part of the subjectivity of human beings is the solution to this problem. Human beings are extremely good at recognising sameness in their sensory data, and they do this by a process of assignment (see Chapter 7). In computer speech recognition, the problem is extreme for the simple reason that computers are much more objective than people – they have to be taught how words are similar to prevent them recognising every single word they 'hear' as different. Computers are extremely good at recognising difference. This is the main reason why getting a computer to behave like a human being is very difficult (see Chapter 9 where we talk a little about applications).

MODELLING ASPIRATION – THE CLASSICAL PHONETICS AND COARTICULATION SOLUTIONS

EVALUATION

There are difficulties associated with the aspiration concept as used in classical phonetics. Aspiration in that model refers to the period of aperiodic sound immediately following a voiceless plosive [p, t, k] release in languages such as English. This is the third phase of a three-phase stop consonant. This third phase does not occur in phonologically voiced stops [b, d, g].

Some researchers prefer to model all stops as two-phase. This leaves the problem of what to do with the aspiration period. In Coarticulation Theory this third period is modelled as a failure of intended vocal cord vibration at the beginning of the vowel (or other phonologically voiced consonant) following the plosive. The argument goes like this: the speaker's intention is to produce just two phases for the stop consonant – stop and release phases. But with voiceless plosives the considerable intraoral air-pressure drop following the release is such that the delicate balance required for spontaneous vocal cord vibration and for the subsequent voiced segment (consonants like [l] or [r], or vowels) is violated and the voicing fails until the balance is restored. This can take between 10 ms and perhaps 100 ms. During this time all we hear is aperiodic sound associated with the escaping air. But what has failed is the vocal cord vibration for the start of the subsequent voiced sound – it is not a part of the stop itself.

The competing models can be tested. When there is aspiration, is the duration of the vowel less than when there is no aspiration? The second, more modern model above

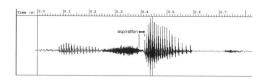

Figure 2.4 Waveform of the utterance *he sa*t. Notice the brief period of aspiration following the frication for [s]. The increase in air pressure during the fricative is sufficient to create a brief period at the beginning of the vowel during which vibration fails.

would predict a *yes* in answer to this question. Look again at Figure 2.3 above; you can see that the period of vocal cord vibration following the release of [p] has less duration than the period following [b]. This tends to indicate that aspiration has *used up* a portion of the vowel. An added advantage to this more recent model is that all stops can now be regarded as symmetrical: all have now just two phases.

The coarticulation-based model rests on the build-up of intraoral air pressure (behind the stop and above the larynx). It would predict that any build-up would produce a similar result proportional to its extent. So even fricatives would produce the same effect; *see* [si] should show a period of aspiration after the [s]; and this is indeed the case (see Figure 2.4).

FURTHER READING

Cruttenden, A. (2008), *Gimson's Pronunciation of English*, Oxford: Oxford University Press.

Hewlett, N. and J. Beck (2006), *An Introduction to the Science of Phonetics*, Mahwah, NJ: Lawrence Erlbaum Associates.

Jones, D. (1918), *An Outline of English Phonetics*, 9th edn 1962, Cambridge: Heffers.

Ladefoged, P. (2003), *Vowels and Consonants*, 3rd edn 2006, Oxford: Blackwell.

Ladefoged, P. (2006), *A Course in Phonetics*, 5th edn, Boston, MA: Thompson, Wadsworth.

Wells, J. (1982), *Accents of English*, Cambridge: Cambridge University Press.

CHAPTER 3 – THE FOUNDATION RESEARCH

INTRODUCTION

There have been a number of important ideas about speech production and perception over the past century or so. In this chapter we have selected a few to look at, some in more detail than others. We take a historical approach, noting especially those researchers and their ideas which have been responsible for significant progress leading to current theories.

THREE EARLY RESEARCHERS

Henry Sweet (1845–1912)

Sweet's *Handbook of Phonetics* (1877) is arguably the landmark publication signalling the start of modern phonetics, certainly in Britain and Europe. One important innovation developed by Sweet was a transcription system he termed *broad romic,* since its symbols were based on the Roman alphabet and were used not so much to represent the detail of the pronunciation of speech sounds but as labels for the way in which various sounds seemed to *group*. A second level of transcription, *narrow romic*, included some additional details enabling the separate identification of members of the groups gathered under the symbols of the broad representation. It could be said that the insight embodied in the idea of grouping sounds, giving the groups labels, identifying members of groups, giving *them* labels, and formally distinguishing between two types of representation foreshadowed the later, more formal concept of the phoneme and its attendant allophones. The actual symbol system Sweet proposed was adopted by the International Phonetic Association as the basis of the IPA (International Phonetic Alphabet).

In Sweet's *Handbook* we find him outlining a two-dimensional 3 × 3 vowel matrix. There are nine fixed cells in the matrix: high front, mid front, low front, high back, mid back, low back, high mixed, mid mixed and low mixed. Each of these cells can be further divided into nine cells. This is an important foreshadowing of Jones' later, perhaps better-defined, but certainly more formal, cardinal vowel system. There is an important difference, however: Sweet's version maps out nine cells in a matrix, while Jones locates a number of points on a grid (see the chart in TUTORIAL

47

– CARDINAL VOWELS). It is Jones' idea which prevails into modern times.

Daniel Jones (1881–1967)

Daniel Jones was a prominent English phonetician and a leader in the development of classical phonetics within a linguistics framework (Jones 1918). He was concerned with the *linguistic* description of pronunciation rather than the theory of speech production and perception. Importantly, he firmed up the concept of *phoneme,* discussed first on a formal basis by the Polish linguist Jan Baudouin de Courtenay (1845–1929) in various publications towards the end of the nineteenth and into the twentieth century (TUTORIAL – PHONEMES AND ALLOPHONES).

In a further theoretically important innovation, Jones realised that the usual way of describing vowels in terms of coordinates on the traditional chart only makes sense if the boundaries of the chart can be formally defined. In a move towards introducing fixed coordinates – at least for a single speaker – Jones proposed the cardinal vowel system for relating vowels to each other and to their oral tongue positions (TUTORIAL – CARDINAL VOWELS).

The obvious difficulty which arises from vowel charts in general is the transfer of the notion of *tongue placement* – something in the physical world – to an abstract, two-dimensional chart. The placing of a dot on a graph by phoneticians – whilst being meaningful within the theory – cannot in the end be anything other than a subjective impression of how the vowels relate to one another in *some* space, though the space is almost certainly a *cognitive*, perceptual one rather than a *physical*, spatial one. The reason for saying this is that although rudimentary X-ray pictures of tongue placement were available at the time, most phonetic data was based on the auditory observations of trained phoneticians. There have been attempts in modern times to relate phoneticians' auditory impressions to measurements of acoustic signals, plotting centre formant frequencies of vowels on a two-dimensional graph using the *x*-axis for the frequency of F2 (the second formant) and the *y*-axis for the frequency of F1 (the first formant) with the origin of the graph in the top right corner. These plots look remarkably like phoneticians' vowel charts.

Nikolai Trubetskoy (1890–1938)

It was Trubetskoy who pointed out that Baudouin de Courtenay had defined the phoneme as 'the psychic equivalent of the speech sound' (1939, 1971: 37). He showed that there could be several speech sounds corresponding to the same phoneme, 'each having its own psychic equivalent', and this *could not be* – strong words indeed. Trubetskoy is pointing out that the members of the allophonic group identified with a particular phoneme can sometimes differ widely. For example, we have noted that in English the phoneme /t/ can have a wide range of allophones which are not just those which are accidental in the sense that they arise because of coarticulatory constraint: an example of this would be the dental [t̪] in the word *eighth* – the coarticulatory influence of the interdental fricative following. Trubetskoy is referring to what we call extrinsic allophones (see Chapter 1), which are derived by cognitive phonological processes and therefore have each a 'psychic equivalent' – that is, each has a corresponding cognitive unit which is not a phoneme. An example of this in English might be the two extrinsic allophones [l̠ⱼ] and [l̠ᵧ], clear [l] and dark [l] respectively, which are used in phonological plans and derived by phonological processes from the underlying unit /l/:

l ⟹ l̠ⱼ at the beginning of a syllable before the vowel;

l ⟹ l̠ᵧ at the end of a syllable or before a consonant at the end of a syllable.

These rules are optional in the sense that we need not apply them; in other words their use is a matter of cognitively driven choice. Rules deriving intrinsic or coarticulated allophones like the dental [t̪] above are phonetic rules which under normal conditions are not optional (but see the explanation of 'cognitive supervision/management' below).

Specifically, Trubetskoy models the process of identifying speech sounds in a continuous waveform by a cognitive process which matches stretches of the speech wave to specific phonemes. Using modern terminology we would say that we use the sound wave to enable us to *assign* appropriate *phoneme labels* to an utterance. These labels must be known to the listener in advance – that is, the listener must know at least the phonological units of the language, and probably the phonological processes as well. Since phonemes are abstract objects it is *not possible* to assign boundaries to the labels by inspection of the sound wave. Trubetskoy is clear that 'the speech sound can only be defined in terms of its relation to the phoneme' (1939, 1971: 38). From our perspective, and using *our* terminology, this means that a stretch of speech audio can only have 'meaning' or be a proper stretch of speech by reference to its ability to have appropriate labels assigned to it.

Trubetskoy was aware of Jones' 1918 definition of the phoneme, but believed that he related the idea too closely to transcription rather than to phonological considerations. We leave Trubetskoy with a quotation:

The phoneme can be defined satisfactorily neither on the basis of its psychological nature nor on the basis of its relation to the phonetic variants, but purely and solely on the basis of its function in the system of language. (1939, 1971: 40)

Trubetskoy distances himself, therefore, from starting with cognitive considerations or – the other side of the coin – from phonetic considerations. For him the idea of the phoneme is simply a notion assisting in understanding the phonological system of language.

SOME LATER RESEARCH

Continuous speech vs. discrete representations

Although it had been known for several decades that articulation and the speech waveform are more or less continuous, it was only around the early 1960s that speech researchers began to consider seriously the relationship between the static, segment-by-segment modelling of classical phonetics and the dynamic continuousness of the speech waveform. What was needed was a formal model which could relate the abstract descriptions of classical phonetics to the waveforms, spectrograms and other representations of the physical side of speech (Tatham and Morton 2010). This was to be the heyday of acoustic phonetics (see Lehiste 1967), with other experimental techniques such as air-pressure and airflow studies also coming forward. Perhaps the biggest single impetus stemmed from the general availability from the end of the 1940s of the SOUND SPECTROGRAPH, able to display fairly quickly spectrograms of short bursts of recorded speech.

SOUND SPECTROGRAPH
A software package or, earlier, a hardware device able to display an analysis of a speech waveform into its constituent parameters of frequency, amplitude and time. Generally the display takes the form of a graph, the *spectrogram*, in which the vertical *y*-axis represents frequency, the horizontal *x*-axis represents time and the *z*-axis represents amplitude. The *z*-axis is shown on the two-dimensional screen (or, before computer screens, on paper) as variations in colour or levels of grey.

What was becoming obvious from the dozens of experiments being conducted on the acoustics of speech was that the traditional classical phonetics descriptions were no longer adequate for characterising our observations about speech dynamics, let alone explaining them formally. It seemed necessary to have a new way of reconciling the discontinuous symbolic or alphabetic representations such as the IPA with the continuous appearance of spectrograms, waveforms and images of other parameters such as airflow, air pressure and electromyography signals (see 'Electromyography', Chapter 10).

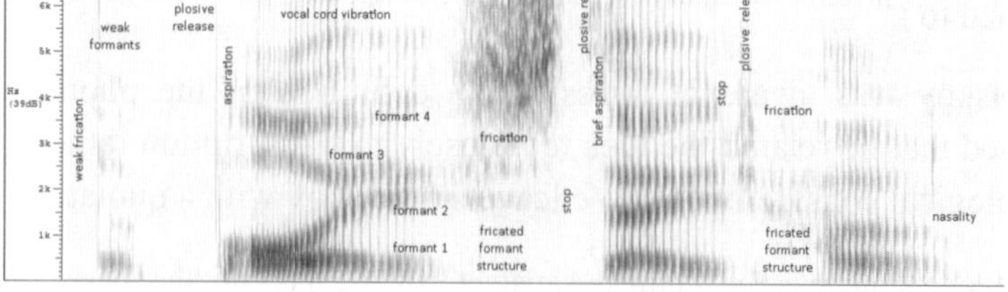

Figure 3.1 Spectrogram of the utterance *The boy stayed home.*

As with the development of any science there was a natural reluctance to reject the traditional views altogether, and instead theorists began to examine ways of linking the abstract representations with the experimentally observable physical facts, rather than simply reject the SEGMENT-BASED REPRESENTATIONS of classical phonetics.

SEGMENT-BASED REPRESENTATIONS

Segment- or symbol-based representations like the IPA for phonetics–but in fact all spelling systems which use letters to represent sounds-have been retained for a very important reason: human beings seem to represent speech in their minds using discrete segments. There is a great deal of evidence for this (see Chapters 7 and 8), and the idea carries through in both linguistics and psychology.

To our knowledge it has not been seriously claimed that representations of speech in the mind are other than basically segmental, and this is probably why most writing systems use the segmental approach. There *are* some writing systems that identify syllable-sized (e.g. Japanese *kana*) or morpheme-sized (e.g. Mandarin Chinese) segments as basic units of representation, but even here it is claimed that there is evidence of discrete sound segments in the way speakers of these languages think of speech. Any apparent discrepancy between the physical world and the cognitive world underlines the need for us to try to understand how the two relate.

Syllable-based writing systems tend to derive from a language's phonological *structure*, whereas morpheme-based systems tend to derive from morphological *structure*. Sound-segment-based-systems emphasise the phonological and phonetic *inventories* of the language. Inventories reflect the set of available units in phonology or phonetics, but do not of themselves reveal much of its structure. For example, a list of sounds does not itself tell us how such sounds may be continued.

The beginnings of a theory

The most obvious way forward in the 1960s was to elaborate on a theory which was based on the following formal idea:

String of underlying   Transformation →   Continuous derived
discrete symbols →   waveform

The hypothesis was that speech begins in the mind of the speaker as a representation involving a linear sequence of discrete SYMBOL-type objects, but that on their journey through the speech production process (later to be called *rendering*) they become continuous, acquiring the transitions seen in spectrograms. Notice that in this first shot at a model, we still identify discrete objects, but speak now also of transitions between them. The idea was that the transitions provide the continuousness. If the transitions can be linked to processes external to the system, then they *explain* the continuousness. This was what Coarticulation Theory tried to do (see the TUTORIAL – COARTICULATION THEORY).

SYMBOL

A symbol is an abstract representation of something else – in our case an abstract representation of physical speech, in which each symbol represents a speech sound. The term is ambiguous, meaning on the one hand the symbols which phoneticians use (for example, the alphabetic symbols of the IPA) and on the other the objects found in symbolic representations in the minds of speakers. Remember at all times that the symbol is *not* the object itself: it is an *abstract representation* of that object. So, for example, [i] is *not* a sound or an articulation: it is a *representation* of these, and is therefore distinct or detached from them.

51

The idea of transformation is also found in the linguistic theory prevalent at the time: Transformational Generative Grammar. Linguistic processing in a speaker's mind was seen as a cascade of processes reflecting progressively less abstract levels until we end up with a speech waveform. Theories incorporating this idea were later to be referred to as *translation theories* (see 'Action Theory' in Chapter 4), where the cascaded processes linked representations as they moved from one level of abstraction to another (TUTORIAL – TRANSLATION THEORIES).

Deep/underlying
representation
↓
Translation
process
↓
Surface/derived
representation

The linguistic derivation of surface intrinsic allophonic representations

Abstract phonological and phonetic processes are used to derive a fully specified representation from the underlying minimal phonemic representation in two stages, one phonological and one phonetic, shown in the table below.

Phonology				*Phonetics*		
Underlying representa-tion →	Phonological processes →	Derived representation		Underlying representa-tion →	Phonetic processes →	Derived represen-tation
STRING of UNITS	RULES	STRING of UNITS – the UTTERANCE PLAN	Abstract/physical interface	Copied STRING of UNITS	RULES	STRING of UNITS
Phonemes		Extrinsic allophones		Extrinsic allophones		Intrinsic allo-phones

The underlying representation of the phonology, as well as the derived representation, comprises a timeless or static description of a string of abstract segments. Although we have used the term 'phoneme' to name the deepest units for the sake of some compatibility with classical phonetics, other terms have been used: underlying segments, morpho-phonemes, systematic phonemic units. The derived representation shown here using extrinsic allophone units is copied across to form the entry-level representation of the phonetics.

- The derived representation in the phonology is the UTTERANCE PLAN in the model we favour, since it specifies how the speaker *intends* the utterance to sound. In effect, the utterance plan is the blueprint for PHONETIC RENDERING.

> **UTTERANCE PLAN**
>
> In dynamically focused approaches to speech production modelling (see Chapter 4) the utterance plan is a formal abstract statement of what a speaker intends to offer up for phonetic rendering. The utterance plan contains all the necessary information for
>
> 1. segmental rendering to proceed, and
> 2. careful monitoring and supervision of the rendering process to achieve an optimum acoustic signal.
>
>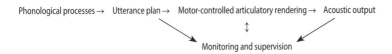
>
> Phonological processes → Utterance plan → Motor-controlled articulatory rendering → Acoustic output
>
> $\updownarrow$
>
> Monitoring and supervision
>
> The effects of articulatory rendering are monitored and used to supervise the rendering process. This ensures that the acoustic output is suitable for perception by the listener (see 'Production for Perception' in Chapter 7). The supervising *agent* has access to the plan and to the overall result – the acoustic output. An on-going iterative process ensures a suitable acoustic output for perception to take place.

PHONETIC RENDERING

Phonetic rendering is a modern cover term for the processes which convert an utterance plan into an acoustic signal. In classical phonetics the term phonetic realisation was often used; it is an informal equivalent to the more formal rendering. So classical phonetics phoneticians might have said something like:

> *The /l/ is realised as a dark [lˠ] in final position in English words, and as a clear [l] at the beginning of words immediately before a vowel*

if referring to the planned phonological variants of /l/, or

> *The /t/ is realised as dental rather than alveolar if it precedes an interdental fricative*

as in the word *width* /wɪdθ/, which has the surface representation [wɪt̪θ].

Following traditional generative linguistics, phonetic processes govern the translation of the underlying representation of the PHONETICS into its derived representation. Like the other components of the grammar, phonetics is itself multi-layered. Thus we recognise that

- at the start of phonetics the representation is abstract and mental (or cognitive), and comprises a string of phonologically derived segments;

- after appropriate phonetic processes the output takes the form of a string of intrinsic allophones.

There is need for care here. The phonetic output is *characterised* as a string of intrinsic allophonic segments. These are not sounds. They are labels which linguists assign to stretches of articulation or sound wave, and unlike the sound wave itself they are an abstract representation of the output of the human phonetic processes. We repeat that it is often helpful to distinguish between phonology and phonetics as parts of the descriptive system of linguistics, and the phonological and phonetic processes which human beings undertake. The human processes are called phonological and phonetic because phonology and phonetics are those areas of linguistics which we use to describe them – helpful in one way, but confusing in another.

PHONETICS

In generative linguistics, at least originally, phonetics played a minor role. Phonetic realisation of the output of the phonology was seen as largely an automatic process of little or no linguistic significance, in the sense that no linguistic or meaning-related information could be added during this component. This approach was fairly typical, and is exemplified in publications such as *The Sound Pattern of English* (Chomsky and Halle 1968). Later, phonetics was seen as helping explain some phonological processes, such as assimilation (see 'Unifying the Approach' below). In more recent times phonetics has had a more important explanatory role in phonology. Meanwhile in contemporary phonetic theory phonetic processes are seen as extending meaning-related information, especially in terms of pragmatics and expressive content (see Chapter 6).

- It is important to realise that the final representation in phonetics – a string of intrinsic allophones – is still abstract and symbolic: it is *not* the articulation or the sound wave, but a symbolic representation of the *potential* of these.

In taking a mentalistic or cognitively based approach to knowledge, linguistics enumerates all the knowledge necessary for characterising all possible sentences in the language, and a phonetic component built in the same way would characterise all possible utterance renderings of those sentences – *not* a rendering of any one utterance in particular. Many allied disciplines which need the support of linguistics (see Chapter 9) find that this constraint is too severe, and call for a linguistics and phonetics which enable *selection between sentences*, and therefore are able to characterise what happens for a *single* chosen sentence. The strength of linguistics lies in its generality, but this does not always suit particular potential applications of the discipline.

In the physical world we believe there is a series of processes which accounts for the translation of the string of discrete abstract segments – the extrinsic allophonic representation of the utterance plan – into a representation of a continuously changing pattern of sound. The overall process is a complex one, particularly because *in our model* a transition from abstract to physical is included.

Phonology in the diagram above (p. 52) is a characterisation of the cognitive processes *known* by the speaker, and then, by extending the knowledge-based model, *used* by the speaker to convert the underlying representation into the representation of a plan for a specific utterance. The utterance plan is then used as the basis for controlling the musculature to produce the aerodynamic and acoustic effects which form the acoustic speech signal itself – the rendering processes.

This is a difficult and complex part of speech production theory. The diagram on p. 52 is a model using a symbolic representation of the speaker's static knowledge irrespective of whether or not it is currently being used. Remember: a symbolic representation of an object or event is not the object or event itself, just a representation of it.

In the phonetics part of the diagram, there are several incompatibilities between the input (a string of extrinsic allophones) and output (a string of intrinsic allophones):

- The input is a representation of something cognitive and the output is a representation of something physical (or, respectively, abstract and concrete).

- Time is introduced somehow during the phonetic encoding, since it is essential in understanding some phonetic processes such as coarticulation.

- The discrete character of individual segments at the input becomes lost to the representation of a continuous sound wave at the output, in which it is not possible to find much indication of earlier separate segments.

Phonetics has the job of accounting for these discrepancies, and explaining how the various mechanisms we have been discussing play a role in this translation process – including the addition of time, still rather vague in contemporary speech production models (but see – 'Action Theory' and 'Cognitive Phonetics' in Chapter 4).

Time in translation theories

The introduction of *real time* (as opposed to the abstract notional time of phonology) is very controversial: we are by no means sure how to place this in the model. One idea is that a rhythm generator is incorporated into the production system. It is suggested that the signal provided by the rhythm generator is used in phonetic processes to control the timing of SYLLABLE-sized strings in the incoming phonological representation. There is evidence to suggest that the cerebellum (see definition, Chapter 9) generates rhythmic processes or signals which might be used in speech production timing (Corr 2006).

> **SYLLABLE**
>
> The syllable is an abstract linguistic unit in the phonological component of a grammar. Syllables are defined in terms of how classes of segment sequence. In a language like English, a syllable consists of a consonantal *onset* consisting of up to three consonants, a vocalic *nucleus* consisting of a single vowel, and a consonantal *coda* consisting of up to four consonants. Languages vary as to how many consonants might be involved in the onset and coda parts of the surface syllable; there are usually language-specific constraints on the order in which consonants can sequence, as well as general constraints. The syllable is generally modelled in terms of a structure behind this surface manifestation. In classical phonetics some researchers attempted to define a physical phonetic syllable, but no physical definition has been really successful.

The rhythm generator appears to pace the articulation of the vocalic (or vowel-based) syllable nuclei, allowing the consonants to take care of themselves, but this is controversial and by no means certain. The *phonetic* process of timing requires the identification of individual syllables within the phonology, some have argued, and those models of phonology which do not say much about the syllable would clearly be of little use feeding the phonetics. Several comparatively recent phonological models, however, do characterise in some detail the syllabic structure of the derived-level representation. Syllables are the basic units of speech prosody (see Chapter 10).

Coarticulation

The blurring, running together or overlapping of individual segments to produce a smooth, continuous sound has received considerable attention since the early 1960s (Bell-Berti *et al.* 1995). Various models have been proposed, mostly centring on the phenomenon known as *coarticulation* (Daniloff and Hammarberg 1973). In earlier phonetic theories, coarticulation referred to the simultaneous articulation of certain segmental features, but in the modern theory COARTICULATION is about the overlapping of

> **REMINDER: COARTICULATION**
>
> Coarticulation is the blending together or overlap of adjacent segments when they are spoken, or phonetically rendered. Phonology tends to keep segments distinct, even within the syllable structure, but when we come to speak they blur into one another to produce a near-continuous sound wave. A major contributor to coarticulation is the inertia in the mechanical system of the vocal tract and organs of speech, and since inertia is time-dependent the degree of overlap of segments appears to be usually greatest when the speech is being delivered fast (TUTORIAL – COARTICULATION THEORY)

discrete segments to produce a continuous signal (**EVALUATION – COARTICULATION OF SEGMENTS VS. SYLLABLES**).

The input to motor control appeared to be a string of discrete units, but its output – articulator movement – appeared smooth or continuous, as did the resulting aerodynamics and sound wave. The answer was Coarticulation Theory (TUTORIAL – COARTICULATION THEORY), which appeared in the first half of the 1960s.

Much of coarticulation is thought to result from mechanical effects, especially inertia in the movement of the organs of speech. Since these have mass and their movement is in real time, there is always going to be some INERTIA. The peripheral mechanical system of the vocal tract is almost certainly going to be more cumbersome than the brain's physical correlates of the mental processing which controls it. Abstract MENTAL PROCESSING correlating with the brain's physical electrochemical system is fast and can accommodate rapid and abrupt changes from one segment to another, but the vocal system requires much more time to move from one segment to another because of the mechanical inertia of the system and the mass of its component articulators. The theory assumes that the mental system drives the mechanical system just a little too fast for it to accomplish these abrupt changes from segment to segment satisfactorily, resulting in a blurring together of segments, and consequent loss of their boundaries and distinct individual identities. On occasions so much of a mismatch may occur that articulations bear little resemblance to, say, the leisurely (but quite artificial) articulation of a single isolated segment (Keating 1990).

> **INERTIA**
>
> Inertia is a technical term expressing the reluctance of an object to change its motion state, either from no motion to some motion, or to slow down, or speed up.

> **MENTAL PROCESSING**
>
> The question of cerebral vs. mental processing is not being addressed here, though of course it is important. The simple position being taken by proponents of the coarticulation model sees the physical brain's neural system as *accommodating* the mind's abstract cognitive processing.
>
> *Cognitive processing* can be understood as an abstract perspective on *neural processing*. One of the advantages of using the newer network-based models (see explanation of 'neural networks', Chapter 4) is that the model framework (the mathematical formulation or the net) is common to modelling *both* cognitive and neural processes.

So, for example, in the planned sequence /əki/, for the phrase *a key*, we might find the rendered [k̟] so far fronted that it is more like the palatal plosive [c], which does not occur in English.

- If [c] did occur in English there might well be an ambiguity arising between the phrase [əki] and the supposed phrase [əci] because the places of articulation associated with [c] and [k] are so close that reliable separation is not really possible. A general principle here is that phonological and phonetic systems do not undertake to include articulations and sounds which are difficult to keep separate in either production or perception. This principle is explicitly included in cognitive phonetics (Tatham 1986b, and see Chapter 4).

It is claimed in Coarticulation Theory that the tongue is literally pulled forward to produce the fronted stop. A similar situation occurs round the other way in the phrase *a car*, /əkɑ/, in which the rendered [k̲] is retracted or pulled right back on the velum. The displacement of the tongue position is not planned – it is an involuntary effect explained by a combination of the inertia in the tongue's movement and the available time for the gesture.

One obvious question arises here: what is the upper limit of acceptable blurring? This is usually answered by suggesting that in normal speaking the dominant mental control drives the articulatory system as fast as possible consistent with enabling efficient decoding on the part of any listener. This is quite a claim, for it implies that the speaker is mindful of the listener's perceptual system and takes this into account as an integral part of speaking. In the theory this is referred to as production for perception, implying that no speech is produced without intending it to be perceived and without adjustment based on the speaker's knowledge of the processing properties of the perceptual system (see 'Production for Perception' in Chapter 7).

Some researchers have attempted, with more or less success, to show that there are coarticulatory effects taking place at the neurophysiological level and at the acoustic level, but mechanical and aerodynamic effects continue to be thought of as mostly responsible for the loss of distinct segments somewhere between phonology and sound. In phonetics the term *target* refers to the articulatory segment which would have been produced (i.e. the one intended) had it not been for coarticulatory effects preventing its full realisation (see TUTORIAL – TARGET THEORY in Chapter 2). Those coarticulatory effects which are thought of as mechanical are described in a detailed model using equations derived from mechanics, and are therefore seen as non-linguistic.

Where in speech production does discrete become continuous?

In investigating the mismatch between underlying discrete segment representations and surface continuous speech representations one of the main questions is:

- *Where* in the translation process from underlying representation (corresponding to the phonemic representations of classical phonetics or the underlying systematic phonemic representations of the transformational phonologists of the time) to waveform did discreteness give way to continuousness?

There are several candidate areas where this could happen, because the translation process is multi-layered, and each is open to scientific investigation, as shown in the table below.

Area of investigation	Field of study	Result
Underlying phonemic string		
↓ Phonetic string – utterance plan	Linguistic intuition – psychology	Discreteness
↓ Motor control of the articulators	Control of the articulators – neurophysiology	*Discreteness/ continuousness*
↓ Aerodynamic processes	Airflow patterns – aerodynamics	Continuousness
↓ Acoustic processes	Acoustic patterns – acoustics	Continuousness
Surface waveform		

It was clear when this question was first seriously addressed in the 1960s (Cooper 1966) that underlying cognitive areas of speech production seemed to involve discreteness: speakers do not feel that their thoughts involve anything other than discrete objects; lay listeners have little or no awareness of the continuousness of the signals we hear. It was also clear that in the physically measurable areas of aerodynamics and acoustics, discreteness was almost impossible to detect. It had to be the case that the translation occurs around the area of the motor control of the articulators and their subsequent movement. Consequently there was a considerable experimental investment between the mid-1960s and the mid-1970s in trying to find out as much as possible about how the articulators were actually controlled. This work was in effect a continuation of earlier 1950s experiments on formant transitions (TUTORIAL – FORMANT TRANSITIONS) in plosive + vowel sequences.

Task Dynamics

Task dynamics in speech production theory is a model which focuses on the way in which a speaker achieves the goals of rendering gestural requirements detailed in the utterance plan. Linked elements in the production system – articulators or muscles – behave in a dynamic, coordinated way to achieve these goals.

Articulatory Phonology

Action Theory (Fowler, from 1977) and Cognitive Phonetics (Tatham and Morton, from 1980; see Chapter 4 for an explanation of both) attempted to redefine the scope of phonology and phonetics (detailed in Tatham and Morton 2006).

On the one hand, Action Theory had taken many of the phenomena previously associated with purely cognitive phonology and relocated them to the periphery: they now became intrinsic to the motor control system and lost their direct relationship with cognitive processing. In particular many of these now low-level processes became part of the internal functioning of coordinative structures. Fowler argued that the model of motor control which allowed for individual control of muscles directly from the motor cortex should be superseded by a model which groups muscles and enhances a relatively simple central control by detail *known* at the periphery. Fowler described an appropriate mathematics for characterising coordinative structures, timing and *coproduction* (the new version of coarticulation). Tatham described an appropriate computational paradigm (the object-oriented model (TUTORIAL – THE OBJECT-ORIENTED PROGRAMMING PARADIGM)) for simulating the processes by computer.

On the other hand, cognitive phonetics introduced *cognitive* processing – previously reserved for physical processes – into the domain of phonetics. The point here was that there are many phonetic phenomena which are intrinsic to the physical mechanism (coarticulatory or coproduction processes) which are nevertheless open to limited COGNITIVE SUPERVISION. Cognitive supervision or management could be used to modify low-level *physical* coarticulatory processes either to provide systematic alternates (variation, for example, in the way different dialects of English succumb to such phenomena at a purely phonetic level – e.g. inter-nasal nasalisation of phonologically oral vowels) or even to provide contrastive phonological segments (the systematic manipulation, for example, of aerodynamic constraints on vocal cord vibration following plosives – e.g. the provision of different 'lengths' of aspiration for contrastive purposes).

COGNITIVE SUPERVISION

Some physical processes which would otherwise proceed automatically can be constrained or even enhanced by the process of cognitive supervision or management. If physical processes like coproduction are predicted and on-going rendering is generally monitored, decisions can be taken to constrain these processes if they are predicted to make for less than optimum perception.

Cognitive supervision can be taken further. By systematically interfering with coproduction processes it is possible to add to a language's phonological inventory: that is, make newly produced sounds usable systematically at a phonological level. An example of this would be the constraining of the coarticulatory delay introduced into vocal cord timing following initial [–voice] plosives. English probably has the delay unconstrained, as in the word *peep* (/pip/$_{Eng}$ → [p^{h}ip]), but the theory would suggest that the delay is constrained in the French word *pipe* (/pip/$_{Fr}$ → [pip], with no or very little aspiration). The possible French word *bipe* (/bip/$_{Fr}$ → [bip]) has some enhancement leading to *pre-voicing* – the vocal cord vibration begins before the release of the [b].

Still the problem remained, though, of the continuing separation of phonology and phonetics. Browman and Goldstein (1986) sought to unify phonological and phonetic descriptions in speech production by the introduction of a common mathematics, and in particular a common graphical representation of the two. Some progress was made towards solving the problem, but unfortunately their theory, Articulatory Phonology, still fails to meet the goal.

Unifying the approach

There are a number of fronts on which the problem of unification of the phonological and phonetic models needs to be tackled. It is not a simple matter to unify two such different theories: on the one hand phonology is entirely abstract (though it does attempt to derive some explanation from the phonetic area to account for processes like assimilation – contemporary phonological theory goes further than this simple example), and deals with cognitive processes associated with what we know of the sound patterning of our languages. These processes contribute to how we plan the phonetic execution of an utterance. Phonetics, on the other hand, is almost entirely physical, while at the same time obtaining its 'instructions' concerning what articulatory gestures are required from the phonological area in the form of the utterance plan.

Units

One area where unification is essential is in the choice of units of representation. Traditionally, generative phonology uses a number of units of different sizes, such as feature, phoneme, extrinsic allophone and syllable. Processes which are characterised in phonology involve one or more of these units: they are concerned with the manipulation of either:

- features, as in the characterisation of what is and is not possible in terms of feature combinations – you might want to say, for example, that in English all segments which are [+nasal] are also [+voice] (e.g. /m/, /ŋ/); or

- phonemes/allophones, as in accounting for alternates in particular contextual environments – in English we like a clear or palatalised /lʲ/ before a vowel, but a dark or velarised /lˠ/ at the end of a word or before a consonant at the end of a word (e.g. *leaf* /lʲif/, *feel* /filˠ/, *milk* /mɪlˠk/) (the transcriptions here represent utterance plans, and the symbols therefore represent extrinsic allophones); or

- syllables, when expressing the units of prosodic phenomena or the behaviour of stress patterning; for example, we might want to say that the word *content* is pronounced in two different ways depending on whether it is a noun or an adjective (e.g. noun /ˈkɒn.tɛnt/ – stress on the first syllable, adjective /kən.ˈtɛnt/ – stress on the second syllable) (the transcriptions here use ' to represent a following stressed syllable, and . to represent a syllable boundary).

Features used in describing segments in phonology are a mixture of articulatory (e.g. [±high]), acoustic/perceptual (e.g. [±strident]) and psycholinguistic (e.g. [±consonantal]); the choice of particular features is not transparently principled. Linguistic units such as features and syllables are highly abstract, making it as impossible to locate them in a sound wave as it is the more usual articulatory or sound segments.

Browman and Goldstein addressed the question by going back to basics to consider alternative units of phonological representation. They started by conceptualising phonology as a set of goal-driven processes. This idea accords well with task dynamics (effectively a more formal development of Action Theory) and the object-oriented computational model of production. The next task was to consider how those goals might be represented in terms of plausible psycho-physical units. The researchers chose a very simple model of speech production which centred on the aerodynamic production of sounds: the overall task of phonology is to specify at what places in the vocal tract airflow is to be impeded – these are *points of constriction* and can be made anywhere in the vocal tract where there is at least one mobile articulator to move towards another mobile or fixed articulator. Possibilities range from bilabial constriction at one end of the tract to glottal constriction (vocal cords touching under tension) at the other end. These areas of constriction were named *tract variables*.

Unification with phonology is achieved by expressing phonological goals (for us, the plan) in terms of these tract variables, and then by describing subsequent phonetic phenomena resulting from rendering in terms of the aerodynamics/acoustics of airflow impedance.

- Notice that these units are on a level with the kind of features found earlier – either the *abstract* phonological features or the *physical* features of classical phonetics. They are not features which have anything to say about segments. For Browman and Goldstein, segments are ruled out of the model.

Ruling out explicit segmentation

Focusing the speech production model on the sequencing of phoneme-/allophone- or even syllable-sized objects is explicitly ruled out of articulatory phonology. Traditionally, both phonology and phonetics are about sequencing of such segments – even non-linear phonology, which seeks to set up underlying structures to account for linear surface phenomena (as phonetics had done since the middle 1960s), cannot resist segment 'chunking' of speech. Chunking is the way the continuous stream of audio signals *appears* to segment into concatenated chunks of sound. The reason for this is that on a perceptual/cognitive level, segment chunking has a certain PSYCHOLOGICAL REALITY – the mistake had been to infer the transfer of the *perceptual* phenomenon into the overall model of speech production and assume it also had *physical* reality.

PSYCHOLOGICAL REALITY
Objects or processes are said to have psychological reality if it can be shown that for the speaker/listener they can be readily identified and referred to. Thus, a listener can refer to the three sounds they 'hear' in the word *cat* even if in the accent in question the final [t] may be unreleased and therefore completely silent. For the listener, these sounds appear to have an objective reality even if an objective measurement of the word reveals something else.

Browman and Goldstein reorient the model away from chunking into a parametrically based account in which the continuous behaviour of the parameters or features is emphasised irrespective of how this behaviour does or does not synchronise into chunks. The notion of continuous behaviour implies, of course, that progression through time now becomes central to the model – a foreground consideration, and the notion of segment chunking is relegated to being just a background consideration. Several phoneticians in the 1960s had pointed out that as soon as you go behind the actual acoustic signal and the vocal tract configurations that produce them, speech production *cannot* be thought of in terms of a sequence of segments (Tatham and Morton 1969). These researchers suggested that the only sensible thing to do was to consider how the various parameters of speech worked together asynchronously to produce the resultant sounds for the listener. Browman and Goldstein picked up this idea, and at the same time defined very precisely what those parameters should be.

- It must be pointed out, though, that the idea originates from much earlier. In the 1930s and 1940s it formed the basis of prosodic analysis – a phonological model proposed by John Firth at the School of African and Oriental Studies in London University (Firth 1957). The model also had much in it which foreshadowed modern non-linear phonology.

The gestural score

The graphical notation of articulatory phonology makes much of the idea of parallel parameters – the tract variables – unfolding in time. The term used by Browman and Goldstein to describe the notation is 'gestural score', by analogy with a musical score, which uses parallel staves running from left to right across the page to indicate how the various instruments in a band or orchestra are playing together. Browman and Goldstein call their staves 'tracks', and these are the parameters of their model – the 'tract variables', which, as we have seen, enumerate those places in the vocal tract where constriction can occur. The way in which the tracks unfold in time reveals the temporal, gestural nature of speech. Much earlier, in classical phonetics, the term 'gesture' had been introduced to describe articulations, particularly those in which there was time or movement of the articulators.

So, we have a graph of tracks running from left to right in time (Figure 3.2). In this example illustration you can see scores for the utterances *a pan* and *a ban* showing the highest-level phonological representation. There are five tract variables shown: lip aperture, tongue tip, tongue body, velum and glottis – these are the points of constriction in the vocal tract. The blocks indicated on the tract show the 'plans' for the utterances – notice that they are not particularly synchronised. Try to work out what's going on in more classical terms.

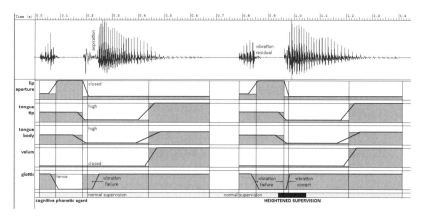

Figure 3.2 Waveform and partial articulatory score of the utterances *a pan* and *a ban*. Shaded grey areas represent abstract phonological requirements (equivalent to the utterance plan). Black lines are notional physical achievements of the relevant parameters. Vertical lines stand for phonological (not phonetic) segment boundaries. The track along the bottom of the figure is an addition derived from cognitive phonetics, and not in the original Browman and Goldstein formulation. Here the black area represents cognitive intervention to prevent aspiration or devoicing following [b].

The grey blocks in the gestural score above are only one part of the graphical representation. Browman and Goldstein superimpose on this a tracing of what is happening at the phonetic level. This captures the gradual (integrated or smoothed) tracts of the trajectories of the same parameters – but this time in the physical world. At the phonetic level these trajectories are idealised or represent just one rendering occasion. As with all actual renderings there will be considerable variation from occasion to occasion and from speaker to speaker.

We have added a track along the bottom of the diagram: this represents cognitively driven supervision of the rendering process – an important concept in cognitive phonetics (Chapter 4). The grey areas here represent normal supervision of the actions, but the black area represents heightened supervision designed to prevent the coarticulatory aerodynamic process normally resulting in failed vocal cord vibration at the start of the vowel. You can see that this has occurred following [p], where no enhanced supervision was applied.

In summary, we could say that articulatory phonology was another attempt, after Action Theory and cognitive phonetics, to bring phonology and phonetics into closer contact – something that had been lost since the beginning of generative phonology in the late 1950s, a model which tended to emphasise *differences* between the two areas of study. Articulatory phonology focused on the idea that phonology exists to drive phonetic rendering, and indicated a way in which this might happen.

PHONEMES AND ALLOPHONES

For Jones and most of his contemporaries working in the field of classical phonetics the phoneme was taken to be the *name* of a group of sounds which all shared the same phonological *function*. An example of a phonological function would be the way the phoneme /t/, and its group members, contrasts with the phoneme /d/, and its group members, by distinguishing words like *mat* /mæt/ and *mad* /mæd/, *rider* /raidə/ and *writer* /raitə/, *ton* /tʌn/ and *done* /dʌn/, and so on. Each pair has words which are identical except for the change in the *single* phoneme; they are often referred to as *minimal pairs*. So, phonemes function to distinguish between words (more technically, morphemes) in languages. Round the other way: differing sounds which do not distinguish words are not contrasting phonemes (Ladefoged 1965).

Sounds which can distinguish phonemic pairs in one language may be found in other languages where they do not distinguish morphemes. So, for example, the pair /l/ and /r/ in English are phonemes (e.g. in *light* and *right*), but not in Japanese, where they are allophones of a single phoneme. Similarly, in Spanish and Greek the pair /s/ and /ʃ/ are not used to distinguish words, whereas in English they do (as in *see* and *she*). The last sound in the Greek name *Níkoς* (*Nikos*) is somewhere between [s] and [ʃ] and has more variability than either in English.

Members of a phoneme group are, in classical phonetics, called *allophones*, each being a contextually dependent realisation of the group, and as such able to signal the morphemic contrast needed to differentiate between words. It is important to realise that the contrast is provided by membership of a particular group, not by the actual sound of the allophone. As an example, we can say that in the word *ton*, the initial sound is the aspirated allophone [tʰ], a member of the phoneme group /t/. Aspirated [−voice] plosives (e.g. [pʰ, tʰ, kʰ]) are the allophonic realisations of phoneme /t/ at the start of stressed syllables or monosyllabic words. This aspirated [tʰ] signals the phonemic /t/ vs. /d/ contrast between *ton* and *done*, and there is no equivalent [dʰ] in English, or indeed any aspirated [+voice] plosive. However, at the beginning of a word, but when preceded by /s/, the allophone is [t] with no aspiration – hence *stun* /stʌn/, realised as [stʌn]. Again it is membership of the /t/ phoneme, rather than the allophone itself, which enables us to identify the word. It so happens that in English we cannot have /sdʌn/ because a [t] following an [s] sounds exactly like a [d] and the two words would therefore be indistinguishable.

- Remember we presented an alternative to the classical phonetics model of aspiration in Chapter 2, and compared both in the **EVALUATION – MODELLING ASPIRATION – THE CLASSICAL PHONETICS AND COARTICULATION SOLUTIONS.**

Take another, more complicated example. In Estuary English and several other accents, the isolated word *tap* has the phonemic structure /tæp/ and the word *tab* has the structure /tæb/. But there is a difficulty: in final position /b/ and /p/ are both realised in articulatory terms as an unreleased plosive and acoustically as a silence, with the difference between the words being transferred to the vowel: [æː] in *tab* is longer than [æ] in *tap*, hence [tæːb˺] and [tæp˺] respectively. Cockney has a similar problem with words like *tad* and *tat*, phonemically /tæd/ and /tæt/ and allophonically [tʰæːʔ] and [tʰæʔ].

In general the context for determining allophonic variants for a phoneme group in classical phonetics is the surface linear phonemic environment. Thus in English a phonologically [–voice] plosive is said to be realised as an aspirated allophone at the beginning of a word and before a stressed vowel, as an unaspirated allophone before a stressed vowel if preceded by /s/, or as an unreleased allophone at the end of a word, and so on. Although in a sense equivalent, the idea was more of a *label* placed on a collection of equal-status allophones (shown in the diagram below) rather than of the name of a hierarchically dominant node such as we might find in more modern phonetic theory.

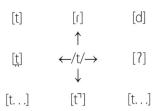

In the classical model the phoneme /t/ is little more than a label identifying allophones as members of its group. The allophones are pronounced variants. In classical phonetics little distinction was made between phonological (extrinsic) and phonetic (intrinsic) allophones. This contrasts with a more contemporary hierarchical arrangement in which the dominant relationship becomes clear, as shown below.

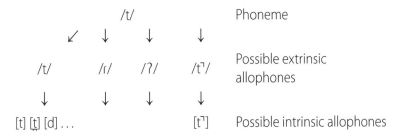

Note that in neither approach is the phoneme, as a symbolic label, itself pronounceable: physical pronunciation is achieved only by realisation through one of the member allophones.

In Jones' cardinal vowel system the extremes on the vowel chart were defined as eight placings of the tongue around the periphery of the oral cavity, starting with the two extremes – highest, most front possible, and lowest, most back possible; then low front and high back, with two equally spaced points between high front and low front, and similarly two equally spaced points between low back and high back. These locations set the two-dimensional vowel space for the speaker in question; their actual native language vowels will fall within this space and so be formally related to the boundaries formed by the cardinal vowels. Jones made at least two sets of audio recordings of his own cardinal vowels to guide apprentice phoneticians.

In the diagram below we see a quadrilateral representing a cross-section of the oral cavity, and showing the eight extreme positions of the primary cardinal vowels [i], [e], [ɛ], [a], [ɑ], [ɔ], [o] and [u].

	Front		Back
High	i		u
	e		o
	ɛ		ɔ
Low	a		ɑ

Compare this diagram with the chart of the English vowels in Figure 1.1 above. In the cardinal vowel chart the symbols occupy extreme positions in their cells, indicating that the tongue location is as far to the extremes of its possible positioning. In the English vowel chart the positioning falls back from the extremes (Figure 3.3). This sensitivity to positioning is used differently in different languages; for example, [i] in French is higher and more front than [i] in English – and for this reason is closer to the corresponding cardinal vowel. Similarly in French the low front vowel [a] is lower and more front than the English [æ] – making French [a] nearer to the corresponding cardinal vowel.

For those wanting to use the cardinal vowel system for making decisions as to the placement of the tongue for vowels in any language, the idea worked just fine, and much progress was able to be made towards describing the vowel sounds available in many of the world's languages. Phoneticians practising descriptive classical phonetics make use of the system even today to provide what we might call tongue reference points to try to define formally how the vowels of a language relate to one another.

Although some writers have described the cardinal vowel approach as more art than science (Abercrombie 1967), this was in fact an important, rigorous attempt

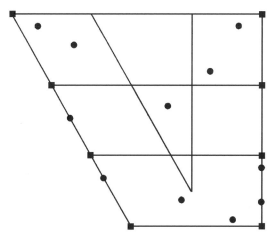

Figure 3.3 Cardinal vowel chart showing the eight primary cardinal vowels (small squares) and a number of English vowels (small circles) (compare with Figure 1.1). You can see that the primary vowels are used to define the extremities of the grid within which the vowels from individual languages can be placed. Anti-clockwise from the top left the cardinal vowels are: [i], [e], [ɛ], [a], [ɑ], [ɔ], [o] and [u]; and, also from the top left anti-clockwise, the English vowels are: [i], [ɪ], [ɛ], [æ], [ʌ], [ɑ], [ɒ], [ɔ], [ʊ] and [u], with [ə] in the centre. Notice an ambiguity in the use of symbols here: [i], for example, stands for both a cardinal vowel and a vowel of English. These have different positions on the chart.

(given the lack of instrumentation and analysis techniques available at the time) to improve the objectivity of vowel description. There is no doubt that Jones' cardinal vowel system advanced phoneticians' ability to describe and compare vowels usefully both within a single language system and across languages. The idea of cardinal vowels was a true landmark in the development of phonetic theory.

TRANSLATION THEORIES

TUTORIAL

Classical phonetics gave us an important aoristic, or timeless, static descriptive model for characterising speech. There was little attempt to tackle dynamic events, except for prosodics (See 'Prosody and Suprasegmentals' in Chapter 10), or to move beyond simple description towards an explanation of what phoneticians were observing. The theory provided us with a linear, flat or surface model, which did not go behind the observations. Ideally we would see the development of a theory as proceeding from observation to explanation, as in the table here.

Theory level		Data handling	If done well meets the criteria for
Observation	↓	Gathers data systematically	Observational adequacy
Description	↓	Characerises patterning in the assembled data	Descriptive adequacy
Explanation	↓	Explains the patterns drawn out by description	Explanatory adequacy

The new Coarticulation Theory of the middle 1960s introduced both a dynamic perspective – the characterisation of time-governed continuous events – and a hierarchically based model paving the way for explanation of the data, going beyond simple description. The proponents of Coarticulation Theory were the first to address seriously the question: *why* are speech articulation and the consequent waveform the way they are, and not some other way? The adoption of a hierarchical model similar in structure to that recently devised for linguistics introduced the *translation* approach to speech research. Arguably Coarticulation Theory begins a new age in speech production theory where the focus shifts from simple surface description of what we observe experimentally to an attempt to explain what we observe.

Take an example: in producing the English word *eighth* we would in the 1960s have begun the process at a cognitive level with a *phonemic string* /eitθ/. This translates using phonological processes to the *extrinsic allophonic string* /eitθ/ – yes, the symbols are all the same, reflecting a major ambiguity problem with the transcription; not even the brackets tell you what level we're at. The extrinsic allophonic string is the plan used as the basis for rendering the word into an articulation and hence an acoustic signal. In effect this plan says that the speaker wants a sequence of segments, but says nothing about how they are to be conjoined. At this point *time* is added as the representational segment string is again translated into a string of motor targets, probably specified in terms of motor or articulatory parameters. However, when the speaker's phonetic system tackles the rendering it finds that, under the imposed time constraints – only so much time is allowed for the utterance – the target alveolar ridge constriction specified for the /t/ is unable to be met, and that, because the tongue blade is en route towards the interdental /θ/, the intended alveolar [t] turns out to be an *unintended* dental [t̪] – an intrinsic allophone. Thus the explanation for the final dental rendering of the underlying planned /t/ rests on (1) the constraints imposed on the tongue blade's positioning and trajectory by the motor targets of adjacent segments, and (2) the time allowed to execute the articulation. Other similar examples include the fronted or advanced [k̟] before [i] in the word *key*, but the retracted [k̠] before [ɑ] in the word *car*. It is safe to say that most motor targets will get altered in some way along these lines in normal running speech. In general, the faster the rate of delivery the more the ideal targets will be missed.

- A frequent exception to general target missing occurs with angry speech. Angry speech is often faster than normal, but at the same time usually more precise with less target missing than we usually expect with fast speech (See 'Experiments with Emotive and Expressive Hypotheses' in Chapter 6).

The major distinguishing characteristic of translation theory in general is that information flows from the system's entry point to its exit point, and is successively translated or transformed along the way. We speak of cascading levels of representation. This process can be described in several ways for language and speech. We say that thought is translated or encoded as sound, or thought is mapped onto sound. The encoding is seen as a multi-layer process in which at each layer there is a representation of the information translated from the previous layer's representation and to be translated to the next layer's representation. The original information or thought is thus carried along through the various layers, undergoing translation after translation to give representation after representation as far as the final acoustic signal. This has been the general model in linguistics since Chomsky's first work in the mid-1950s (see Chapter 5).

Thus, for example, in phonology the underlying representation of a sentence (or any other string, like a phrase or a word) at the entry point to the phonology is mapped onto the derived representation by rules – the final derived representation being at the exit point of the phonology. These rules govern changes to or modifications of the underlying representation.

FORMANT TRANSITIONS

TUTORIAL

Researchers at the Haskins Laboratories observed in the mid-1950s that FORMANT transitions or formant bending occurred systematically at the beginning of vowels immediately following stops (Liberman *et al.* 1957). In particular, they noticed that whatever the vowel's usual formant distribution, each formant appeared to start from a particular position or locus (Latin plural: loci). They hypothesised that it was the tongue's position for the stop which determined the frequency of the locus; it was as though the vowel had begun at the point where the stop had left off – with the vocal tract configured not for the steady-state vowel, but for a vowel *where the stop was*. What is happening is that the air in the vocal tract is resonating as the tongue moves from its target position for the stop to its target position for the vowel – this is the period of the formant transition, during which bending is observed on the spectrogram.

> **REMINDER: FORMANT**
> A formant is a resonance in the vocal tract, visible on a spectrogram as a grouping of harmonics with an overall bandwidth of around 100 Hz on average. Vowels can be seen to have at least four such groupings or formants, and each vowel is unique in the combination of their centre frequencies. Generally vowels can be identified by the centre frequency values of the first three, or lowest in frequency, formants.

Figure 3.4 shows spectrograms of the English vowels [i], [ɪ], [ɛ], [æ], [ɑ], [ɒ], [o] and [u], and Figure 3.5 shows a selection of plosive + vowel utterances. Notice that in the isolated vowels the formants are more or less steady – they have formants parallel to the graph's baseline. The centre frequencies of the

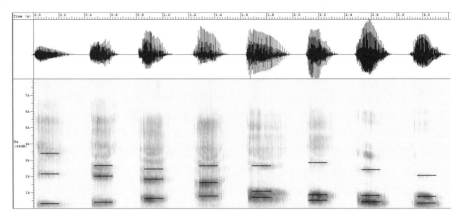

Figure 3.4 Spectrograms of isolated renderings of the English vowels [i], [ɪ], [ɛ], [æ], [ɑ], [ɒ], [o] and [u]. The centre frequencies the first three formants of each vowel have been drawn in by hand.

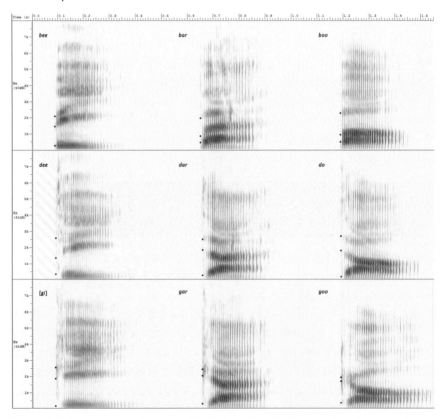

Figure 3.5 Spectrograms of nine combinations in English of [+voice] plosive + vowel. Notice the formant bending at the start of each vowel, eventually settling to the expected steady values as the tongue finally reaches its target position.

first three formants of each vowel have been drawn in to exaggerate this. But notice in the plosive + vowel combinations that the formants bend from immediately following the plosive release to well into the vowel. Eventually they settle to expected steady-state values. This formant bending is caused by the movement of the tongue from its position for the plosive to its target position for the following vowel. Inevitably there is a movement transition between the two positions, and because there is vocal cord vibration present in this period (particularly in the case of [+voice] plosives) this will appear as sound – part of the vowel rendering.

What is interesting is that listeners are not aware of this movement of the formants during what can be an appreciable period of time as far as the speech domain is concerned – perhaps as much as 200 ms. They seem to perceive the stop and the vowel as segments abruptly conjoined in sequence, as the diagram below shows.

Stop burst ↘

Formant loci →   Formant transitions →   Vowel target formants

The nature of the STOP BURST – its spectral content due to the tongue position within the oral cavity – determines the loci from which transitional formants seem to move in time towards their final expected frequency values for the following vowel. In the rendering of phonologically [+voice] plosives like [b, d, g], the formants in the transitional phase are just like regular formants with a periodic source, except that their centre frequencies are changing as time unfolds. In the rendering of phonologically [–voice] plosives like [p, t, k], the formants in the transitional phase have an aperiodic source because of the delay in vocal cord vibration onset associated with these plosives – called *aspiration* in classical phonetics.

Although as listeners we are not directly aware of formant transitions, the Haskins researchers hypothesised that the transitions themselves were being used as cues to identify the preceding stop. The hypothesis was that the loci and the movement of the formant values away from them in some way characterised the stop for listeners. The researchers set up a series of experiments using an early form of synthetic speech in which they played listeners only the formant transitions followed by their settled or steady-state vowel values - that is, with no direct acoustic cues for the stops, no stop phase and no burst. The results were surprising: listeners invariably perceived the stops correctly, although in fact none was present in the signal.

The conclusions of this landmark experiment are still with us:

1. In rendering the speaker's utterance plan, an appreciable amount of time is spent on transitions from one target to another.

2. Although listeners are unaware of these transitions and report only their perception of speakers' target segments, the transitions themselves are providing important cues to the target values.

STOP BURST

In classical phonetics stops are modelled as having either two or three phases:

- Voiced stops begin with the stop period (which may or may not have some vocal cord vibration) followed by the burst phase – a very brief (3–4 ms) period of aperiodic, relatively high-amplitude signal marking the release of the air pressure behind the stop as the articulators are pulled apart. Note that it is not the case that the air breaks through the constriction – there is a deliberate pulling apart of the articulators by the speaker.

- Voiceless stops have three phases: the stop phase, then the burst (at rather higher amplitude than with voiced stops), then a period of aspiration before the vocal cords began vibrating.

We prefer to recognise the two phases of stop and burst, but with voiceless stops assign the following period of delayed vocal cord vibration to the vowel rendering. As far as the speaker is concerned, in this approach the vowel begins (as with voiced stops) immediately after the burst.

FEATURE TRANSFER

Feature transfer occurs when the identity of a segment is deduced by a listener from some other - usually adjacent - segment.

3. A segment's perception can be, and often is, triggered by what is happening in adjacent segments: this phenomenon is called FEATURE TRANSFER. In the case of initial stop perception, it is what is happening to the formants of the following vowel (in the case of [+voice] plosives) or the formants in the initial devoiced section of the vowel (in the case of [−voice] plosives).

The consequence of these results for classical phonetics was the need to revise the now theoretically unsafe idea that speech is a sequence of steady-state sounds and that it is these which provide listeners with the necessary perceptual cues. The move away from this idea and towards understanding the perceptual importance of transitions paved the way for the development in the 1960s of coarticulation theory (TUTORIAL – COARTICULATION THEORY). Later, for more modern theories like COGNITIVE PHONETICS (see Chapter 4), it means that speakers and listeners have knowledge of a great deal more than just the target values of individual segments - they know how they glide from one to another, using this knowledge to help towards assigning to the signals they hear symbolic representations matching up with the speaker's planned utterance.

In the mid-1960s Öhman conducted experiments to determine the way in which vowel formants showed transitions into stops and then again out of stops in VCV (vowel + consonant + vowel) sequences such as [ɑpɑ], [iti], [ɑkɑ], etc. Öhman showed that the transitions were not symmetrical about the central stop. He devised a simple mathematical model of how the transitions worked, and this was set out in his papers 'Coarticulation in VCV utterances: spectrographic measurements' (Öhman 1966) and 'Numerical model of coarticulation' (Öhman 1967).

COGNITIVE PHONETICS

Cognitive phonetics is an integrated theory of speech production and perception, developed in the early 1980s, which focuses on cognition rather than the more physical aspects of speech. Speech production is seen as the rendering of the speaker's utterance plan which is carefully managed by a cognitive *supervisor*, constantly referring to the original utterance plan; via feedback, to the rendering results and the environmental conditions (such as background noise); and, via a predictive perceptual model, to how the signal might be perceived by a listener. The idea of the supervisor is to make continuous adjustments to the rendering to optimise the signal for the listener's benefit (see diagram below).

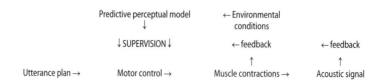

The supervisor is modelled as an autonomous agent, with knowledge of the properties of the system and its potential and limitations.

COARTICULATION THEORY

Close examination of the speech waveform in the 1950s, using instruments such as the sound spectrograph, failed to reveal the physical existence of discrete segments corresponding to those found in the representations of phonology and classical phonetics. No linear string of objects corresponding to the representational symbols of phonetics could be identified in the acoustic signal, despite the fact that speakers often believe they speak in a string of sounds and listeners believe they hear a string of sounds. These sounds are perceived as joined together with abrupt boundary changes between them. The facts of the acoustic signal could not be further from this: the sound is characterised by continuousness, *not* discontinuity, and rarely are there any boundaries visible in waveforms or spectrograms.

It follows that an account of speech production and perception needs to explain a number of observations:

1. Speakers *think* of speech as a string of isolable and permutable sounds.
2. We *feel* we can rearrange the sounds to plan and speak different or new words.
3. Listeners *feel* they can hear and recognise the individual sounds within the speech signal.
4. But the *speech waveform* is rarely a sequence of discrete sounds; it's more often a continuous event – revealed in analysis of the acoustic signal.
5. The *articulation* preceding the sound wave is rarely discrete – revealed in the analysis of video X-ray sequences.

And in addition:

6. We can often utter the sounds in a word separately if asked to – although this is not how we would normally speak words.

Coarticulation Theory focused on trying to understand how speakers' and listeners' confidence in their feelings about the discontinuity of the speech signal (both articulatory and acoustic) could be reconciled with the continuousness of the physical facts as measured (Hammarberg 1976).

THE OBJECT-ORIENTED PROGRAMMING PARADIGM

Object-oriented programming is characterised by its data structures, called objects, which consist of data and methods. Methods are functions and procedures which describe the behaviour of the data within the object, setting up a local structure within an overall program which might include other, similar objects.

As an example in speech articulation, consider the musculature of the tongue, and let us call this the *tongue object*. The tongue's muscles usually work in a way which indicates some cooperation between them – they constitute a *coordinative structure*; the term was coined by Easton (1972). Methods or procedures within the tongue object spell out how the muscles work together to perform this or that function. So, for example, a group of functions will ensure that the muscles contract in such a way as to produce a raised blade for contact with the alveolar ridge to form the stop phase of English [t]. Other functions will ensure that the same muscles cooperate to lower the back of the tongue for a vowels like [ɑ]; while others, by the inclusion of time, produce a gesture appropriate for [l] or [r]. An object can dominate a set of nested objects. So, for example, such an object, associated with tongue/jaw collaboration to achieve tongue raising and lowering, would include the tongue object and also a jaw object, taking in muscles and methods for jaw lowering/raising.

In this way an object can be said to 'know' certain behaviours appropriate to its role in producing the gestures for speech. The knowledge of how the object is to achieve certain goals is held within the object itself. This means that detailed information about performing certain tasks need not be computed in the brain or be sent from the motor cortex to individual muscles. The signal from the motor cortex to the tongue object, for example, could be a symbolic coding of a required gesture, such as *perform a complete tongue/alveolar ridge constriction*, or perhaps in some extremes *perform a [t]*.

Obviously such gestures will often or even usually be appropriate for a particular language, and so they need to be learned by the child in the case of native languages or by the adult in the case of later language learning. What the child does *not* learn is the existence of the structures and the communication pathways between the muscles: it is the specifics of the methods (the equations of constraint) which need to be learned. The mechanism which is being programmed in the learning procedure is genetically determined, it is hypothesised.

Methods can be accessed and altered to change the behaviour of an object. Action Theory allowed for tuning – adjustment of the coordinative structure from outside the structure itself. Similarly, methods in the object-oriented model used to simulate speech production are capable of being accessed for on-the-fly tuning, or *supervision* as it is called in the cognitive phonetics model (Chapter 4). This same mechanism is needed for learning new behaviour for the structure.

COARTICULATION OF SEGMENTS VS. SYLLABLES

EVALUATION

Any model which incorporates the notion of coarticulation begs the question as to the nature of the input to the phonetic rendering process: it assumes it is segmental. That is, the decision to account for the coarticulation of segments presupposes that there are segments to be coarticulated. Although there is general agreement that we should model the speech production system around the notion of segment, there is little hard evidence to support the idea.

There are also models which propose the syllable to be the basic unit of articulation. In these models it is sometimes assumed that *within* the syllable, segment transitions are largely already specified; most blending which occurs at the coarticulatory level would be between syllable units – that is, at the syllable boundaries.

The fact that prosody (and the use of prosody in conveying expressive content) adopts the syllable as the basic unit, rather than the single articulatory segment, certainly contributes to the idea that the syllable is a basic organisational unit of speech. There is much evidence in phonology supporting this idea. However, there is simply not enough evidence yet to dismiss theories based on coarticulated segments.

Keating's research (e.g. 1990) has made a major contribution to coarticulation studies. We discuss her 'window model' at length in Tatham and Morton (2006).

FURTHER READING

Hardcastle, W. and N. Hewlett (1999), *Coarticulation: Theory, Data and Techniques*, Cambridge: Cambridge University Press.

Ladefoged, P. (1965), *The Nature of General Phonetic Theories*, Georgetown University Monograph on Languages and Linguistics 18, Washington, DC: Georgetown University.

Sweet, H. (1877), *Handbook of Phonetics*, Oxford: Clarendon Press.

Tatham, M. and K. Morton (2006), *Speech Production and Perception*, Basingstoke: Palgrave Macmillan.

Trubetskoy, N. (1939), *Grundzüge der Phonologie* (TCLP VII): Prague. Trans. from 3rd edn, Göttingen: Ruprecht, by C. Baltaxe (1971) as *Principles of Phonology*, Los Angeles: University of California Press.

CHAPTER 4 – CONTEMPORARY MODEL BUILDING

INTRODUCTION

This chapter discusses the cusp of the change from classical and static models to the modern search for dynamic models which more certainly reflect the on-going process of spoken language communication – itself a dynamic process. Muscle control over the articulators is discussed, and Action Theory, with its underlying concept of coordinative structures, is introduced. The cognitive control over speech production is discussed under the construct 'cognitive phonetics'. The importance of a suitable phonological model is introduced, emphasising the need for invariance at this level. Invariance here reflects unchanging elements of speech, such as the vowel system, which must remain constant for both speaker and listener to enable communication to work.

You will have noticed that understanding speech production and perception involves looking at a number of different disciplines; for example, psychology, neurophysiology, aerodynamics and acoustics. These are scientific fields which exist in their own right and which perhaps develop at different rates. There is no guarantee that they are in step with each other when we consult them from our speech perspective: they may be primarily concerned with different areas of focus. See the explanation: ARE THE RELEVANT DISCIPLINES SYNCHRONISED?

ARE THE RELEVANT DISCIPLINES SYNCHRONISED?

You can readily see by examining the phonological feature labels in Distinctive Feature Theory, for example, how often one discipline or part of a discipline can lag behind another. Thus, even in *The Sound Pattern of English* Chomsky and Halle (1968) base their feature set partly on the early anatomical model, although both theoretical and experimental phonetics had already progressed to a more dynamic control model (TUTORIAL – DISTINCTIVE FEATURE THEORY). In fact, in phonology even as late as the 1980s, we find little to reflect the changes already apparent in the approach of phonetics. This is not a criticism of phonology, for indeed the reverse is also true: too much of 1980s phonetics had not taken account of the considerable developments in phonology since 1968. Phonology and phonetics are much more in tune these days, though they approach unification from different starting points (Hayes 2008).

ARTICULATOR CONTROL

The ANATOMICAL MODEL of CLASSICAL PHONETICS said nothing about how vocal tract ARTICULATORY CONFIGURATIONS are achieved. Equally the early model said nothing about the mechanism or functioning of any CONTROL SYSTEM for articulator movement. Until the 1950s and 1960s it seemed enough to leave the whole matter of articulation at the descriptive anatomical level, creating a completely STATIC MODEL focusing on articulatory shapes for individual sounds.

REMINDER: CLASSICAL PHONETICS

Sometimes called traditional or articulatory phonetics, classical phonetics is a descriptive theory of speech within the core theory of linguistics. Linguists these days distinguish between phonology, which is speech at a cognitive level, and phonetics, which is speech treated as a physical phenomenon. Up until around 1965 the approach of classical phonetics dominated, and was largely concerned with anatomical perspectives on speaking – what configurations of the vocal tract are used to produce this or that sound. The approach was, by modern standards, rather informal and subjective, and relied heavily on perceived observations of speech made by phoneticians who had to be trained in listening, and labelling what they perceived with phonetic symbols. A phonetician's training attempted to minimise subjectivity, but this can never be completely removed. In modern times the phonetician's perception is replaced by objective and specialised experimental work in which detailed measurements of speech phenomena can be made (see Chapters 10 and 11).

CONTROL SYSTEM

Speech sounds are produced by the aerodynamics of the vocal tract as it assumes particular configurations. The vocal tract itself has both movable and fixed elements – the various articulators – and it is necessary for these to be set up in the configurations demanded by the sounds the speaker has chosen to use. It is important for us to understand how this is done, and how the control system which organises articulator movement works, including how it is controlled by the speaker's brain. We shall see later that it is also important to know how the sound production is turning out while speaking, how its progress is *monitored* and *supervised* (see 'Cognitive Phonetics' below).

ARTICULATOR SHAPE AND MOVEMENT

Articulator movement and configurations have *shape* which changes in time during an utterance. They also have *movement*, and indeed X-ray videos show almost *continuous* movement during an utterance, especially with articulators like the tongue and jaw, which are involved in articulating almost every segment. The articulators rarely hold perfectly still even in slow or deliberate speech.

We must be very careful about what exactly we mean by an articulator and its movement. We can see, using X-rays or other imaging techniques, that the tongue, for example, moves. But in fact 'tongue' is the name given to an anatomical organ whose movement and shape are not *directly* under control. Beneath the surface of the tongue and other articulators lies a complex musculature, and it is this which is controlled to produce movement and shape.

Even the contraction or tensing of a single muscle within a speech organ like the tongue is more complex than it might seem. A MUSCLE consists of a skin-like sheath or outer covering beneath which are hundreds of individual MUSCLE FIBRES. It is these which are ultimately under control from the brain's motor cortex (TUTORIAL – MUSCLE CONTRACTION AND

MUSCLES AND MUSCLE FIBRES

The muscles which control articulator shape are packed with hundreds of individual muscle fibres. Muscles themselves are not addressed directly – their movement and shape depend on addressing the muscles fibres within them. Simply, the unit of control is the muscle fibre, not the whole muscle. Put another way, muscles are not indivisible objects; they consist of bundles of muscle fibres. It is the muscle fibres which contract to alter the size and shape of their muscle, and which are also responsible for its movement.

ARTICULATOR MOVEMENT; TUTORIAL – MOTOR CONTROL OF
THE ARTICULATORS – AN EARLY CONSIDERATION).

FEEDBACK

FEEDBACK

A feedback system is one designed to report back information which can be used to assess the effectiveness of control signals. This information is used to calculate any adjustments that may be necessary to improve the output. For example, if a speaker hears, using auditory feedback, that they are competing with high background noise they will speak louder, more slowly and with increased precision. It is hard to imagine any speech control system which does not take into account feedback of some kind.

It is generally agreed that the control of articulation involves some monitoring subsystem. This means that *FEEDBACK* mechanisms must be available to perform the monitoring and report back to the control centre. In speech production we can identify three major feedback mechanisms which seem to play some role in governing control: auditory, tactile and intra-muscular.

Auditory feedback

Auditory feedback detects information about how the production system is doing by monitoring the resultant audio waveform. We hear the sound via two pathways: it can be either air-borne or conducted through the bones of the jaw and head to the auditory mechanism. Feedback of this kind is characterised by being comparatively slow and usable over only fairly long periods of time (i.e. longer than syllables or words). We would predict, therefore, that any effects based on this mechanism or its failure would involve long-term aspects of speech above the level of segment.

Experiments show that if people are deprived of auditory feedback there is some deterioration of their ability to control *suprasegmental* phenomena like intonation. That is, deprivation of auditory monitoring encourages *monotone speech* or speech with no recognisable or apparently relevant intonation pattern. Long-term timing control also suffers, giving rise to loss of rhythm and of the correct relationships in the timing of segments.

Tactile feedback

Tactile feedback is provided by pressure sensors. There are nerve endings on the surface of the speech organs which are sensitive to pressure variations, and which generate feedback signals when pressure changes occur. Such pressure changes mostly result when articulators touch. However, there are even very sensitive sensors in the oral cavity capable of responding to small changes in air pressure. All this tactile information is continuously fed back to the 'control centre' in the brain to improve the effectiveness of control. It is, however, still comparatively slow (though not as slow as auditory feedback). Experiments depriving subjects of tactile feedback by application of mild surface anaesthetics show a segment-by-segment (sounds and syllables) deterioration of speech resulting in a drunken-like slurring. Timing is affected here too, but now it's the timing of individual segments, rather than the longer-term timing of suprasegmental rhythm associated with auditory feedback.

Intra-muscular feedback

Intra-muscular feedback is the fastest of the three types, and is potentially usable within the time span of a single segment, though there has been some argument on this point. The fast response time is achieved by having sensors *within* the muscles themselves, and by the fact that the response is reflex or automatic, with only a minimal secondary role being played by any cognitive processing of the feedback information. The mechanism for the reflex intra-muscular monitoring and response is the *gamma loop*.

The Gamma-Loop Feedback System

Within a muscle, besides the normal muscle fibres discussed earlier, there are special fibres called *muscle spindles*. A primary role of these muscle spindles is to sense the rate of stretch of the muscle. They *generate* signals proportional in number and frequency to any stretching that occurs, and these are sent from the muscle by specially designated nerve fibres called *gamma fibres*. These gamma fibres, taking feedback signals *away* from the muscle, contrast with *alpha fibres*, which are responsible for bringing control signals *to* the muscle.

Before reaching any area of the brain where cognitive activity might occur, the gamma-loop reflex signals are automatically turned around (in the spinal cord) to travel down the alpha fibres back to the muscle – thus modifying the normal enervator signals. The entire loop for the feedback signal is called the *gamma loop*, and is an example of what is called a *reflex arc*. A defining characteristic of a reflex arc is that its operation is automatic, requiring no cognitive supervision or recalculation – hence the speed. Experiments based on deprivation of gamma feedback in speech are difficult to design and carry out, and results have been relatively inconclusive as to the actual role intra-muscular feedback might be playing in speech production. However, contemporary theories of speech production, including Action Theory, task dynamics and cognitive phonetics, assume both the existence and usefulness of the gamma reflex arc.

The gamma loop is central to the notion of coordinative structure because it provides the necessary messaging system. The gamma fibres are also responsible for providing (in Action Theory) the tuning mechanism and (in cognitive phonetics) the mechanism used by the supervisor agent. Both of these use the gamma pathway from the brain down to the muscle spindles;

in cognitive phonetics this pathway conveys the messages responsible for cognitive supervision.

THE ABSTRACT THEORY OF ARTICULATOR CONTROL

The overall physical model of dynamic articulation involves a range of areas from anatomical and mechanical description of the speech organs through to the computations which must be achieved cognitively to feed a control system seen in neurophysiological evidence. This is a complex *system* drawing on various disciplines for its characterisation. The model is essentially a *mechanistic* one; that is, it is built around what we can learn by experiment of the nature and functioning of the mechanisms concerned.

But there is another kind of model which can be built. This is a more abstract model, focusing much less on mechanisms, and attempting to arrive at a plausible abstract explanation of the results of the mechanisms' functions. For the most part linguistics itself is just such an abstract theory: the mechanistic counterpart is neurolinguistics, which seeks to describe and explain language from the point of view of the neural mechanisms involved. For the moment very little is known of these mechanisms because of the difficulties of experimental work involving the brain. But since the early 1950s there has been increased activity in the modelling of neural mechanisms in general, using NEURAL NETWORKS.

NEURAL NETWORKS

The modelling of neural networks in the brain has been paralleled by important developments in the modelling of cognitive processes, also using networks. The more usual term in the cognitive sciences is *connectionist modelling* or *parallel distributed processing*, and the techniques involved abandon rule-based systems in favour of the network paradigm, using a different mathematical approach. The cognitive aspects of linguistics and phonetics are included in the areas of cognitive science that many researchers are investigating using the new techniques. A neural network takes the form of a complex arrangement of neurons or nodes associated with connections between them and arranged in layers. By means of 'exposing' the network to data taken from experiments it is possible, using a system of weightings attached to the connections between nodes, to arrange for the network to 'learn' associations between input and output data. For example, the network can learn to associate a particular formant distribution with a particular phonological symbol. Thus 'low first formant AND high second formant AND high third formant' might be associated with the symbol /i/, whereas 'high first formant AND low second formant AND low third formant' might be associated with the symbol /ɑ/. Networks are trained on large quantities of data to learn such paired associations.

ACTION THEORY

Comparatively recently (since 1975, and gathering momentum since the early 1980s) it has been suggested that translation theories, as described in Chapter 3, are unsatisfactory because they fail to account for some of the observations made of speech production. In particular, translation theories cannot give a satisfactory account of *compensatory articulation*, as when speakers readjust their articulations to take account of some external mechanical constraint like trying to talk with a pipe held in the mouth, or talking while doing a handstand – that is, with gravity pulling the tongue, for example, *towards* the palate rather than away from it. These and other observations led to a PARADIGM CHANGE in speech production theory in the mid-1970s.

PARADIGM CHANGE

At certain points in the development of any science, when enough observations have been made which the extant theory cannot account for, the science undergoes a paradigm change. That is, quite suddenly a new approach and accompanying theory are proposed which do account for the new observations. The replacement theory will usually be a significant extension of the earlier one, or it might be completely new. After debate among researchers and testing to make sure the new theory is adequate, it replaces the old one. Although the proposal of the new theory is usually sudden, the replacement process can often be protracted. It is almost always the case too that the earlier theory lingers in those areas where it has already proved adequate and productive.

A new theory of speech production control was proposed around 1975 by a group of researchers at the *Haskins Laboratories* in New Haven, Connecticut. Acceptance of the new theory has been gaining ground as it is modified to the point where it can satisfactorily account not just for the new observations which prompted its development, but also everything covered by the earlier translation theories which it replaces.

The new theory, which draws on parallel changes in the theory of neurophysiology, is called *Action Theory* (Fowler 1980). It criticises translation theory on the grounds that:

- speaking does *not* consist of the handing on of information for re-encoding, layer after layer through the process, beginning deep in the phonology and ending with the sound wave;

- the amount of information that would have to be added during such a translation process is just counter-intuitively too great;

- the neurophysiological mechanisms for action and the way they function in speaking have been misunderstood and wrongly modelled.

These claims form not just a weak departure from established theory, but the basis of a radically new way of looking at speech production – hence the signalling of a paradigm change.

Action Theory suggests that information processing at the cognitive levels of phonology and early in the phonetics is not in terms of the detailed representations (e.g. bundles of distinctive features) we have been used to in linguistics. More, it is a comparatively simple handling of broadly based labels (not unlike the acoustic targets of Target Theory, described in Chapter 2) characterising *gross* rather than detailed effects of articulation. One might imagine instructions like *Do vocal cord vibration!* or *Do vowel-ness!* A characteristic of such instructions is that they lack detailed information about *how* to do the actions specified. Action Theorists would claim that this detailed information is contained in

- the way in which the articulatory system itself is structured and organised – so the information does not need to be specified as part of the higher-level instruction;

- the detail of low-level messaging between muscles within muscle groupings.

The articulatory mechanism, which includes both the anatomy and the neurophysiology of the system, is said to be arranged into organised groupings. These are invoked in the theory as COORDINATIVE STRUCTURES. The idea of the coordinative structure was borrowed into speech theory in the mid-1970s, and was developed by Kugler *et al.* (1980) and Fowler *et al.* (1980).

The individual muscles in a muscle coordinative structure cooperate with each other, using the structure's built-in messaging system to fill out and perform the appropriate details of a gross instruction issued by the brain's motor cortex.

Exactly how this cooperation or coordination within the structure operates is described in the model by equations governing the working relationships between the component parts (in our example the muscles) of the structure. These equations are called *EQUATIONS OF CONSTRAINT*, and they characterise the constraints inherent in a coordinative structure's functioning.

> **REMINDER: COORDINATIVE STRUCTURE**
>
> A coordinative structure is usually taken as a grouping of muscles incorporating well-defined working relationships between them. The muscles within a coordinative structure are linked by nerves which conduct messages between them, describing their current behaviour. The balance between the messages expresses the *knowledge* which the structure has to perform certain tasks. An example might be messaging between the muscles of the tongue to achieve an overall high front position for making the sound [i], or between the muscles controlling tension in the larynx to achieve, in conjunction with the right subglottal air pressure, spontaneous vocal cord vibration.
>
> Coordinative structures can be nested; that is, grouped together for the purpose of performing certain operations. For example, the tongue muscle coordinative structure and the jaw muscle structure can be linked to perform tongue raising and lowering: this is not performed solely by the tongue.

> **EQUATIONS OF CONSTRAINT**
>
> Here is an example of a simplified equation of constraint:
>
> $$K = m_1 \times w_1 . m_2 \times w_2 . m_3 \times w_3 \ldots m_n \times w_n$$
>
> where K is the task goal (the movement required), m_x is the required contractile state of a particular member of the set of muscles in the structure, and w is a weighting factor associated with the particular muscle.
>
> The equation reads: *The goal is achieved by interacting contractions of a set of muscles, each of which contributes towards the goal in the specified way.*
>
> The point about the way the equation is formulated is that so long as K, the goal, is achieved, then there is leeway in setting up the muscles involved. In principle, it is possible to alter the contractile value of one muscle, and adjust one or more of the others to make sure that the equation is still true, and that K is achieved; K is the CONSTANT GOAL. In practice, the extent to which this compensatory principle can be applied is limited – and this is expressed partly by the value of w for each member muscle. This idea is incorporated into the operation of coordinative structures to allow for phenomena like being able to speak while
>
> - holding something between the teeth, like a pipe;
> - moving the he ad – even standing on the head – and thereby interfering with the direction of gravitational pull on the articulators.
>
> Interference of this kind with normal articulation is common, and our model of speech production needs to be able to explain how it is possible to continue talking under abnormal conditions – something we readily do. No previous account of speech production had even come close to explaining these observations. In a model which computes everything in the brain there would, we imagine, be an impossible amount of computational overload implied. For researchers in the 1970s it was important to alter the theory to move the heavy computation away from the brain and into peripheral operations (see **EVALUATION – TRADITIONAL APPROACHES TO MOTOR CONTROL VS. ACTION THEORY**).

Using the familiar terminology of computer modelling, we would say that a coordinative structure is *internally* programmed to behave in a particular way. The component parts are not directly or independently controlled. Each operates in conjunction with its associated muscles in a well-defined way which can be described using the equation of constraint.

CONSTANT GOAL

The equations of constraint which govern the behaviour of a coordinative structure are expressed in terms of a goal (as an example, this could be a particular tongue position to be achieved) and a number of interacting variables to achieve that goal. Thus

$$\text{goal} = \text{variable}_1 \times \text{variable}_2 \times \text{variable}_3 \times \ldots \text{variable}_n$$

In this very simple version of the equation, the goal is the desired position, and the variables are the contractile states of the various muscles involved. The point is that if you change (say, by altering the direction of gravity) one variable, say variable_2, then the others will automatically change to make sure the goal remains the same. The messaging system automatically takes care of all this without referring to the brain for additional computation. To illustrate the point more simply, consider the following equations:

$10 = (x \times y) + z$ the general case, and a specific case:
$10 = (4 \times 2) + 2$ but change the 4 to a 3 and we get
$10 = (3 \times 2) + 4$ to hold onto the same goal of 10, or
$10 = (6 \times 2) - 2$ achieving the constant goal of 10, or
$10 = (2 \times 3) + 4$ achieving the same goal

We have a slight modification for how the system works in cognitive phonetics (see below):

- The overall speech control system *already knows* that the appropriate muscular contractions will take place according to local or low-level arrangements, as defined by the equations of constraint which govern the relationships between the coordinative structure's components. So the control system need only issue very gross instructions designed to *trigger* the coordinative structure's own internal program. In this way, information about rendering is added to the underlying utterance plan. Structures, along with their pre-programmed abilities, are said to be marshalled by the system to execute the simple linguistic requirements of the utterance plan.

In addition, structures are nested: that is, one structure may itself, together with other structures, form some *super coordinative structure*, as shown in the diagrams below.

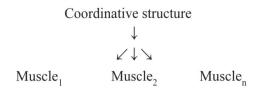

Coordinative structure

Muscle$_1$ Muscle$_2$ Muscle$_n$

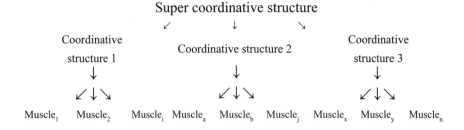

Although the behaviour of a coordinative structure is governed by its equations of constraint, the behaviour of the individual elements within the structure can be altered during an utterance, or on a more long-term basis. This process was called *TUNING* by the researchers who proposed Action Theory. Tuning involves direct access by the brain *into* coordinative structures; the mechanism for this calls for fast transmission of signals to the coordinative structure using gamma fibres. Gamma fibres (see 'The Gamma-Loop Feedback System' above) take signals from the motor cortex to the musculature at a faster rate than the normal alpha fibres which are used for the main controlling signals. The tuning mechanism is invoked to explain how

- the detail of an equation of constraint is learned initially by the speaker;

- speakers can modify their behaviour to adjust to the requirements of a new language;

- speakers might adjust to external conditions like unexpected constraints on articulator moment beyond the abilities of the self-compensating nature of coordinative structures – *even while an utterance is on-going*.

Because of its abstract, phonologically oriented nature, classical phonetics invokes TIME only notionally in observations like comparing the relative lengths of different vowel sounds: *clock time* (real time) in, say, milliseconds was never invoked in the theory. For example, in English [ɪ] is *shorter* than [i] and [ɑ] is *longer* than [æ]. In Coarticulation Theory the dynamic nature of speaking became the centre of focus, with clock time being properly introduced into the model. So we would now say, for example, that in English [ɪ] has *less duration* than [i] and [ɑ] has *greater duration* than [æ].

Action Theory reintroduces time within the coordinative structure itself, making the relative timing of actions more a low-level property of the system rather than something elaborately calculated in the brain **(EVALUATION – USEFULNESS OF THE ACTION THEORY MODEL)**.

TUNING

The individual muscle components of a coordinative structure, and also low-level structures which form a superstructure stand in a well-defined relationship to other components of the structure; but at the same time they are capable of being *tuned*. That is, they can be adjusted if necessary, on an individual basis: their internal programs can be *interfered with* both on a long-term basis and on the fly. However, because of the way in which any one element within the structure relates to all the others, tuning will result in some correlating or compensatory adjustments made automatically among the remaining components of the system. It is a property of each local structure's program that external interference is internally compensated for.

TIME

Cooperation between muscle groups or between mechanically linked portions of the vocal system is certainly not a new concept, but had, up to the 1970s, been little more than a relatively vague idea in speech production theory. Action Theory adds an important new element: one of the crucial dimensions of a coordinative structure is that of time. In Action Theory much of the timing detail of an articulatory gesture which had hitherto in translation theories been assumed to be calculated (and therefore the result of cognitive activity) is treated as a property of the workings of the structure itself. The notion that time is added at such a comparatively low level in the system was new to speech production theory.

COGNITIVE PHONETICS

If mechanical and aerodynamic inertial, rather than linguistic, effects were responsible for apparent segment blending, then the phenomenon would be universal – all people would do it no matter what language was being spoken. Coarticulation was seen as a property of the *human* vocal system, not a property of languages. But in the 1970s it became clear from careful experimental work that coarticulatory phenomena could not be entirely accounted for using the mechanical inertia model of Coarticulation Theory (Tatham 1969, 1986b; Lindblom 1990; for a discussion see Tatham and Morton 2006: ch. 3). It was also observed that the *degree* of coarticulation seems to vary from language to language even when the juxtaposed segments are similar. Later it was noticed too that the *degree* of coarticulation between segments varies *within* a language, and even within a single sentence.

There had been an early, comparatively simple attempt to account for the cross-language observation in the 1960s, suggesting that coarticulation was *not* in fact a universal effect as the coarticulationists were suggesting, but language-specific and therefore under voluntary control. Thus this explanation explicitly denied the universal and automatic explanation of the phenomenon. The proposal included the notion that all intrinsic ALLOPHONES are in fact stored mentally to be used whenever the mechanical context called for them. The proposal, made by Ladefoged (1967, 1971), was based on the observation that some languages appeared to break the claims of universality, and concluded that these claims were therefore false. One or two researchers, however, pointed out that in fact there were errors in the analyses of the apparent contradictory data – thus removing the need to deny universals of coarticulation (Tatham 1969). Insufficient attention had been paid to the distinction between intrinsic and extrinsic allophones – the apparent anomalous intrinsic allophones turned out instead to be extrinsic or phonological, and under the control of the speaker rather than automatic or mechanical in origin.

REMINDER: ALLOPHONE

The term 'allophone' was used in classical phonetics to categorise a variant of a phoneme class. Thus, the phoneme /t/ could be, using classical phonetics terminology, realised in a number of different ways depending on linear articulatory context: in word-initial position in English it could be aspirated (e.g. *tack* [tʰæk]); in final position in US English or Estuary English it could be unreleased (e.g. *cat* [kæt̚]); it could have nasal or lateral release (e.g. *button* [bʌtⁿn̩], *metal* [mɛtˡl̩]); it could turn into a voiced alveolar flap in some US accents (e.g. *later* [leiɾɚ]); it could be realised between vowels or in word-final position as a glottal stop in Cockney (e.g. *matter* [mæʔə], *mat* [mæʔ]); and so on.

Later, allophones were split into two subsets. One was the subset of those explicitly derived as the result of voluntary, phonological processes; these were called *extrinsic allophones*. The other was of those derived as the result of involuntary coarticulatory phonetic processes; these were called *intrinsic allophones* (Ladefoged 1967; Tatham 1969). The new model of sub-phonemic variants set these two types of allophone in a hierarchy, shown below.

Phonemes ↓	Deep phonological units
Extrinsic allophones (phonologically derived) ↓	Surface phonological units used in specifying the utterance plan
Universal effects ↓	
Intrinsic allophones (phonetically derived)	Surface phonetic units used to describe symbolically either the articulation or the acoustic waveform

In theories such as cognitive phonetics, extrinsic allophones are the symbolic phonological units used in specifying a speaker's utterance plan. They also form the basis of the targets used in Target Theory (see Chapter 2) at the beginning of the phonetic rendering process.

Although in the original definitions intrinsic allophones were seen to be entirely automatic and involuntarily derived largely by mechanical and aerodynamic coarticulatory processes, it was later recognised that many could be voluntarily constrained (see below).

Remember that in classical phonetics we dealing with a static (no time), flat (no hierarchy) model. The concept of hierarchical derivation comes later with the introduction of Coarticulation Theory. All subsequent models adopt the hierarchical approach. Some are dynamic and emphasise time (Action Theory, cognitive phonetics), while others focus on parametric specifications for their units (Articulatory Phonology).

A more sophisticated model was proposed which accounted for coarticulation as a two-layer process (Tatham 1969, 1986b, 1990; Morton 1986). The deeper layer was said to be universal and mechanical, but the surface layer somehow overlaid cognitive or voluntary adjustments on these mechanical effects, thereby constraining them using a supervisory or managing mechanism called the *Cognitive Phonetics Agent* (CPA; Tatham 1995), shown below.

Language-specific
phonemes
↓

Language-specific
Extrinsic allophones
↓

Universal effects   ← Language-specific
↓   cognitive supervision

Constrained
intrinsic allophones

This model had an advantage: it preserved the earlier idea of the universality of coarticulation, but at the same time accounted satisfactorily for the observation that the overall effect (both layers together) is indeed language-specific. It was noted that sometimes the involuntary effect was *constrained* by special effort, but that sometimes it was actually *enhanced*. Enhancement adds a degree of *negative* constraint. The example often given for enhancement is the situation where normal coarticulation processes predict a certain amount of nasality applied to [æ] in the word *man* [mæ̃n] in *all* accents of English, with the nasality on a second level deliberately enhanced in *some* accents. For example, in some US social accents, and often among urban teenagers in the UK, the word *Man!* as in *Man, did he ever!* has enhanced nasalisation on the inter-nasal vowel. Note, however, these are strictly *not* nasal vowels, since phonologically there are no nasal vowels in English to contrast with oral, or [−nasal], vowels – they are *nasalised* vowels with different degrees of nasalisation.

It was not until the late 1970s and early 1980s, though, that the two-layer model addressed the problem of explaining the mechanism by which constraints on universal coarticulation could be applied (Tatham 1986a). It was at this time that the theory became known as cognitive phonetics, since it was also being developed to take into account other, non-physical phenomena observed at the phonetic level. By this time few researchers were still denying the universality of the lower layer of coarticulation, but the theoretical question which needed to be resolved was whether the upper cognitive layer should in fact be the final part of the phonology. Some researchers were able to show conclusively that the cognitive effects being characterised were in no sense wholly phonological: they are at most phonologically (i.e. cognitively) driven modifications of *phonetic* coarticulatory processes. This is because the constraint does not – in the English examples – contribute to morpheme differentiation: the basic function of phonological contrast. A similar, alternative theory involved the notion of adaptive variability (Lindblom 1990), whereby an articulation is varied along a 'hyper–hypo continuum' of decreasing phonetic contrast. The model encompasses less than cognitive phonetics, and in particular makes no provision for management using a supervising agent.

Sometimes, however, cognitive supervision of this kind can be used to enlarge a language's phonological inventory, contributing to the specification of *additional* phonemes not otherwise possible. For example, it is usually held that Korean has two sets of [−voice] stops. /kʰ/ is lightly aspirated, perhaps less than normally expected for /k/ in English, but /kʰʰ/ is strongly aspirated, perhaps more than English /k/. Compared with the English plosives, the lightly aspirated version in Korean constrains the aerodynamic coarticulatory effect which causes aspiration – though not as much as it is constrained in English /b, d, g/ or French /p, t, k/ (just 2 ms or 3 ms of aspiration). The /k^{hh}/, on the other hand, has somewhat enhanced delay in the vocal cord vibration for the following vowel. These uses of constraint to enlarge a language's phonemic inventory are only possible because cognitive supervision on an otherwise universal and involuntary function of coarticulation is systematic and repeatable. A necessary property of any phoneme's specification is that it must be repeatable to avoid coding confusions leading to morphemic ambiguity.

- Remember: the rendering of an extrinsic allophone is usually subject to all sorts of coarticulatory constraints. On most occasions, these simply produce a range of intrinsic allophonic variants which have to be recognised and negated in some way during a listener's perceptual processing; indeed the listener is usually not aware of them. But, perhaps surprisingly, sometimes cognitive supervision in the rendering process can so reliably modify coarticulation as to make the result usable in a systematic way to enlarge the language's phonemic inventory. This is the mechanism whereby what might otherwise be *just* a simple, variable phonetic coarticulatory effect becomes a consistently usable phonological object – a phoneme or extrinsic allophone.

Explaining how the two layers of coarticulation interact to enable one layer to constrain the universal effects of the other layer unites the theory of cognitive phonetics with the general principles expressed in Action Theory. Specifically, the tuning mechanism proposed in Action Theory was just the device cognitive phonetics had been looking for to perform the role of supervision of motor control, and to enable the cognitive supervision we have just discussed. Coincidentally the coarticulatory phenomenon provided a perfect example for the Action Theorists of a use of the tuning mechanism, which up to that time they had played down a little because of insufficiently convincing examples of its use.

TUTORIAL

DISTINCTIVE FEATURE THEORY

INTRODUCTION

As we saw in Chapters 1 and 2, classical phonetics used the place–manner classification system for consonants and the high–low/front–back system for vowels. The main purpose here was clearly to enable the phonetician to specify how particular sounds were made with respect to their articulation. There was, however, an important spin-off from these systems: it became possible to use the features or parameters of the classification system to label whole sets of sounds or articulations (Fant 1973). Thus we might refer to: *the set of all plosives* (seven in English), *or the set of all voiced plosives* (three in English), or *the set of all voiced alveolar plosives* (one only in English) – and so on, cutting horizontally and vertically around the consonant matrix. Similarly, for vowels, we could speak of *the set of all front vowels*, or *the set of all rounded vowels*, and so on.

As a consequence of being able to label sets of sounds in this way it became possible to describe the aspects of the *behaviour* of particular sets. So, for example, it was possible to say that the set of voiced plosives devoice in word-final position, or that all vowels lengthen before voiced plosives in the same syllable, and so on. So rules no longer had to be about the contextual behaviour of individual sounds; they could be in terms of how *sets* or classes of sounds behave. We now had the ability to capture and express generalisation – an important theoretical principle in linguistics: generalisations *must* be expressed whenever possible.

It was not until transformational generative grammar came along, though, that these generalisations became formalised in phonological theory. Halle's *The Sound Pattern of Russian* (1959) was really the first influential textbook in contemporary phonological theory (just two years after Chomsky's 1957 *Syntactic Structures*, the first influential textbook in contemporary syntactic theory). The generative phonologists adopted the theory of distinctive features from the earlier Prague School of Linguistics, which was under the leadership of Trubetskoy (see Chapter 3) – a much more formal representation than that of the classical phoneticians.

Remember that in this book we are using a relatively non-controversial version of phonological theory for our examples. Up-to-the-minute phonological theory (including, for example, Optimality Theory) introduces some exciting new ideas which we cannot deal with here. However, the earlier version is stable (even if somewhat dated) and serves us well to illustrate some enduring *principles* of phonology.

THE THEORY OF DISTINCTIVE FEATURES

The use of distinctive features in phonology enables us to capture *natural classes*, and, by extension, to generalise regularly occurring phenomena, formulating predictions about the behaviour of class members. If we wanted to hypothesise about human processing of phonology, we would use this idea to suggest that human beings process the patterns of phonology as part of speech planning in terms of these classes rather than in terms of individual segments. The regularity of patterning in phonology is part of the evidence for this claim – but the claim is more solid when based on the evidence that when the users of a language make up new words they do so by producing utterances which obey the rules of the natural classes their sounds fall into.

There have been various sets of distinctive features proposed as the parameters of segment description and classification. One of the original sets used in transformational phonology appeared in Jakobson, Fant and Halle (1952, reprinted 1963), and consisted of around fourteen features. Chomsky and Halle (1968) had around forty-five features, explaining that they found the original set of fourteen inappropriate for characterising some subtleties in phonology.

Like Jakobson, Fant and Halle, most modern phonologists have argued for a binary system of indexing features: a segment either possesses or does not possess any one particular feature. Clearly, with a binary system of indexing, the maximum number of features needed to classify uniquely the sounds of a language like English (with around forty-five phonemes) would be six, to give us 2^6 or sixty-four different segments. More would be needed to classify uniquely the sounds of all the languages of the world or indeed all possible human languages. However, larger sets of features were actually chosen because it was felt that it was appropriate to sacrifice mathematical simplicity in favour of a feature-labelling system which appeared to relate these phonological features to the phonetic set of classical phonetics. In this way, it was claimed, the *meaning* of the features became more transparent.

These ideas are embodied in three principles surrounding the distinctive feature set – it should be able to

1. *characterise* all contrasting segments in human languages;
2. *capture* natural classes in a clear fashion;
3. be *transparent* with regard to phonetic correlates.

A claim inherent in the first principle is that the feature set somehow embodies the humanness, rather than the language-specific nature, of features. It is predicted that if this set is correctly specified no other features will be needed even for future languages, so long as human beings do not change how they make and handle language – that is, so long as human beings remain human.

The second principle refers not just to classes, but to *natural* classes. The idea here is that the classes themselves reveal something of what is 'natural' in human language behaviour, once again referring to the fact that phonological processing is a human activity; they will therefore contain elements which are truly universal.

The third principle enables us to establish phonetic similarity - that is, to group sounds which are phonetically similar by feature. There is a very good reason for doing this: it becomes possible to explain some phonological processes in terms of the behaviour of their phonetic correlates.

The distinctive feature set most usually found is often that of Halle and Clements (1983), which is based on the Chomsky and Halle set. Chomsky and Halle (1968) have a lengthy description of their own set. In the late 1980s Ladefoged (1989) presented a formal method of representing what he called 'phonetic structure' using a hierarchically organised set of *phonetic* features. The work is important because it debates carefully what it is that we actually want to represent using abstract symbols, what the content of these symbols might be, and how phonological and phonetic representations are related.

MUSCLE CONTRACTION AND ARTICULATOR MOVEMENT

TUTORIAL

Muscle fibres within a muscle are *recruited* to participate in its overall contraction (Toates 2001). When a muscle fibre receives a neural instruction to contract, three interrelated events occur:

- mechanical contraction;
- chemical reaction;
- electrical discharge (resulting from the chemical reaction).

The mechanical contraction is *all-or-none*. That is, whenever contraction occurs it is total: a muscle fibre cannot partially contract. Usually this contraction results in a physical shortening of the muscle fibre by around one third its normal length. The apparent paradox of all-or-none contraction of individual fibres and the graded (or analogue) contraction of the whole muscle is explained by the operation of two mechanisms:

1. There is control of fibre *firing* rate. That is, the firing or response rate of individual fibres can be varied from occasional firing up to an upper rate determined by the fibre's speed of recovery from the previous firing. Immediately following firing the *recovery period* begins, during which the muscle fibre returns to its original mechanical, chemical and electrical states. Firing cannot recur (even if a new control signal arrives) before near-completion of the recovery period.

2. There is progressive *recruitment* of muscle fibres. The number of fibres recruited (or brought into play) for a particular overall muscle contraction can be varied. Thus 50 per cent of the number of fibres available might be recruited to achieve roughly 50 per cent overall contraction, 20 per cent to achieve roughly 20 per cent contraction, and so on.

In practice both mechanisms operate together, though the relationship between them is not fully understood.

The neural signals innervating muscle fibres have an all-or-none character: they take the form of pulsed electrochemical activity. These signals have special characteristics:

- The width or *duration* of each pulse is comparatively short and does not vary.
- The height or *amplitude* of the pulses does not vary.

ANALOGUE, DIGITAL

Analogue systems are characterised by their smoothness of behaviour and output. This contrasts with digital systems, whose behaviour takes the form of serial, pulsed activity. An analogue signal is technically a special case of a digital signal with the individual pulses infinitely close together. The pulses in a digital signal are called samples, and the rate at which they occur is called the sample rate. The closer the samples are together (or, the higher the sampling rate) the more closely the digital signal resembles an analogue signal and the more accurately it encodes the analogue signal.

- The required *degree* of muscular contraction is coded by how often these pulsed signals arrive: increased frequency signals more contraction, decreased frequency less. That is, the required *amplitude* of the contraction is coded as the *frequency* at which the signals are sent to the muscles.

The signals controlling muscle contraction are said take a digital or binary format because of their discrete, on/off, all-or-none nature. Likewise the behaviour of muscle fibres is DIGITAL in nature. But the behaviour of the *overall* muscle is clearly not pulsed and not binary: smoothness and continuous variation, typical of an ANALOGUE system, characterise whole-muscle behaviour. What has occurred is digital-to-analogue conversion (DAC): the digital behaviour of individual muscle fibres has been converted to the analogue behaviour of the whole muscle. The DAC is accomplished mechanically by an arrangement of the system which permits asynchronous firing of the muscle fibres – they are firing *out of sync*. This, coupled with the elasticity of the muscle contents, has the effect of smoothing the abrupt, jerky nature of the firing of the individual fibres.

TUTORIAL

MOTOR CONTROL OF THE ARTICULATORS – AN EARLY CONSIDERATION

Two basic types of general control system are possible contenders for modelling articulation control:

1. The *comb model:* Assemble very detailed information about how to perform the required effect (in this case articulatory movement), and use this information to send carefully organised and accurately detailed control signals to the musculature, knowing that these signals will be sufficient to achieve the desired objective.

2. The *chain model:* Send coarse signals which are less detailed and which rely on local checking (monitoring) and adjustment by the device itself (in this case the musculature). Early versions of the model sent feedback to the motor cortex for revision of the control signals if necessary.

In the comb model, the results of the control signals are not monitored: the system simply assumes that the calculations which form the basis of the signals are accurate and that the signals themselves will be suitably interpreted by the peripheral device. By analogy with navigation at sea, such a system is sometimes referred to as *dead reckoning*.

In the chain model, constant monitoring provides feedback of the results of control signals, and leads to continuous correction of any signal or peripheral device errors. Errors might arise because the relatively coarse signals lack detail. Such a system minimises the overhead needed for advance calculation of detailed control signals, but involves the additional workload or overhead of having to monitor the results.

Between around 1965 and 1970 there was much discussion among researchers as to which of these two models most appropriately described the behaviour of the speech musculature control system. Ultimately it seemed that the chain model (with its monitoring and feedback systems) was the most appropriate, though some comb-model-based control was not ruled out, particularly when the speaker is learning new sounds.

TRADITIONAL APPROACHES TO MOTOR CONTROL VS. ACTION THEORY

EVALUATION

Equations of constraint work in a way that seems to explain our abilities in the area of compensatory articulation. Imagine, for example that we want the tongue to make the vowel sound [ɑ]:

1. In *classical phonetics*, the vowel is described as requiring normal vocal cord vibration together with the tongue set in a low back position in the oral cavity. In pre-Action-Theory control models, achieving this phonetic rendering of the vowel would require first a cognitive search to find the specification of the vowel in terms of the several muscles involved and just how much each needs to be contracted to take the tongue to the required position. The computation in the brain would be exhaustive, and would then trigger the sending of the appropriate signals from the motor cortex to each individual muscle.
2. In *Action Theory*, the vowel is also described as being a low back sound with vocal cord vibration. However, rendering begins with a cognitive search to find only a very general specification: say,
    a. there shall be basic vowel-*ness* – i.e. the vocal cord vibration shared by all vowels in most languages;
    b. there shall be general tongue positioning, to set up the resonance system in the oral cavity – shared by all vowels;
    c. the tongue should be set in a low back position, unique to this vowel, let us say.

The above three features are in decreasing generality – vowel-ness applies to all vowels, as does tongue positioning, but specific tongue position applies only to *this* vowel. Points (a) and (b) would be the same for all vowels, with (c) differing, so as to specify *which* of the available vowels is to be set up. The detail of how to achieve all this is not cognitively searched or computed. Gross instructions with this outline specification are sent to the vocal-cord-controlling coordinative structure and to the tongue coordinative structure. Now the internal messaging systems take over to complete the detail of the specification and finalise the rendering.

The net result is that the right [ɑ] vowel sound will be the same, no matter whether the classical phonetics model is used or the Action Theory model. So what is to be gained by using the Action Theory explanation of motor control?

1. Greater generality is achieved – showing what it is that the vowel sounds or their subsets have in common. This is important to the scientist because maximum generality is one of the goals of scientific description. The principle of maximum generality is also important in the context of the human speaker/ listener because it contributes towards explaining why we *feel* certain sounds to be similar: they *share* certain abstract properties *and* also certain physical rendering mechanisms.

2. The low-level filling out of the specification can be achieved much faster than if the entire specification is computed in the brain, and with much less *central* computational load. Detail of the computation has been moved to the *periphery,* away from the brain. This will have a bearing on setting the upper limit on how fast or efficiently we can speak.

3. Suppose you try to make the vowel sound [ɑ] while standing on your head. Instead of the tongue moving from some central neutral position in the middle of the oral cavity downwards – assisted by gravity – to a low back position, it now has to be moved *upwards* against gravity! This means that articulatory control must compensate for the headstand. Although it is possible that the brain could calculate all this, it is much more plausible to suggest that the coordinative structure system has in-built compensation mechanisms via its messaging system to retain a constant goal (the specified position) whatever the gravity environment.

EVALUATION

USEFULNESS OF THE ACTION THEORY MODEL

In its original 1970s formulation, Action Theory was rather vague about concepts such as tuning and timing, and the effect it might have, as a new theory of speech production, on phonology and its place within linguistic theory. Would Action Theory, for example, virtually eliminate phonology by moving most of its processes from cognition into the physical world of motor control? The proponents of Action Theory were for the most part neurophysiologists and psychologists rather than linguists, and what they had to say was therefore of much more importance to phonetics than to abstract linguistics.

The simplicity of Action Theory is attractive, and once we are prepared to allow that detailed information can be added *during* a process without the need for constant re-representation of information from top to bottom, as had been the case with earlier translation models such as Coarticulation Theory, then much of the difficult data which these models could not deal with satisfactorily can easily be explained.

For example, classical phonetics and its successor, Coarticulation Theory, still could not explain that the various articulatory parameters of an articulation – such as the tongue's sections, the lips, the velum, the larynx – never quite SYNCHRONISE or succumb equally to coarticulatory effects at apparent boundaries between segments. Action Theory moved to a parametric approach and largely abandoned, in effect, the notion of syllable: this novel idea at the physical level was developed extensively in articulatory phonology in the 1980s. This parametric approach minimised the synchronicity of articulator groupings and defocused the notion of boundary between segments – thus leading to coproduction, a parametrically oriented version of coarticulation.

Arguably, Action Theory is basically a *physicalist* (current term: *biological*) theory of speech production in that it is attempting to take into account more of the detail of the actual mechanisms involved, and show that when this is done it has serious consequences for the way the input to the system (and therefore the higher levels as a whole) is to be specified. The antithesis of a physicalist theory is a *mentalist* theory, which places the bulk of the processing in the cognitive rather than physical domain. There have been developments which partially reinterpret the physical model *abstractly* to accommodate some of the observations in the area of cognitive phonetics – the area of phonetics which models how the constraints of the physical system can be modified.

SYNCHRONISING OF PARAMETERS AT SEGMENT BOUNDARIES

In classical phonetics, analysis and description proceeded linearly or segment by segment through an utterance. Coarticulation Theory drew attention to what was referred to as boundary blending or blurring between segments, and explained the phenomenon largely in terms of mechanical, aerodynamic and motor control inertia. Neither theory, though, focused on parametric modelling of an utterance. In a parametric approach, the focus is on the linear behaviour of individual parameters as an utterance unfolds, with little attention to any notion of segment boundaries. The reason for this is simple: the behaviour of the individual parameters appears not to be well synchronised. It is easy to see why this would be the case: articulators such as the tongue body, the tongue tip, the lips, the velum or the vocal cords are very different in terms of their masses and their controllability. The tongue tip is much more subtly controllable than the tongue body, for example. This means that synchronisation of their behaviour to achieve a neat boundary between segments would be difficult, if not impossible. But above all, it may be the case that synchronisation is not necessary and that boundaries are perhaps irrelevant. The reason for this would lie in the perceptual ability of the listener to assign neat, segment-style labels to the continuous, parametrically varying waveform without difficulty: the signal need not itself contain the boundaries since they would be assigned by the listener as part of the perceptual decoding process (see 'The Associative Store Theory of Speech Perception' in Chapter 8).

FURTHER READING

Chomsky, N. and M. Halle (1968), *The Sound Pattern of English*, New York: Harper and Row.

Halle, M. (1959), *The Sound Pattern of Russian: A Linguistic and Acoustical Investigation*, 's-Gravenhage: Mouton.

Jakobson, R., G. Fant, and M. Halle (1952, reprinted 1963), *Preliminaries to Speech Analysis, Technical Report B. Acoustic Laboratory MIT*, Cambridge, MA: MIT Press.

Ladefoged, P. (1989), *Representing Phonetic Structure*, UCLA Working Papers in Phonetics 73, Los Angeles: University of California Press.

Tatham, M. and K. Morton (2006), *Speech Production and Perception*, Basingstoke: Palgrave Macmillan.

Toates, F. (2001), *Biological Psychology: An Integrative Approach*, Harlow: Pearson.

CHAPTER 5 – THEORETICAL CONSIDERATIONS

INTRODUCTION

This chapter is about defining linguistic study – the various current points of view, and a brief history of how these views developed and coalesced into different approaches. We shall note that the area is still very fluid.

THE SCIENTIFIC STUDY OF LANGUAGE

Linguistics is often called the *scientific study of language*. This suggests that the usual principles of science are part of the methodology of studying language. That is, linguists make *observations* about language, noticing patterns such as repeating sounds – *words*; sequences of these words – *grammar* or *syntax*; common associations between words as representing similar events – *meaning* or *semantics*; and repeating patterns of sound within the word level – *phonology*. There are other types of observation, such as repeating usages in particular situations – *pragmatics* – and the production and perception of the sounds of the language – *phonetics*.

Those observations have been systematised into *descriptive* systems; for example, classes have been established, such as nouns, verbs and adjectives, and refer to the recurring type-usage of words (syntactic categories). When a new word comes into the language, it finds a place in the descriptive system of word classes. Recurring patterned sequences of words can be described by grammatical *rules*. For example, generally in English a subject noun is followed by a verb, and adjectives come before the nouns they qualify. The concept of rule does not imply such ordering is irrevocable, but tells us that the pattern that has become the conventional way of constructing sentences. These conventions can and do change. Just as with any science, the ultimate aim of language study is to provide *explanations* for these observations of units and how they pattern. An explanatory model or a theory suggests, or hypothesises, *why* things occur the way they do, or *how* they came to be as they are.

Current research in language studies involves a two-fold approach:

- *describing* language construction, establishing classes of words, features of sound, meaning, usage, combinations of features;

- *modelling* the nature of the human mind to provide a possible *explanation* for language systems.

Put another way, one point of view looks at language as the *output* of the production system and the relationship among the units of this output: this is termed *language* behaviour. The second viewpoint considers HUMAN LANGUAGE BEHAVIOUR – how human beings deal cognitively and biologically with the production and perception of language.

WHAT THEORETICAL LINGUISTS STUDY

In the original transformational generative model (Chomsky 1957, 1965) the individual components of the grammar represent what a speaker/hearer knows about the semantics, syntax and phonology of their language. What was being studied was the underlying language structure from a general perspective. The sets of rules are *not* descriptions of actual procedures during an act of performance. They are a descriptive characterisation only of COMPETENCE – what a speaker of the language must *know* to perform language tasks. Though strictly not theoretically correct, it is nevertheless helpful to imagine an ideal PERFORMANCE grammar which is equivalent to a performed competence grammar, but without any of the special considerations unique to a performance grammar per se. The phonological and phonetic processes referred to here are strictly representations of a speaker's knowledge of the regularities in the language, though it may be helpful to imagine them as steps in some idealised performance. In real performance other facts outside the scope of linguistics come into play, and often degrade this idealised performance to what we can actually observe. Examples of such performance-based degradation include temporary memory failures, short-term grammatical mistakes and hesitation phenomena, articulation problems like running out of breath, background noise interfering with communication, and so on.

COMPETENCE, PERFORMANCE

Competence is a *static model* of what a language user knows or perhaps needs to know about how language *in general* works and about how their *particular* language works within the general framework. A static model is one which does not incorporate clock time, referring to time only in a notional way. The knowledge consists of the language's basic units and the rules restricting their combination. Such units include grammatical categories and the syntax needed to combine them, and phonological units like phonemes and the rules which modify them in particular environments (like their placement within a syllable). At the phonetic level, a slightly different type of knowledge is needed: e.g. 'How do I make this or that particular sound requirement?'

Performance is a *dynamic model* of the actual use of competence in a real situation involving communication using language, where many other factors will be involved. These factors are often environmental, taking into account the purpose of a conversation, for example, or the mood and feelings of speakers and listeners. Performance often involves introducing non-linguistic considerations, therefore, and the need for selection between various otherwise linguistically equal possibilities for communicating thoughts. Some models (see 'Cognitive Phonetics', Chapter 4) introduce the idea that performance needs careful supervision to succeed. Dynamic models usually focus on clock time and the timing of events being described.

Besides the fact that competence and performance are models, the terms are often used ambiguously to refer to actual properties of the human being. That is, the models and what is being modelled converge in some accounts by researchers.

In modern times, different approaches have been taken to that put forward in the early work by Chomsky. These are too wide-reaching and complex to discuss here, but any good modern textbook on linguistics should give an idea of how the subject is developing (for example, Givon 2005; Jackendoff 2002). When we speak of phonological theory in this book we say each time which particular approach we are using. Remember that in general when one discipline (say, speech production and perception theory) refers to another (say, linguistics or psychology) it is quite usual to refer to the last or most recent *stable* theory to avoid confusing the non-expert reader. Rehearsing current controversies in these allied disciplines only confuses the issue – though, of course, we *do* present controversial or competitive positions when it comes to speech production and perception.

GENERATIVE LINGUISTICS

Up until the 1960s, most descriptions of language were made according to methods laid down by descriptivists and structuralists. The approach classified and described language(s) without reference to the nature of the human mind. But in the latter part of the twentieth century one of the major established points of view is known as GENERATIVE. The approach has given rise to productive research on the nature of mind. However, it is worth remembering that the relationship between language and properties of the mind had been suggested by various earlier schools of thought, and notably by John Locke (1690).

> **GENERATIVE LINGUISTICS**
>
> Generative linguistics is a method of characterising knowledge of a language, and relating this *knowledge* to language *expression* by a set of rules.

During the late 1950s and early 1960s there was a marked change in the direction of linguistic research. The initial proposals for the generative grammar model began by noting many descriptions of individual instances of language production which could be generalised in successive layers of abstraction. A set of mapping rules related the very general descriptions to less general ones – deep to surface structure. Attached to the initial grammars were two *interpretative* components – *semantics*, dealing with adding meaning, and *phonology*, dealing with adding speech to the core syntax.

This approach led to seeking generalised descriptions characterising principles about some basic features of human language called *universals*, and the assumption that these features or, sometimes, principles arise from common cognitive features. Later, the question of relating language patterns to cognitive functioning was pursued within the Chomskyan approach. Other questions at the time were:

- Do common features in language express characteristics of the cognitive *structure* of the mind?

- Just as sound systems vary, so do syntactic and semantic descriptions; but do they vary in a *systematic* way?

More recently, it has been proposed that cognitive *features* are themselves constrained by biologically based *structures*, a process called embodiment (Lakoff and Johnson 1999).

Deviations from general principles are accounted for by rules expressing variation. For example, in English adjectives usually occur before the noun they modify, while in French the usual pattern is that adjectives occur after the noun. In both cases, adjectives are closely associated with nouns sequentially (Matthews 2003), but variation leads to the rules sometimes being violated.

Central to later study were queries about the nature of phonological and phonetic data. Attention became focused on the cognitive and biological divide, since in speech it is not possible to avoid attempting to reconcile the cognitive and physical aspects of the theory. The questions here are:

- Can models of the speech production system provide evidence supporting cognitive/biological models?

- Do language models contradict cognitive models? (This was a later consideration.)

- Can language models be accounted for by cognitive models?

- Does the biological base associated with mental activity give rise to certain mental structures? (This is now referred now as EMBODIMENT.) Can language help model such a relation?

EMBODIMENT, EMBODIED COGNITION

The term *embodied cognition* involves a hypothesis suggesting that cognitive structures are constrained by biological structures. This includes all thought, concepts, metaphor, intuition and so on. *Knowledge* arises as the product of biological system activity, and also the result of interacting with the external world. On-going research into the influence of sensorimotor models on the formation of concepts and words provides some evidence of the importance of the embodiment model (Lakoff and Johnson 1999; Damasio 2003). Note that embodiment is *not* the same as correlating a biological base of activity with cognitive activity. One view suggests that cognition is *shaped* by biological structures, though another simply suggests, cognitive and biological activity can be *associated*.

FUNCTIONAL GRAMMARS

In functional grammars of models of language, the underlying theory is based on data from language *use*. The suggested language structures in the model are a result of investigation by specialists in discourse – communication interaction – with contributions from cognitive and physical studies.

Later models are sometimes referred to as being in the *Chomskyan tradition*. More recently, the formal Chomskyan approach to language description is contrasted with FUNCTIONAL GRAMMARS, arising from work on typology by Joseph Greenberg (2005), among others. The emphasis is on how language is used by speakers and how they are successful in a communicative setting (Givon 2005, for a current model). The objective is to build linguistic models based on language *use*. Theories in this approach seek explanations of language structure and language change, and from various areas such as cognitive studies, physical potential, discourse analyses, cultural studies and sociology. It should be noted that there also are other types of language model, for example structural, systemic functional and Minimalist, among others.

COGNITIVE RESEARCH AND LANGUAGE

Outside the field defined as linguistics/phonetics, a number of disciplines study language, or use language tokens as stimuli for experimental work. In fact, teams of researchers from different disciplines are working to model different aspects of language; speech researchers are often part of these teams. We outline four major areas developed from the 1950s onwards that might increasingly include speech research, in terms of what they want to do, the method used, and some of the results.

> **COGNITIVE**
>
> The term *cognitive* refers to activity of the mind, in contradistinction to physical activity. Some cognitive activity can be associated or correlated with brain and other physical activity.
>
> *Cognitive behaviour* refers to mental processing as distinguished from physical processing. Mental processes are not directly observable and require special experimental techniques. *Cognitive activity* is not directly measurable either, and relies on behavioural experiments or subjective reporting

At the same time as Chomsky (1957, 1965), psychologists such as Miller (1967) questioned the prominence of behavioural models in psychology which focused on measuring observed stimuli and observed responses, but said nothing about internal representations of knowledge or mental processing. Increasingly at that time, psychologists began to develop ways of constructing mental models, or COGNITIVE models, of internal processing – models suggesting what might happen *after* the stimulus was detected but before a response occurred.

During the 1970s, with the rise in computational modelling, interest developed in simulation of cognitive PROCESSING and in applications such as artificial intelligence. The researchers were known as cognitive scientists, and grouped naturally with linguists and psychologists. During the 1980s, linguists began to address ways of modelling the relationship between language and thought within the developing area of cognitive linguistics. Growing from this field, in the 1990s, research interest focused on suggesting constraints on cognitive processing arising from biological systems; the hypothesis was referred to as *embodiment* (Lakoff and Johnson 1999). Also during the early 1990s, cognitive neuroscience gained ground, based on novel developments in techniques in brain imaging – particularly the ability to display an image assumed to be directly related to brain activity. The following four areas are a very general outline that might be of interest to speech researchers concerned with the nature of mental representations and how these might be investigated.

> **PROCESS**
>
> In science in general, a process involves a series of changes in a dynamic system; usually the input and output of the process are known. In psychology, 'process' is a general term characterising changes within an organism, which are not usually directly observable, but are often hypothesised to account for experimental results; examples are areas such as memory and vision.

Cognitive linguistics – the interdisciplinary relationship between language and thought

In the 1970s, many linguists turned their attention away from formal linguistics to the relationship between language and thought, as a response to the innateness hypothesis proposed by Chomsky. Innateness suggested that humans are born with mental structures specific to language. With the major focus on syntax, generalisations based on descriptive linguistics were said to reflect this INNATE capacity.

> **INNATE**
>
> As used in linguistics, the term *innate* refers to the capacity, or the potential, to produce and understand language as a result of exposure to a language environment, but not necessarily the result of a clear learning process.

Some linguists, however, suggested that linguistic forms – specifically in the area of semantics (meaning) – reflected cognitive abilities that were properties of the mind and not solely confined to mental language structures. Fillmore in the 1970s and early 1980s, and Lakoff in the 1980s and early 1990s, initiated much of this work. The area gained ground in the early 1990s, and became known as cognitive linguistics (Lakoff and Johnson 1999; Evans *et al.* 2007).

Currently, cognitive linguists continue to see language as providing evidence to account for plausible models of cognitive processing. Cognitive structures may be modelled as innate, which suggests that although some aspects of language might *seem* to be innate, the essential innateness would not be *specific* to language. Lakoff and Johnson, among others, suggested that behind language lie conceptual representations that may occur within limits set by the biological system and by our psychobiological and social interaction with our environment.

> **REMINDER: COGNITIVE ACTION**
>
> Higher cognitive action is generally thought to occur as a result of interaction between whatever innate capacities there may be and exposure to the environment. That is, events in the environment, such as those created by social context, reading, television, etc., can trigger cognitive activity. In this case, it might well be that the capacity to learn language is innate, requiring consistent presentation of language patterns from the language spoken in the environmental context to learn a specific language. Cognitive action is thought to occur mainly in the cortex, with some activity occurring in other areas.

It might be useful to ask whether the proposed biological constraints could apply to areas other than language production. Can such limits be seen in other expressive areas such as music, art, literature, and science, and be *modelled in the same way*? Questions are asked such as:

- If common underlying structures can be established, how are their manifestations in literature, art, music, etc., similar?

- How does the nature of language fit within such categories?

The embodiment construct refers to modelling the relation of biological structures and the type of cognitive activity we seem to perform. For example, perception, instinctive reactions, thought and the decoding of types of sensory information, among other COGNITIVE ACTIONS, are formed and limited by *biological* structures.

Within cognitive linguistics, methods of investigation will vary depending on the background of the researchers. Methods range from experimental work to mathematical modelling to philosophy. Important questions are asked:

- Is language different from the symbolic means to compose music?

- Or is language indeed a special feature of the mind?

- If storage and retrieval are principles of the functioning of the mind, then if a disorder appears in language use, is it accompanied by similar disorder in storage and retrieval in other areas such as art or music?

When it becomes the case that strong links with researchers in psycholinguistics, pragmatics, metaphor and language description develop more fully, we may see a productive cognitive METATHEORY which can describe and perhaps explain aspects of human cognition. One developing area is a move away from modelling lexical items as collections of features isolable from other lexical items; the suggestion is that, however represented, these items have wider connections to other cognitive representations (Myers and Blumstein 2008; Holle *et al.* 2010).

Cognitive psychology and mental models

The name 'cognitive psychology' can be seen as overarching a number of divisions in psychology (Eysenck and Keane 2005). Areas such as memory, thinking, perception, reasoning and so on fall within the general area. The objective of the study is to conduct well-controlled experiments producing replicable results according to standard experimental and statistical methods in psychology research – standardisation enables viable and efficient comparison of research results.

Cognitive psychology was developed during the 1950s and 1960s as a way of investigating mental properties rather than looking solely at observable responses. Until around 1950, behaviourism predominated, requiring careful measurements of both stimuli and subjects' responses (Skinner 1957). The behaviour of the mind as it deals with changing environmental circumstances is not directly observable, whereas a response by the organism can be observed and correlated with the change in the environment, including presenting stimuli in an experimental situation. But it became increasingly difficult to work within the behaviour paradigm when constructing cognitive models of mental processing.

George Miller and Jerome Bruner (www.Harvard.edu) are credited with initiating research in cognitive psychology; they established the Harvard Center for Cognitive Studies in 1960. The purpose was to focus on research into cognitive or mental activity, concentrating on processing features. Miller was especially interested in bringing information-processing MODELS into psychology and built an early model of memory processing; he is known for the *chunking model*, which established the number of

METATHEORY

A metatheory (literally: a theory beyond a theory) formally links different models or theories together, since it prescribes for each a shared or linked abstract theoretical approach. Speaking and perception as yet do not have a reliable metatheory linking the theory of the capacity to plan utterances with speech production and with perceptual models of the acoustic waveform.

REMINDER: MODEL

The term *model* usually refers to a coherent set of statements derived from sound experimental work within a formal theory. The implication is that the statements can be accepted until new work provides a more plausible explanation of the observed phenomenon, and can take into account a wide range of events.

separate instances of objects or events that can be stored and recalled in short-term memory as seven. Of more interest to linguistics/phonetics is that he collaborated with Chomsky in early experiments testing some implications of the generative model for a possible processing model of language.

This type of research began to address questions such as how knowledge of our world and prediction about new events affects perceptions. For example, given the beginning of a sentence or word, we can often guess what the rest of the sentence or word might be even if we have never heard that particular sentence:

- Using PHONOTACTICS (tacit knowledge of possible phonological sequences in the language) we can predict the end of the word.

- Using knowledge of allowed syntax constructions (the grammar), and knowledge of environmental context, we can often guess the end of an utterance or sentence.

PHONOTACTICS

Phonotactics refers to the patterning of permissible sound sequences in an individual language. For example, in English, knowledge of the language's phonotactics enables us to invent a new word *blick* with the appropriate sound structure /blɪk/, but not the word *bnick*, /bnɪk/, since the word- or morpheme-initial sequence /bn/ is not permitted in the phonotactics of the language. This means that some nonsense words can be invented, but others cannot, and that they can be correctly devised by following the appropriate allowed phonotactic pattern. This has implications for experiments using nonsense words as stimuli, since words that follow the form are possible words of English, while words that do not conform to the pattern are not only nonsense words but nonsensical patterns and could never occur; their use in an experiment would perhaps introduce an unexpected variable.

There is some evidence from studies of speech errors for the validity of phonotactics. On occasion, we all make errors. For example, *big flan* can be produced as *fig blan, thunder and lightning* can be *lunder and thightning.* In these cases, the speaker keeps to the phonotactic rules of the language. Although *blan* is not a word in English, it could be one, and is acceptable to a speaker of the language as a potential word.

Cognitive psychologists have subdivided studies of cognitive processing into areas of research such as perception, attention, memory, problem solving, reasoning, learning, etc. By focusing research effort on these areas, model builders have derived plausible systems of *function*. These separately studied areas are beginning to be put together into a coherent system of cognitive activity (Mather 2006; Eysenck 2009). Language is studied with reference to these areas.

Psycholinguistics

PSYCHOLINGUISTICS is regarded as a subcategory of cognitive psychology focusing on language production and PERCEPTION, with an emphasis on information describing categories conveyed by language. For example, language conveys statements, feelings, requests and commands, queries and opinions about the world, and fantasy and fiction about imagined worlds. Experiments are conducted according to standard methods in psychology using language stimuli (Garnham 2001).

Psycholinguists specifically address questions of how to account for the speaker/listeners' ability to produce and understand language cognitively. A main question asked by psycholinguists, contributing to building plausible cognitive models, might be 'Are there analogous but different levels of cognitive language processing depending on level of representation – e.g. corresponding to linguistic levels such as phonology, morphology, syntax, pragmatics, or some other linguistic division?' The psycholinguist must decide to test cognition or language description but not both in the same experiment. Additionally, psycholinguistics asks 'Are linguistic levels processed separately or in parallel, or by some other method?' At some point, there may be an overlap with cognitive neuroscience (see below) in looking at timing relations in biological and cognitive processing.

> **PSYCHOLINGUISTICS**
> Psycholinguistics studies the cognitive (sometimes neurobiological) processes involved when a speaker/listener acquires, understands or produces a grammatical and appropriate sentence or utterance. Psycholinguistics is interdisciplinary, and is studied by researchers in several fields, for example psychology, cognitive science, linguistics or neuroscience. Applied areas include developmental studies on children's language learning ability, bilingual studies, and word recognition in reading studies.

REMINDER: PERCEPTION AND THE PLAN

The relationship between perception or decoding of the signal (as opposed to hearing it – see Chapter 7) and triggering recognition of the speaker's underlying utterance plan is not clear. It is possible for a listener to report perception of, say, a word or sentence, but this does not mean that the recognition of the speaker's *intent* as represented in their *utterance plan* is necessarily successful. How the listener assigns contextual meaning to the result of perception, or whether perception itself has happened only if an understanding of the speaker is reported, remains to be clarified. Several models of perception fail to address this particular question (see Chapter 8).

Cognitive Science

Cognitive science proceeds from the assumption that language is a subset of cognitive activity in general (Harré 2002). Around the mid-1950s, interdisciplinary teams began to study cognitive activity as *processing*. Researchers from psychology, computational modelling (in particular, artificial intelligence), philosophy and linguistics (among others) realised they had common interests in this area of study. They wanted to investigate properties of the mind that could reasonably be *computationally* modelled. Ultimately, the goal was to develop an overall theory of cognition by bringing together disparate linguistic and psychological models and their experimental design within a *computational framework*. The value of computational modelling when simulating properties of cognitive processing is that results from the computer model can be compared with results from psychological experiments with human subjects. If the results do not contradict each other, there is a calculated probability that the modelling need not be rejected – that is, can be provisionally accepted (following Popper 1934) – see Chapters 10 and 11 for how hypotheses are formulated and their results interpreted. Sometimes the computer model is ambitious, and attempts a simulation of the corresponding human processes.

Multi-disciplinary research has provoked questions about the nature of representation and about what constitutes good explanations. One area that developed from early cognitive science is computational linguistics, which has had many applications, such as machine translation and data-retrieval/ processing systems. Some computational approaches have been used in automatic speech recognition and speech synthesis (Chapter 9).

Cognitive Neuroscience

One of the objectives of the interdisciplinary area of cognitive neuroscience is to investigate what brain activity can be recorded and measured when the subject is carrying out cognitive functions (Gazzaniga 2009). Currently, most of the work consists of correlating a known stimulus input with imaging or other types of recording such as functional magnetic resonance imaging (fMRI), magnetoencephalography (MEG) or electroencephalography (EEG). A probability rating is assigned to the correlation which points to the reliability of the association – whether or not the two events can reasonably be accepted as co-occurring. The paradigm is: an external event results in brain activity and associated mental activity, resulting in behaviour change. The reliability of associating these events is not yet established, though in the future it may be possible to bring cognitive psychology, cognitive linguistics and cognitive neuroscience into a comprehensive model of mind-brain behaviour (Gazzaniga 2008; Poeppel *et al.* 2008).

A serious potential flaw lies in drawing conclusions from activity in a particular brain area as *directly* related to the stimulus item or the response. Relevant or observed cognitive activity may not be localised but may occur as a network-based activity, or sequentially, or in other areas in parallel with the area being looked at. It seems that currently only a small part of relevant activity may be recorded by the investigating technique.

The experimental procedure is similar to psychology experiments in which cognitive tasks are presented to subjects, and both task and responses are measurable. In imaging studies, the behaviour *response* is associated with the *image* of brain activity. Inferences are drawn about the relationship of brain activity to behaviour – although these inferences must be carefully made (Uttal 2001; Raichle 2003; Frith 2007). However, it must be remembered that the associated and assumed concurrent cognitive activity is not directly observable.

Ultimately some researchers hope to show

- how cognitive representations (concepts) can be associated with neural activity;

- that language constructs could be discussed in terms of neurological functioning.

Other researchers, however, hesitate to relate cognitive and biological activity – feeling these are two levels of representation that cannot be related as cause and effect. The most that can be done at the moment is to note some association between these levels. Nonetheless, clinicians have found these images useful in building empirical applications models; language disorders can sometimes be shown to be associated with brain dysfunction. In these cases, correcting the biological fault may result in more effective cognitive function.

THE FUTURE

The areas of study described above are predicted to remain viable research areas. One direction which may become more focused is how the nature of language may be constrained by properties of the human mind, and how much of the nature of the human mind might be modelled taking into account constraints and properties of the biological system (embodied).

And of course it is also possible to see and study the results of cognitive activity with no reference to biological underpinning. We can discuss music theory, for example, without taking into account the biological imperatives that might give rise to our cognitive capacity to think in musical terms. Or we can discuss interpersonal relationships without reference to possible underlying biological constraints. It depends on the question being asked.

RELATING SPEECH STUDIES TO COGNITIVE MODELLING

Spoken language research has its place in the cognitive areas, as well as in applications work (Chapter 9). Speech production is ultimately the result of cognitive processing – with different theories sometimes producing different accounts of the processes. Speech perception is active detection and decoding of the speaker's intent, and can also be modelled from different approaches. However we look at things, we assume that before speaking, and during perception, knowledge about language is accessed, and that separately linguistic descriptions characterise that knowledge. All models of production and perception incorporate cognitive and biological structures relevant to language. In some linguistic descriptive systems, biological and physical phonetic data is used to support cognitive phonological claims. For example, Optimality Theory in phonology (Hayes *et al.* 2004) incorporates phonetic data, and cognitive phonetics (Chapter 4) requires knowledge of the physical system in order to use the articulators optimally. It will remain useful for speech researchers to take linguistics and cognitive modelling into account, since speaking and understanding language are ultimately linked with models of language production and perception.

CONCLUSION

Linguists try to externalise and make explicit features of language that we as speakers and listeners have internalised and employ implicitly (Matthews 2003). As human beings we do this easily, usually without being aware of what we are doing or how we are doing it – and usually with few errors and reasonable success. Linguists are continually developing descriptions with a view to accounting for observations made in languages which vary considerably, and, in some approaches, they are interested in establishing linguistic universals. They also develop models which look at language from differing points of view, resulting in different approaches such as functional grammar, grammars in the Chomskyan tradition, Minimalist grammars, etc.

- It must always be remembered that the model is not reality – it is not itself the process or object being modelled. We implement ideas about language and construct model systems that seem to work; these models change down through the decades. The arrival of more detail about languages, gathered according to principles set out by the model, modifies the existing model until it is no longer useful in accounting for the phenomenon. Simply, the model needs careful changes to account for data it can no longer deal with. This procedure results in a new model, based on some new principles, and development of new methods.

One very important point: we must remember that *talking about* language involves *using* language, and thinking about language probably requires some sort of symbolic system and manipulation. Is it possible to discuss the result of cognitive activity in cognitively derived terms? That is, can we truly investigate the mind using the mind itself as one of our tools of investigation? To date, there seems be no resolution of this query – we see the problem, but not the answer. It will be interesting to see whether, in the future, a *metatheory* will be developed into which all describable cognitive functions could be placed, and where different kinds of behaviour such as human language usages could be subsumed. Such a metatheory would ensure that the different branches of study would collaborate effectively and without theoretical conflict.

EVALUATION

DESCRIPTIVE LINGUISTICS AND COGNITIVE MODELS

Descriptive linguistics and cognitive models look at language with different aims. The first describes language *without* reference to underlying cognitive or biological structures. For applications work (Chapter 9), descriptions with no reference to the nature of cognitive language production are usually adequate. The second approach, explicitly rooted in cognitive studies, is useful for understanding the nature of language as human activity and how language study can contribute to understanding the nature of mind.

FURTHER READING

Chomsky, N. (1957), *Syntactic Structures*, The Hague: Mouton.

Chomsky, N. (1965), *Aspects of the Theory of Syntax*, Cambridge, MA: MIT Press.

Damasio, A. (2003), *Looking for Spinoza*, Orlando: Harcourt.

Evans, V., B. Bergen, and J. Zinken (eds) (2007), *The Cognitive Linguistics Reader*, London: Equinox.

Eysenck, M. and M. Keane (2005), *Cognitive Psychology: A Student's Handbook*, Hove: Psychology Press.

Frith, C. (2007), *Making up the Mind*, Oxford: Blackwell.

Garnham, A. (2001), *Mental Models and the Interpretation of Anaphora*, Hove: Psychology Press.

Gazzaniga, M. (2009), *The Cognitive Neurosciences,* 4th edn, Cambridge, MA: MIT Press.

Givon, T. (2005), *Context as Other Minds*, Amsterdam: John Benjamins.

Greenberg, J. (2005), *Universals of Language*, The Hague: Mouton de Gruyter.

Guendouzi, J., F. Loncke, and M. Williams (eds) (2010), *The Handbook of Psycholinguistic and Cognitive Processes*, London and New York: Psychology Press.

Harré, R. (2002), *Cognitive Science: A Philosophical Introduction*, London: Sage.

Hartsuiker R., R. Bastiaanse, A. Postma, and F. Wijnen (eds) (2005), *Phonological Encoding and Monitoring in Normal and Pathological Speech*, New York: Psychology Press.

Ladefoged, P. (1965), *The Nature of General Phonetic Theories*, Georgetown University Monograph on Languages and Linguistics 18, Washington, DC: Georgetown University.

Ladefoged, P. (1971), *Preliminaries to Linguistic Phonetics*, Chicago: University of Chicago Press.

Lakoff, G. and M. Johnson (1999), *Philosophy in the Flesh: The Embodied Mind and its Challenge to Western Thought,* New York: Basic Books.

Locke, J. (1690), *An Essay Concerning Human Understanding*, 2004 edn, Harmondsworth: Penguin.

Matthews, P. (2003), *Linguistics: A Very Short Introduction*, Oxford: Oxford University Press.

CHAPTER 6 – ESSENTIALS IN DESCRIBING SPEECH

INTRODUCTION

There are a number of basic considerations to take into account when describing speech.

In speech *production*:

- Is the focus the cognitive properties of speech?

- Is the focus the physical properties of speech?

- Is the focus the interaction between cognitive and physical properties?

In speech *perception*:

- Are we concerned with hearing or perception?

- Are we concerned with the physical or cognitive properties of listening/perception?

DISTINGUISHING BETWEEN PHONOLOGY AND PHONETICS

Speech can be approached from several different viewpoints: linguistics, psychology, philosophy, computer science, aerodynamics, acoustics, anatomy, neurophysiology, neurology, electronic engineering, clinical linguistics and hearing impairment studies, among others. Researchers, teachers or therapists in all these areas have their own reasons for studying speech, and for the most part these mesh well. Often the approach starts with phonetics, usually regarded as a subdiscipline of linguistics. Theoretical linguistics itself is about either

- examining language with a view to spotting the patterns or procedures which can adequately describe the data we observe and note, or

- formulating hypotheses about the nature of the mental processes which might be involved in producing, perceiving or sometimes understanding language.

In the second of these aims we are ultimately interested in explaining why language is the way it is, whereas in the first aim the goal is less ambitious: the straightforward description of what we observe in human language behaviour.

The term *language* is itself ambiguous. In the past linguists have tended to mean by the word *language* something which we can hear spoken by users of language or read as their writing. This meaning goes along with the more simple and descriptive of the two aims above. But language can also mean the entire process by which a speaker produces a sound wave or some written text, all the way from having a deep-seated *notion* of something to communicate, right through to formulating sentences and ultimately either making a sound wave or producing some writing. Both the sound wave and writing constitute RENDERINGS of the intended meaning.

This characterisation of language can be extended to the processes by which a listener derives an *understanding* of what they hear or see written down. The main distinction between the two views of language is therefore between language as something produced with little interest in how it is produced, and language as the set of processes by which what is spoken or written is *created*. The two definitions can be thought of as mutually exclusive:

> REMINDER: RENDERING
>
> A rendering is a realisation or instantiation of some underlying thought or idea. So, for example, we can have a plan of what we want to say, and then proceed to render that plan as a speech articulation and ultimately an acoustic signal.

1. Cognitive		2. Cognitive		3. Physical		4. Acoustic
development of a thought	→	processes *encoding* the thought	→	processes creating either sound or writing	→	signal or written text

1. Most linguists are not concerned with *how* notions or thoughts are developed, but they *are* concerned with how the cognitive processes in (2) and the physical processes in (3) encode these thoughts into the acoustic or written medium suitable for conveying to listeners or readers. So, for example, if someone has a mental image of a small, furry animal, how does this get turned into the word *cat*, the pronunciation plan /kæt/ and the rendering [kʰæt]? (Remember: we are using the International Phonetic Alphabet (IPA) here to show only *representations* of what is actually happening; so, for example, [kʰæt] is a symbolic representation of the actual sound wave encoding the word *cat*.)

2. This stage in the overall process of encoding thoughts into sound or writing takes in the areas of linguistics known as semantics (concerned with meaning), syntax (concerned with words and their ordering into sentences) and phonology (concerned with planning how the words are to sound). These processes are cognitively based

and, importantly, abstract in nature – they cannot be heard or seen or measured in any physical sense. Psycholinguists *can* measure, in a relative sense, some aspects of a human being's behaviour when using these processes, but these measurements are not physical in the sense, for example, that we can provide a detailed quantitative analysis of speech sounds. In our task of understanding more about speech we are particularly concerned with phonology, because it is here that speakers work out in their minds how they are going to give acoustic rendering to what they want to say or the thoughts they want to communicate to listeners.

3. Phoneticians (as opposed to phonologists) focus mainly on the physical processes involved in creating a sound rendering of words or words strung together as phrases or sentences. Traditionally, for well over a century, phonetics has modelled the articulatory configurations of the vocal tract involved in producing speech sounds (articulatory phonetics) and later, to a certain extent, the aerodynamic and acoustic processes involved in the final production of the sound wave (acoustic phonetics). But in the last fifty or so years, a lot of attention has been paid to how we move the articulators, using motor control involving nerves and muscles. In the last twenty-five years or so, one focus of attention has been on how cognitive processes are used to make sure that motor control works efficiently and effectively (see Chapter 4, especially 'Cognitive Phonetics'). This cognitive supervision in physical motor control should not be confused with the cognitive processes involved in formulating what is actually to be said – this is phonology and strictly part of (2) above.

4. The acoustic signal is within the domain of acoustic phonetics, and provides much of the data for both phonetics and phonology. Phonologists are interested in discovering how underlying *plans* for what is to be spoken actually work out when it comes to the sound wave generated. Phoneticians frequently research the acoustics of speech because, compared with motor control and aerodynamics, it is so easily accessed. Quantitative measurement of the acoustic signal is available using waveforms, spectra and spectrograms (running spectra).

We can see that the abstract areas of core linguistics – semantics, syntax and phonology – involve modelling patterning of units for descriptive purposes, and modelling of aspects of human cognitive processing for more explanatory purposes. Phonetics is different: it is principally concerned with modelling physical aspects of speech, overlapping a little with more abstract processes when we deal with some of the detail of speech production and its motor control (Chapter 4).

- Physical modelling follows closely the principles and methods which are central to disciplines like physics or acoustics (a branch of physics).

- Cognitive modelling, on the other hand, involves often the more complex research techniques developed by psychologists.

One of the most interesting reasons for studying phonetics is that in this branch of linguistics both types of modelling are needed, and reconciling the two approaches becomes an important and difficult consideration.

THE RELATIONSHIP BETWEEN PHONETICS AND PHONOLOGY

Introduction

Until around fifty or sixty years ago phonetics was thought of as encompassing phonology. Phonetics was about the sounds of speech and how they are made, and phonology was about the way in which these sounds function together in languages. The model was primarily a surface treatment, examining only the observable data (what could be seen of the articulation or heard of the sound wave) without looking *behind* this data to discover possible underlying explanations. The model was also static in the sense that the focus was on the individual segments rather than on the dynamics of their sequencing. Since the beginnings of transformational generative grammar in the 1950s there has been a divergence of phonetics and phonology (Clark *et al.* 2007).

Phonology

These days, phonology *underlies* phonetics in the sense that phonological operations come logically earlier than phonetic ones. In modern terms, we think of phonology as characterising the eventual sound shape of words and sentences; and as such it is formulated and planned in some detail. Formulating and planning are, of course, cognitive activities – thus the phonology underlying phonetics now takes in decisions (again, cognitive) about how we want our sentences to sound. We think of phonology as being associated with a set of cognitive processes, or in the linguistic model a set of descriptions of processes, which come together to organise the speaker's plan for creating a sound wave appropriate for a listener to take in and decode back to what the speaker intended. Note the ambiguity: terms like 'phonology' or 'phonetics' refer, on the one hand, to sets of formalisms set out in linguistics, and, on the other hand, to the processes in the human being that they describe.

Once again, 'thinking about', 'planning', 'formulating', 'organising', 'deciding', 'encoding', 'decoding' – these are all terms which are strictly within the cognitive domain. After this cognitive processing the end result is the plan; and this is handed over to the phonetics for appropriate rendering. The phonology plans what the succeeding phonetics will attempt to render, and in doing so expects a certain level of success in making the right sound waves. Obviously, though phonology is constrained within itself, it is constrained also in the sense that it is not going to ask the phonetics to perform an impossible task, or generate a sound wave that listeners cannot handle for some reason. There are several stages involved in turning the plan into an acoustic realisation involving neurophysiological, aerodynamic and acoustic processes characterised in phonetics.

Phonetics

Phonetics is the component responsible for rendering the abstract phonological plan into a physical entity. There are several stages involved in doing this:

- *controlling* motor aspects of the musculature;

- *establishing* an appropriate vocal tract configuration, which is dynamically changing as utterances unfold;

- detecting and using feedback for *supervising* the rendering process as it proceeds.

We are developing the detail of contemporary phonetics as we go along in this book, but we must not forget the previous model, which overlaps with current ideas. To repeat: before modern developments about motor control, the role of cognition and so on, phonetics alone was the core discipline for modelling speaking. *Classical phonetics* as a theory incorporated phonology as a subcomponent dealing with the way in which speech sounds function in a language. In other words, phonology was able to tell us something about such systems as *phonotactics* – how sounds pattern on the surface, or *linearly*, in words; but the primary function of phonetic studies remained to account for how sounds are made from an anatomical, vocal tract perspective.

Abstract vs. physical – some examples from English accents

We have been discussing how, in linguistics, the phonological component underlies the phonetic component. This means that phonological processes logically precede phonetic processes. This is obvious if we define the task of phonology as the preparation of a plan for the required spoken output, as the diagram below shows.

Phonology		*Phonetics*	
Phonological processes →	Utterance plan →	Supervised rendering →	Sound wave

Take a simple, monosyllabic word like *cat*. A very abstract representation of this word in phonology recognises that it is made up of three *potential* speech segments – they are potential because they are still abstract and not yet rendered as physical sounds. These segments group into a hierarchically organised syllable. In traditional IPA notation we might use /kæt/ to indicate a linear sequence of three phonemes, with the / brackets meaning that the representation is phonological rather than phonetic. Speakers of different accents of English tend to pronounce this word differently, particularly on the last segment. The alveolar plosive might be fully released (as in a southern English accent), or unreleased (as in Estuary English), or rendered as a glottal stop (as in Cockney English). These different versions are *decided* by the speaker and, since decision is a cognitive process, we model the changes as *phonological* processes contributing to the utterance plan. This can be expressed as a set of simple descriptive phonological rules:

$t \Rightarrow t_{normal}$ / – # (educated southern English)

$t \Rightarrow t_{unreleased}$ / – # (Estuary English)

$t \Rightarrow ?$ / – # (Cockney English)

- Technically, these rules are of the type *context-sensitive*; that is, the process indicated by the arrow occurs only in the stated context. Thus the first rule is read as 'When /t/ precedes a word boundary in educated southern English it is to be pronounced as /t_{normal}/.' Notice that we say that 'it is to be pronounced' because the object to the right of the arrow constitutes the desired *plan* for the /t/'s pronunciation.

The symbol to the left of the double arrow is the underlying or deep phoneme /t/ and the symbol to the right is the derived extrinsic allophone /t/, /t'/ (using the IPA unreleased diacritic) or /?/. To the right of the /, shown by #, is the context or environment for the process – in this case, the occurrence of the phoneme immediately preceding a word boundary. These rules are stated as *predictive generalisations;* that is, they predict that wherever the underlying phoneme and context are true in a word the appropriate change will apply, as in the three accents illustrated.

Thus words like *sat* /sæt/, *bet* /bɛt/, *kit* /kɪt/, *yacht* /jɒt/, etc. are all specified similarly with respect to their final underlying /t/s. The reason for formulating the rules in this way is that it enables us to say that at some abstract level *known to all these speakers and listeners* the words are pronounced the same in all accents. To repeat: at the deepest level we are referring to the pronunciation of *the language*. The fact that the actual sound waves produced are different for the different accents is of no importance in decoding the intended words, although it is, of course, important in determining which accent is being used. This means that speakers and listeners are aware on the one hand at some level that the surface variants all relate to the *same* words, and on the other hand that the variations are markers not of different meanings, but of *different* accents.

All speakers of a language are aware of, and may even use, several accents, and know the appropriate rules either as speakers or listeners, but all refer back to the underlying form which does not exhibit the variations. Speakers of English may also know enough about the phonologies of other languages to know that, say, a speaker of French whose English pronunciation is not perfect will introduce variants when they speak English which are derived not from another accent of English, but from French – that is, speaker/ listeners can recognise, often mimic, a French accent in English. Similarly we might recognise variants in the pronunciation of young children ([fɪŋ] for *thing*, for example) or non-standard variants among those with speaking difficulties. Notice how useful a symbolic notation is for jotting down such things; researchers into disordered speech have even developed extensions of IPA to cover sounds made by speakers with particular difficulties.

- [fɪŋ] is shown in square brackets because it is probably a phonetic variant caused perhaps by immaturity of the fine tongue control needed for accurate rendering of fricatives; the plan is /θɪŋ/. On the other hand the Cockney pronunciation of *thing* is actually *planned* as a string of extrinsic allophones /fɪŋ/, and then rendered as [fɪŋ] – the underlying phonemic string is /θɪŋ/.

Once a speaker's phonology has come up with a final utterance plan it is handed over to the phonetics to render as actual speech: the acoustic signal. Some cognitive processing in the phonetics will assess how to do this, and set up a supervisory system for making sure that what is intended actually happens as closely to the underlying intentions as possible. We have seen ('Coarticulation' in Chapter 3) that the practical difficulties of creating sound waves using a speaker's musculature to control dynamic or changing vocal tract shapes are such that perfect or ideal renderings of the abstract phonological plan are all but impossible. But the phonetics usually does its best and the result is good: the listener gets the message because the listener is also a speaker and has themselves also met the difficulties. How this all works is covered in 'Production for Perception' in Chapter 7.

One more example of accents at work: consider the word *writer*. In English the underlying phonemic representation of this words in traditional generative-style phonology might be /raɪtər/, but in different accents the utterance plans will be different:

phonemic representation ⇒ extrinsic allophonic representation

gives us:

/raɪtər/ ⇒ /raɪtə/ (southern English)

/raɪtər/ ⇒ /raɪʔə/ (Cockney)

/ raɪtər / ⇒ /raɪɾɚ/ (General American)

Cockney plans a glottal stop extrinsic allophone of underlying /t/, whereas General American plans a voiced alveolar flap extrinsic allophone of /t/. General American also plans a rhotacised version of /ə/ for rendering the underlying final /ə/. The final /r/ is deleted in all three accents.

We have called this section 'Abstract vs. Physical' because we want to contrast the range of variations possible in speaking a comparatively small set of words – for any one word there are numerous ways of speaking it. It only makes sense to have a descriptive system which is able to group together all these variants and pin to them some abstract invariant label. This helps the linguist sort out the variants in order to work out the hidden systems among them; but it also captures an important behavioural property of speakers and listeners – they recognise similarities between the various pronunciations of a single word such that they can declare the variations to have the same meaning. The variations are apparent in the *physical* acoustic signal and also in the way the vocal tract producing the signal is behaving. The sameness between them is apparent in the *abstract* symbolic representation underlying these physical signals. In human speaker/listeners these abstract representations are in their minds. Relating an abstract, ideal, invariant representation to large sets of physical manifestations is a remarkable achievement of human beings, yet somehow so simple and taken for granted – it is the basis of perception (see Chapters 7 and 8).

THE LINK BETWEEN PHYSICAL AND COGNITIVE ASPECTS OF SPEAKING

Experiments with cognitive hypotheses

Many experiments in phonetics are based on ideas coming from PHONOLOGY or from observations of perception. So, for example, we distinguish perceptually (an observation in phonology) that many consonants in most

> **REMINDER: PHONOLOGY**
> Phonology (in speakers) is the cognitive processing which results in utterance plans to be rendered through to sound waves by physical phonetics; and (in listeners) the cognitive processing needed to assign hypothesised underlying utterance plans to heard acoustic signals, resulting in recognition and ultimately understanding of what was said.

languages have voiced and voiceless counterparts. So we find, in English and many other languages, a phonological distinction between voiced and voiceless stops (/b, p/, /d, t/, /g, k/), with speakers and listeners alike perceiving a difference between the two sets. The distinction enables contrasts between different words.

By and large, the most direct phonetic physical-world correlate of the presence or absence of the phonological voicing feature involves vocal cord vibration – present in the phonetic rendering of voiced stops and absent for voiceless stops. *Or at least that's how it seems.* From this observation we could generate the following hypothesis:

- Vocal cord vibration is present whenever the speaker or listener produces or perceives the presence of the voicing feature, especially when words are being contrasted. Thus the words *pat* and *bat* world be symbolically represented phonologically as /pæt/ and /bæt/, and phonetically as [pæt] and [bæt] (all other variations there might be between these words are ignored for the moment in the phonetic transcriptions). We would be hypothesising that [p] with the phonetic [– vocal cord vibration] feature is the direct correlate of unvoiced /p/, and that [b] with the [+ vocal cord vibration] feature is the correlate of voiced /b/

The experiment to support or reject is easy to set up. We just gather a number of native speakers of English (we may want to test several accents in different experiments) and ask them to pronounce the two words in a particular controlled experimental situation. On examining the results, we find that for what is normally regarded as the period in the signal corresponding to the [p] stop there is *no* VOCAL CORD VIBRATION when the word *pat* is pronounced, and that similarly there is also *no* vocal cord vibration during the phonetic [b] in the word *bat* (see Figure 6.1). Despite such experimental evidence, native speakers *think* they produce and hear a difference in the actual sounds; unless they have taken a course in phonetics it is virtually impossible to persuade them otherwise when listening to the words pronounced normally by others or even by themselves.

> **REMINDER: VOCAL CORD VIBRATION**
>
> This is the vibration of the vocal cords when tensed and when there is an egressive airstream, but also the *sound* produced by this mechanism. The sound is typically described as occurring as almost periodic pulses correlating with the opening and closing of the vibrating vocal cords.

To try to understand what is going on we look further. Is there anything unexpected about the waveforms of the two words that might be cueing the perception of difference? Looking at the two waveforms we notice that

- up to the sound of the stop release there is no difference (we are looking at silence during the stop phase of both consonants);

- there is a slight difference in the actual release sound (about 20 per cent less amplitude for [b]);

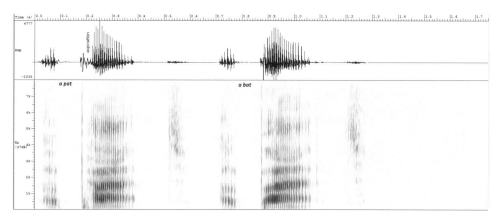

Figure 6.1 Waveforms and spectrograms of a *pat* and a *bat*.

- there is a major difference after the release – vocal cord vibration starts later after [p] than after [b].

Could it be that this delay in vocal cord vibration onset is what is cueing the difference between the two sounds and hence the difference between the two words?

In classical phonetics the delay is called ASPIRATION, a term based on the low-amplitude hissing or frication sound we hear. Classical phonetics modelled this as a property of voiceless consonants: their releases are followed by a period of aspiration, at least in English and languages like German (though not so much in Dutch). In more modern theory we are more likely to model the aspiration as a loss of vocal cord vibration at the start of the vowel, rather than as something tacked onto the consonant (Figure 6.2).

ASPIRATION VS. VOICE ONSET TIME

In classical phonetics the term *aspiration* is ambiguous: it refers both to the period between the release of a plosive and the onset of vocal cord vibration in the following vowel, and also to the aerodynamics and acoustics during this period. Another term, voice onset time (VOT), is strictly the time from the release of the plosive to the onset of the following vowel, where this usually means from the start of the release to the start of the first measurable vocal cord cycle in the acoustics correlating with the vowel.

We can reverse the hypothesis: listeners who are native speakers perceive /b/ when they detect no aspiration, but perceive /p/ when they detect the presence of aspiration. Jumbling up or randomising the recordings and then playing them back to listeners will confirm this, and the effect can be reproduced in a more controlled way by synthesising the sets of words by computer rather than using recordings of human beings. Indeed a [b] can be turned into a [p] as far as listeners are concerned by progressively introducing into the synthesised waveform a longer and longer period of aspiration after the release of a [b].

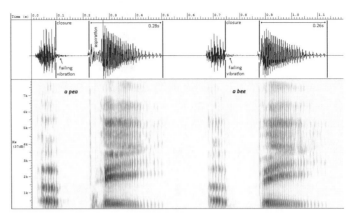

Figure 6.2 Waveforms and spectrograms of *a pea* and *a bee*. The focus of attention here is the period immediately following the release of the bilabial plosive. Notice that the time from the release to the end of the following vowel rendering is similar for both words, indicating that the aspiration is part of the vowel rather than part of the consonant. Classical phonetics claims that the aspiration phase is inserted between the release and the vowel, but if this were the case, how would we explain the consequent apparent shortening of the vowel rendering following [−voice] plosives? A better model is to say that the vocal cord vibration associated with the vowel is apparently shortened by coarticulatory aspiration – devoicing of the vowel – and that the vowel rendering remains relatively constant in duration.

Thus the phonological or cognitive representation of the difference between two potential sounds is conveyed in an unexpected way when those sounds are actually rendered phonetically – the situation being reversed when those same sounds are heard by a listener. We speak of the distinguishing feature (the phonological voicing) being transferred to another segment during the phonetic rendering and being restored back where it belongs during perceptual processing, as the diagram below shows.

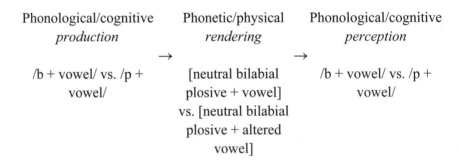

Experiments with physical hypotheses

Experiments with physical hypotheses are usually not based on observations of phonological behaviour. Here we are more concerned with the physical properties of sounds, rather than how they behave linguistically. So we may want to examine the differences in the physical spectra, say, of the set of vowel sounds in a language, or compare them with the vowels in another language. Here's an example of an informal hypothesis:

> Vowels generally have to *sound* different, especially in isolation where linguistic context cannot be used as a cue for perception. The spectral makeup of vowels is based on a pattern of formants, with frequency (rather than amplitude) being the dominant acoustic parameter; so the patterning is hypothesised to be different for the different vowel sounds.

To provide the experimental data, we produce time-free spectra, or time-included spectrograms from the waveforms of some recorded vowels spoken in isolation. We use several speakers for a given accent to make sure speakers behave in more or less the same way. We MEASURE the frequency of the FORMANTS, and arrange the data to reveal any unique patterning which can be correlated with the vowel labels.

What we find is that on the whole we can easily observe four formants (though some are weak, or have low amplitudes, in some vowels) in each vowel, either on a graphical plot of their spectra or in spectrograms; we measure their centre frequencies, since formants are usually specified in terms of their centre frequencies, together with their bandwidths and amplitudes.

FORMANT MEASUREMENT

Formants in vowels and some other speech sounds (for example, [l] and [r]) are specified according to three parameters: bandwidth, peak frequency and amplitude.

Bandwidth	The frequency range of a formant, measured at a point 3 dB down from the amplitude of its peak frequency
Peak frequency	Either the frequency located centrally in the bandwidth, or the frequency with the highest amplitude in the formant band
Amplitude	The highest amplitude reached within the formant band

What we can also observe is that, despite differences in the actual frequencies of formants between speakers, their *relative* patterning is the same. Thus John's large head produces these formant frequencies for [ɛ]: F1 700, F2 1,750, F3 2,400; whereas Mary's smaller head produces: F1 850, F2 1,900, F3 2,600. It is the difference in size of the vocal tracts which produces the different absolute measurements (see explanation, HEAD SIZE, ORAL CAVITY SIZE), not the different pitches of the voices, which is a function of the mass of the vocal cords and their rate of vibration. The ratio between the formants (the pattern) for John is around 1 : 2.5 : 3.4

and Mary's is around 1 : 2.4 : 3.3. It is this ratio which cues the listener to assign a particular label to the vowel sound. The language specifies a relatively invariant *ratio* of formant frequency values rather than the absolute values, which vary much more from speaker to speaker *within* the language community. Experiments often involve considerations of psychoacoustics (TUTORIAL – PSYCHOACOUSTICS).

HEAD SIZE, ORAL CAVITY SIZE

The shape of the oral cavity and the size of individual resonating sub-cavities are what determine a speech sound's formant structure. The absolute frequency values of formants are due to the size of a speaker's oral cavity, in turn reflecting the overall head size. Because people's head sizes vary enormously, the absolute frequency values of formants will differ between speakers. However, when we listen to speech it is not these absolute values which trigger perception, but their *relative* values – or the ratio between them. This is what enables the sounds made by different people to be identified as the *same* – even though they may be very different in terms of absolute formant frequency values.

Experiments with emotive and expressive hypotheses

Emotion and feelings on the part of the speaker are usually events existing quite apart from anything they may want to say. In one sense, anything can be said with any feeling. Thus a speaker may be generally angry for minutes or hours and during that time say things either connected with the anger or apparently unconnected. It may well be the case, though, that the anger inevitably comes across to a listener because the speaker has unconsciously adopted a particular tone of voice. Because the speaker's feelings last longer and are most likely independent of the message to be conveyed, we model the feelings *as they are rendered in speech* as a *wrapper* containing the speech. So, a speaker formulates and utters a sentence *within the context* of feeling angry, happy, etc.

Perhaps during the utterance, or more likely afterwards and during subsequent utterances, the feeling changes (*I'm glad I got that off my chest!*) and the wrapper will evolve, changing its influence on what is being said. As an example, people who are angry generally speak a little louder and faster than usual but with increased precision of articulation and using a narrowed range of intonation. People who are happy also speak faster, but with a greater range of intonation. These expressive wrappers constitute the environment dominating the utterance, and we say that they *evolve* because they change relatively slowly compared with the more immediate semantic content of what is being said (Tatham and Morton 2004).

- It is important to remember that the notion of successive layers of wrappers is a model; the reality is not clear. Models enable us to put together ideas about reality and to express them as formal, testable hypotheses – but they are not the reality itself. What models do is help us to make some sense of what we observe in the real world.

Thinking carefully about how people actually communicate, we might hypothesise that *all* speech is delivered within some wrapper or other. There is really no such thing as speech which does not communicate something of the speaker's feelings at the moment. Or, to put it round the other way, it is impossible not to have feelings, even if they are very bland and neutral. Our model of speech production goes way beyond a consideration of how simple sentences might be spoken in some neutral world, and moves towards attempting to promote an understanding of how speech is altered by these expressive wrappers. Listeners pick up on these wrappers such that their interpretation of what is being said is handled *within* a sense of the speaker's feelings (**EVALUATION – THE REPRESENTATION OF EXPRESSION**).

Expressive speech – that is, *all* speech – has effects within the acoustic signal which are used to communicate the expression to the listener. These effects are usually described as basically prosodic: they are part of the prosodic system which is used to convey other, sometimes linguistic, properties of sentences. For example, rising intonation is used sometimes in English (but more often in French) to convey that the sentence is a question, whereas an overall falling intonation conveys that the sentence is more a statement. The prosody of a language can be modelled in the wrapper theory – a secondary wrapper to the expressive one, shown below. We can say that this is a simple hierarchical model, looking as follows in a practical situation:

Expression   wraps →   *Prosody*   wraps →   *Sentence rendering*

1. I am feeling happy (EXPRESSION), and

2. I want to ask a question using rising intonation (PROSODY), and

3. the sentence I will fit within this environment is *Do you love me too?* (SENTENCE).

Or, more formally, using XML notation (see Tatham and Morton 2004):

```
<expression>                    [begin expression wrapper]
    <prosody>                   [begin prosody wrapper]
        <rising intonation>     [begin intonation wrapper]
            Do you love me too? [utterance]
        </rising intonation>    [end intonation wrapper]
    </prosody>                  [end prosody wrapper]
</expression>                   [end expression wrapper]
```

where <expression> ... </expression> is the expressive wrapper, <prosody> ... </prosody> is the general prosodic wrapper and <rising intonation> ... </rising intonation> is the particular prosodic wrapper.

Thus the acoustic signal embodies and communicates an expression wrapper which is non-linguistic. It is human, but it is not being encoded as part of language. Within this there is the first outer linguistic wrapper, prosody, which is part of the linguistic encoding of what is being said, but at the same time is *independent* of the content within it. Within these wrappers is the sentence, its syntactic and phonological makeup, which contribute to the utterance plan and hence its phonetic rendering.

This model is simple and in this form hides some obvious interactions between wrappers and content. So, for example, a rising intonation can be used to communicate that what is being said is a question rather than a statement with no change of word order. What is important at this stage of the development of this model is the basic formulation and whether or not it is productive in advancing our understanding of what is going on in speech production and perception.

PSYCHOACOUSTICS

Psychoacoustics studies how the acoustic waveform affects the recipient or perceiver. In speech, this refers to the relevant sounds as interpreted by the listener as meaningful speech. The sound signal itself is measurable according to techniques from psychophysics (well-established measurements of intensity, sound pressure and duration). The listener's response varies within the individual at different times because of attention or errors in transmission, and varies among larger populations of individuals. Some of these variations are ascribed to varying ability to detect the sound wave, to the response of the middle ear, or the response of the cochlea. Neural transmission and reception of these signals in the brain can also vary.

Applied areas of psychoacoustics include development of hearing-enhancement aids, signal processing, music, loudspeaker development, cochlear implants, building acoustic design, etc.

THE REPRESENTATION OF EXPRESSION

We should note that the approach to placing expression within a model of speech production which we detail here is comparatively modern. Earlier theories of speech, such as classical phonetics, saw tone of voice – the expression of feelings – as being *added* to or overlaid on speech. These theories begin by modelling a neutral, expression-free rendering of speech, and systematically change that rendering according to the expression being added. So, in this approach, an abstract rendering of a phrase or sentence is the beginning of the process. This contrasts with the more recent approach, which claims that the feelings of the speaker usually *pre-exist* the speech, meaning that the speech comes second and must be fitted into the expressive environment – its wrapper.

FURTHER READING

Clark, J., C. Yallop, and J. Fletcher (2007), *An Introduction to Phonetics and Phonology*, 3rd edn, Malden, MA and Oxford: Blackwell.

Goldsmith, J. (1990), *Autosegmental and Metrical Phonology: An Introduction*, Oxford: Blackwell.

Gussenhoven, C. and H. Jacobs (1998), *Understanding Phonology*, London: Arnold.

Halle, M. and G. Clements (1983), *Problem Book in Phonology*, Cambridge, MA: MIT Press.

Hayes, B. (2008), *Introductory Phonology*, Oxford: Wiley-Blackwell.

Hayes, B., R. Kirchner and D. Steriade (eds) (2004), *Phonetically Based Phonology,* Cambridge: Cambridge University Press.

Tatham, M. and K. Morton (2004), *Expression in Speech: Analysis and Synthesis*, 2nd edn 2006, Oxford: Oxford University Press.

CHAPTER 7 – HEARING AND PERCEPTION

INTRODUCTION

In this introduction we make a number of theoretical points which will be developed in more detail as we work through the chapter. We make an important distinction between hearing and perception:

> **PERIPHERAL PROCESS**
>
> A peripheral process like hearing is one which takes place other than in the brain. Processes taking place in the brain (a physical object) or the mind (an abstract object) are called *central processes*.

- *Hearing* is a PERIPHERAL PROCESS which is largely passive, in the sense that we do not influence its workings by thinking about it either tacitly or with some awareness.

- *Perception* is a central process which is mostly active, in the sense that thinking, or cognitive processing, dominates in the process rather than anything physical.

It is essential to make this distinction between the passive physical process of *hearing* (TUTORIAL – HEARING), which takes place in the ear, and the active, cognitive process of PERCEPTION, which takes place in the mind. The words are often used interchangeably in lay language, and we need to avoid confusion when using the terms technically. We will be repeating this idea as we go along because it is crucial to the distinction we are making throughout the book between cognitive and physical processes.

> **PERCEPTION**
>
> Perception is the *cognitive* process of assigning labels to the incoming signal. This is the case whether the signal is auditory or visual, or derived using any other modality for sensing events in the world outside the human organism. There are several models of perception in the phonetics literature; in Chapter 8 we consider in particular the Motor Theory of speech perception, the Analysis-by-Synthesis Theory and the Associative Store Theory.

At the very least a listener model needs the capacity to detect and examine – or *review* – an acoustic signal, and assign basic phonological labels and patterns to it. These will include segmental, syllabic and prosodic labels. We say this because we can observe that this is basically what a human listener can be observed to do; they can recognise sound segments and syllables from the language, as well as its basic prosodic patterns. The recognition is signalled by externalising a label: a listener might say *I hear the sound [æ]*, or *The first part of* Manchester *is [mæn]*, or *It sounds like he's asking a question* (i.e. using question intonation). Perception of speech does go further than this: it involves not just phonological knowledge (sounds, prosody, etc.) but also some syntactic and pragmatic knowledge.

In addition, listeners can detect and interpret signals revealing a speaker's emotional state – not generally thought to be within the domain of linguistics. We speak of emotional content, or more generally, *expressive content,* as *wrapping* the message the speaker is conveying. Such expressive content *is* within the domain of speech theory because the nature of the wrapper can have an effect on the articulation and acoustic signal. Thus, an angry speaker will perhaps be tense, altering the speed, amplitude and even segmental nature of the signal.

Active and passive approaches to modelling speech perception

We have said that perception is the act of labelling the acoustic signal with appropriate linguistic SYMBOLS; and language processing in the mind is seen in general as the systematic manipulation of linguistic symbols: SYMBOLIC PROCESSING. Speech perception is about sorting out which symbols the *speaker* had in mind when they produced the speech the listener can hear, as the diagram below shows.

Speaker		*Listener*
The speaker has ideas expressed as linguistic symbols, and encodes these as speech sound waves.	→ The sound waves travel between speaker and listener.	→ The listener hears the signals, and perceives them by working out the original symbols the speaker had in mind when the speech was created.

REMINDER: SYMBOLS AND SYMBOLIC PROCESSING

Symbols are the units of a symbolic representation. Speech and language are thought to be indirectly processed by the mind using symbolic representations. The reason for this is that the mind – being abstract – cannot process the physical waveforms of speech directly. Processing works on symbolic representations and re-representations of what is heard by the listener. However, there seem to be physical correlates of many of these cognitive processes.

We take the line that modelling the cognitive process of speech production and perception can cast light on the workings of the brain. One or two researchers have maintained that cognitive perception is much more passive than active. In these theories the mind is seen as a kind of passive *filter* which is used to sort out from the incoming signal the speaker's intended phonological plan – what they wanted to say. Simplistically, these theories hypothesise that the intention is *contained in the signal*, and can be extracted from it. Most researchers seem to feel that this is unrealistic; for example, there are many examples of *identical* sound waves producing *different* and reliable listener responses. By contrast, as we shall see later, the researchers who support the active approach maintain that the speaker's intention has to be *assigned to the signal* by active processing on the part of the listener.

What does seem certain is that listeners need to know the phonology and phonetics of a language before they can interpret a speaker's intentions. We can readily observe that listeners cannot begin to understand a language unless they have acquired some knowledge of its grammatical and semantic systems – as well as its phonology.

Perception and prosody

One question which arises about how listeners detect and process prosodic features of speech concerns whether the interpretation of the segmental structure from the sound wave precedes or follows interpretation of its prosodic structure. That is, do we

- assign a prosodic structure to the sound wave, and *then*

- assign the segmental structure,

or is the ordering of these operations round the other way?

Classical phoneticians would probably assume here either that the two were interpreted *simultaneously,* or that the interpretation of the prosodic structure of an utterance *follows* working out its segmental structure. We support the view, however, that the prosodic structure can be modelled as being assigned first. In this more contemporary approach, the segmental structure is fitted to the prosodic structure, not the other way around. In speech production, expression – often emotive content – comes first, then prosodic content, and then segmental content. We first considered the wrapper idea in Chapter 6 when we were dealing more with speech production. Here, speech perception is going to be about unwrapping the package.

Speech is produced *to be perceived*

We might safely assume that speech is intended to be perceived and that a reasonable hypothesis may be that speaker and listener *know* this and work to help each other out. A simple model along the lines below can be set up.

Knowledge of speech perception		*Knowledge of speech production*
↕		↕
Speech production →	Sound wave →	Speech perception

In this model, part of the process of speech production involves consultation, indicated by the double arrow, of the speaker's knowledge of speech perception, and part of the perceptual process involves consulting the listener's knowledge of speech production. We say that the speaker has *access* to a model of speech perception and that a listener has *access* to a model of speech perception. We can go a little further: these models are fully *predictive*. So, for example, a speaker is able to predict by consulting their perception model how a listener will react, in terms of perceptual difficulty or accuracy, to what they hear. And even further: the producer can modify the speech plan and its rendering in order to complement what is predicted to happen during the subsequent perceptual process.

Briefly, speakers are sensitive to the way perception works and any problems the listener may have. This sensitivity is achieved by *trialling* perception of the intended speech *within the speaker's mind,* before committing to an actual sound wave. Trialling implies access to a predictive model of what will happen.

We can expand the production model as shown below. Here, speech production hypothesises how the output will sound if nothing further is done. This hypothesised output is then passed by the perception model for evaluation. Potential low success ratings cause the rendering to be revised, thus producing a revised output more likely to score success during actual perception. The process could well be iterative until the speaker is satisfied that perception will be perfect, or satisfactory, or adequate.

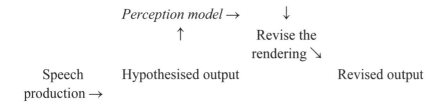

A similar expansion of the perceptual side of the overall process can be made. After an initial shot at perception, the process is repeated by consulting a production model and making adjustments; the result is a revised and more accurate perception which has taken into account something of how the speech might have been produced initially.

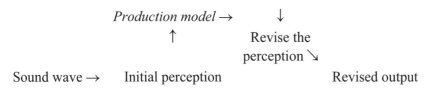

To summarise: it is necessary to make a sharp distinction between hearing and perceiving:

- *Hearing* involves a set of physical processes which convey a representation of a pre-analysed sound wave to the auditory cortex of the brain.

- *Perception* involves a set of cognitive processes which are applied to the results of hearing.

In studying perception we need to account for a number of observations we can make about perceptual behaviour:

1. Perception appears to be categorical – that is, we seem to push what we hear into pre-determined categories which correspond to the set of phonological segments used in the particular language we are listening to. Hence it is hypothesised that we have to have knowledge of our language's phonology. Speakers of different languages use different sets of categories, so these are learned as we learn a language; particularly our native languages (see Chapter 8).

2. Perception involves prior knowledge of at least:

   a. some of the general properties of sounds and how they are used in language in general. For example, sounds occur linearly in sequence and not generally in parallel, and feature searching needs to take several sequenced sounds into account because of the phenomena of feature spreading and feature transfer (the spreading of features to adjacent sounds and the transfer of features completely to different, usually adjacent, sounds). These were discussed in Chapter 6 in connection with the role of aspiration;
   b. the categories of sound used in the language;
   c. the feature specification of sounds, so that they can be fitted to the categories;
   d. the phonotactics of the language – that is, the rules for combining the sound features and the rules for sequencing sounds in syllables (and words).

HEARING – BRIEF INTRODUCTION

Again, we make an important distinction between *hearing* and *perception*:

- Hearing is a PERIPHERAL PROCESS which is largely passive, in the sense that in general we do not influence its workings by thinking about it either consciously or subconsciously.

- Perception is a CENTRAL PROCESS which is mostly active, in the sense that thinking, or cognitive processing, dominates rather than anything physical.

PERIPHERAL VS. CENTRAL PROCESSES

A peripheral process is one which occurs outside the brain, whereas a central process is one which occurs within the brain. Resting on the idea that the brain is *concrete* and is essential for cognitive processing, we also define an *abstract* central process as one which occurs in the mind. In linguistics and phonetics, peripheral processes are generally physical, whereas central processes are generally cognitive. As with many definitions involving human beings there are grey areas, as, for example, when cognitively determined supervision intervenes in some physical processes to make sure all is going well, but in general the definitions here are good working rules of thumb

Speech production

Abstract		Mind – cognitive processing → utterance plans
Concrete or physical	Central	Brain – neural processing → motor cortex
		↕ Connecting nervous system
	Peripheral	Musculature and associated articulators → acoustic signal

Speech perception

Concrete or physical	Peripheral	Acoustic signal →ear – hearing system → pre-analysis
		↕ Connecting nervous system
	Central	Auditory cortex – neural processing → brain
Abstract		Mind – cognitive processing → perceived symbolic representations

1. In speech production theory:

   a. Cognitive phonological processes take place within the mind which result in *utterance plans* – intentions as to how linguistic units should take on physical acoustic rendering;
   b. the utterance plans are interpreted as *target plans* (parametric physical representations of the intended acoustic rendering);
   c. the motor control system renders the targets to produce an *acoustic signal*.
2. In speech perception theory:

   a. the peripheral *hearing mechanism* pre-analyses the acoustic signal parametrically for passing to the central nervous system;
   b. cognitive processing within the mind provides *perceptual interpretation* of the acoustic signal by assigning symbolic representations to it.

The theory and associated model building are discussed more fully in Chapter 8.

The physical hearing mechanism

The following table illustrates the pathway taken by sound (and its analysis) from the environment outside the listener through to its destination in the auditory cortex.

The outer ear

The *pinna* – the external flap of the ear – has the function of collecting sound, particularly from in front of the head. This front bias has the effect of altering the spectrum of the sound coming from behind the head: it has some high-frequency attenuation, providing some rough directional information to the listener. Spectral tilt is used along with relative timing

	Outer ear	Middle ear	Inner ear	Neural transmission	Destination
	Pinna → auditory canal →	Ossicles (malleus, incus, stapes) →	Cochlea →	Auditory nerve →	Auditory cortex
Function	Collect and direct audio signal to the tympanic membrane	Amplify and transmit tympanic membrane vibrations to the oval window	Convert analogue vibrations of the oval window to digital equivalents, using a parametric analysis, to arrive at a neural representation of the audio signal	Transmit the multi-channel digital analysis from the cochlea to the brain, and project it onto the auditory cortex	Receive the digital, parametric representation of the waveform and prepare it for cognitive processing

between the signals from the two ears to help determine the direction the sound is coming from.

The *auditory canal* conducts sound to the tympanic membrane, or eardrum, at its end. The resonant properties of the tube are such that there is an effective shaping of the audio spectrum to provide some emphasis between 3 kHz and 4 kHz. It is partly this that increases our sensitivity to sounds in this area of the spectrum.

The *tympanic membrane* oscillates in sympathy with the auditory air-pressure variations reaching it from along the auditory canal.

The middle ear

The tympanic membrane is the link between the outer and middle ears. The purpose of the middle ear is to conduct the sound vibrations from the eardrum to the oval window in order to introduce them to the cochlea – the inner ear.

The *malleus*, attached to the tympanic membrane, brings the mechanical vibrations of the membrane to the *ossicles* – a set of three connected, tiny bone structures of which the malleus is the first. The other two are the *incus* and the *stapes*. The connection between these forms a lever system providing a degree of mechanical amplification to the vibrations as they are transmitted to the oval window to which the stapes is attached.

The *oval window* is the middle ear's link to the cochlea – the inner ear. The amplification is necessary because vibration in the oval window is resisted by the fluid against its other surface; without amplification there would at best be a significant attenuation of the signal – the viscosity of the cochlea fluid is significantly greater than that of the air on the outer side of the tympanic membrane. The overall process of adjustment of force between the tympanic membrane and the oval window is known as *impedance matching*.

The inner ear

Air-pressure changes in the air outside the ear arrive, amplified by the processes of the middle ear, at the oval window at the beginning of the curled tube known as the *cochlea*. The function of the cochlea is to convert sound energy into neural impulses for transmission to the brain's auditory cortex.

The reality is very complex, but in a simple model suitable for our purpose, rows of hair cells attached to the BASILAR MEMBRANE – and in particular the inner ones – vibrate or move in sympathy with the pressure changes within the cochlea and the vibration of the basilar membrane itself. Differing length hair cells group to vibrate differentially depending on their length, itself responsible for their resonant frequency. The result here is that only specific groupings of hair cells vibrate in response to the spectral energy present in the original signal. The result is a mechanical analysis of the original complex wave.

BASILAR MEMBRANE
This is a relatively stiff tissue running the length of the cochlea and dividing it into two tubes filled with liquid. These tubes are known as the *scala media* and the *scala tympani*. The membrane vibrates along its length, with the highest frequencies occurring where it is narrowest (at the base of the cochlea) and the lowest frequencies occurring where it is widest (at the apex of the cochlea).

The groups of hair cells are attached to platelets which compress slightly as the hair cells vibrate. The function of the platelets is to generate neural signals whose frequency is dependent on the amplitude of the vibrations. Thus a frequency band in the original waveform, having a particular amplitude, will cause a specific group or band of groups of hair cells to vibrate (indicating their position in the frequency spectrum) at particular amplitudes (indicating the amplitude of this particular range of frequencies in the original signal). Since particular platelets are associated with particular groups of hair cells, the compression of a particular platelet is a coding of a frequency component of the original signal. Particular platelets are associated with particular neurons in the complex bundle known as the auditory nerve.

So *which neuron* tells the brain *which frequency band* we are dealing with, and the frequency of the impulse train on that neuron tells us the amplitude of that frequency. It is important to notice that the overall system is converting analogue information (the amplitude of groups of frequencies in the signal) into digital information in the form of neural signals in the auditory nerve – we call this *analogue-to-digital-conversion*. Frequency is signalled by which neuron is activated – we call this *frequency-to-channel conversion*. Amplitude is signalled by rate of firing of the neuron – we call this *amplitude-to-frequency conversion*. Thus the result of the cochlea's analysis of the original waveform is a coding of the amplitudes of specific frequency bands within its spectrum. Remember that sound is described parametrically in terms of its *frequency* and *amplitude*, and how they unfold in time; it is these parameter which are being encoded here.

Speaker's output	Analysed into	Coded as
Original signal *waveform* →	Specific *frequency* bands →	Specific neurons – *channel* encoding
	Amplitude of these frequency bands →	Range of specific neural impulse rates – *frequency* encoding

The ear's separation of the waveform into component frequency bands and their amplitudes approximates to a FOURIER ANALYSIS.

FOURIER ANALYSIS

Fourier theory (named after Joseph Fourier) allows for a complex wave such as speech to be modelled as a series of component sine waves. A sine wave is the simplest form of wave; in the sense that it cannot be analysed into component sine waves or harmonics. Note that we are not saying that a complex wave *is* the sum of some sine waves; rather that it can be *modelled* as such. Fourier analysis is the mathematical procedure which describes the process of deriving potential component sine waves. Spectrograms (graphical representations of the frequency spectrum of a waveform as it unfolds in time) are usually derived using a computational, or computer software-based, version of Fourier analysis, performed on the waveforms.

- A complex wave is one which can be modelled as consisting of a number of simple waves. There may be many of these, and they do not have to have the same amplitudes. A simple or sine wave is one which cannot be modelled in the same way: it already *is* a basic component, which cannot be viewed as consisting of anything simpler.

PASSIVE AND ACTIVE MODEL OF PERCEPTUAL PROCESSING

If speech perception is about labelling the acoustic signal, then one of the biggest problems facing us is the fact that there is no direct, one-to-one or linear correspondence between portions of the waveform and its potential symbolic representation – either in the mind of the listener or for us as investigators (TUTORIAL – THE MAIN PROBLEM IN SPEECH PERCEPTION).

Direct realism theories maintain that we are aware of the outside world directly from information available from our senses – in the case of speech, the auditory information supplied by the ears and the passive hearing processes. On the other hand, *indirect realism* maintains that we are not aware of the external world directly, but that awareness is really dependent on interaction between data from outside (again, through the hearing processes) and stored internal or mental representations of the outside world. We shall be considering examples of both types of theory later (see Chapter 8).

There are several theories of speech perception which rely on internal representations, and some which support the idea of unmediated access to the external world. In general, as we shall see, researchers in speech perception prefer theories which rely on cognitive mediation for INTERPRETATION of the sound wave.

THE ROLE OF THE SPEAKER

Because direct communication of thoughts or cognitive processes between people is not possible, the thoughts and processes have to be encoded into a suitable physical form before they can pass between speaker and listener (Frith 2007). In the case of speech, the physical form is a sound wave – the final representation of a long series of representations and re-representations of thought as part of the overall encoding process. In this book we are not concerned with the encoding of meaning (semantics) or the encoding of words into usable patterns (syntax). What concerns us are two of the final stages of the overall encoding process:

> **INTERPRETATION**
>
> In speech perception, interpretation of the sound wave means the act of labelling the incoming signal using the set of symbolic representations available in the language. These symbols are learned and stored by the listener as part of the process of acquiring the language. These are symbols which the human being uses as part of dealing with language – we do not mean, of course, International Phonetic Alphabet (IPA) symbols.

- *cognitive encoding* of sentences into potential sound shapes according to the rules or conventions of the language, and the building of an abstract speech plan – this is *phonology* in our dynamic model (different from the early static phonology of *The Sound Pattern of English*; Chomsky and Halle 1968);

- *physical rendering* of the speech plan to produce the necessary audio signal – this is *phonetics*; the physical rendering is under cognitive supervision, though we refer to it as the physical part of the speaking process.

THE ROLE OF THE LISTENER

Listeners are involved in decoding the sound wave back into an appropriate cognitive representation of the speaker's original thought – this *is* perception. Once again, there are two main stages involved:

- *physical analysis* of the acoustic signal, pre-processing it into a form suitable for cognitive processing – this is hearing and, from a linguistics point of view, is treated in *phonetics*;

- *cognitive decoding* of the analysed signal, resulting in the assignment of a symbolic representation of the sound wave suitable for syntactic and semantic decoding – this is perception and, within linguistics, is treated in *phonology*.

Speaker		*Listener*
Has an idea expressed as linguistic symbols and encodes these as a speech sound wave	→ The sound wave travels between the two humans	→ Hears the signal and works out the speaker's original symbol representation from it

ACTIVE PROCESS

An active process is one
which involves cognitive
control or cognitive
supervision – opposed to
a passive process, which
is normally uncontrolled,
automatic or involuntary.

To repeat: most researchers have reached the conclusion that perception is an ACTIVE PROCESS and cognitive in nature; it is explained by workings of the MIND rather than the physical brain, although how the BRAIN works is generally felt to constrain how the abstract mind works. This simply means that the physical brain's makeup is to a certain extent responsible for what cognitive processes can be undertaken. We shall take this general line, and discuss a few theories of perception (Chapter 8). So, for us, the active processes involved in speech perception mean that cognitive processing has to occur for speech to be perceived or decoded by the listener; perception for us cannot be a purely passive process.

MIND AND BRAIN

In this book we make the traditional distinction between mind and brain. The mind is an *abstract object* characterised by cognitive activity involved in goal-directed processing of symbolic representations of physical objects. The brain is a *physical object* located mainly in the head and incorporating the spinal cord; it is involved in neural activity which often appears to correlate with cognitive activity. The *precise* relationship between mind and brain, or between the observed cognitive and neural activity, is as yet not fully known or understood, and is largely a philosophical or psycho-philosophical matter.

One or two researchers, however, have maintained that cognitive involvement in perception is much more passive than active. We saw earlier that in these theories the mind is seen as a kind of passive filter which is used to sort out from the incoming signal the speaker's intended phonological plan – that is, what they wanted to say. Simplistically, these theories hypothesise that the speaker's intention is contained or embodied in the signal, and can be extracted from it. Most researchers seem to feel that this is unrealistic.

REMINDER: INTERPRET

Listeners are said to
interpret the sound waves
they hear; interpretation
is performed by layered
or cascaded cognitive
processes which assign
symbolic representations
to the waveform.

What does seem certain is that listeners need to have KNOWLEDGE of the phonology and phonetics of a language before they can INTERPRET a speaker's intentions.

KNOWLEDGE

In linguistics, knowledge is strictly tacit – we are not necessarily aware of what we know or how it is used in language processing. Linguistics is an attempt to model or enumerate this knowledge. In general, the knowledge is of the symbolic representations used in language and the processes they undergo. Only weak claims are made by linguists concerning how the model reflects what happens in the human being – if the model were a true reflection of reality it would not be a model but a trivial copy of the reality itself: models are built to enable us to understand reality, not to copy it. Attempted copies of reality are often called simulations – so, for example, computer speech may sometimes be designed as a simulation of the human process of speaking (see Chapter 9).

PERCEPTION AND PROSODY

The perception of prosody probably follows similar lines to the perception of the segmental structure of an utterance. In linguistics, prosody is a phonological concept and is therefore abstract, participating in building the utterance plan. Just as with segment or syllable units, prosody has ACOUSTIC CORRELATES, and it is these which are available to the listener.

> **ACOUSTIC CORRELATES**
>
> Phonological objects are processed in the mind to build utterance plans – blueprints of how a speaker would like words, phrases or sentences to sound when they are rendered. The plan forms the basis for physical phonetic rendering, and the end result is the articulatory and acoustic signals we can measure. When the acoustic signal has occurred in response to something in the utterance plan, we call it an acoustic correlate of the abstract objects in the plan. Occasionally there are apparently spurious acoustic signals which may be correlates of adjacent objects in the plan; we have already come across this in vocal cord failure at the start of vowels in plosive + vowel sequences – the failure is a correlate of the *preceding* plosive.

The same set of models is available as with segmental perception: direct realist, indirect realist and idealist (see Chapter 8, TUTORIAL – REALISM AND IDEALISM in Chapter 8). There is no need to rehearse the arguments for each of these three again, and it is clear now that our preferred perceptual framework follows indirect realist principles. The Associative Store model (see TUTORIAL – THE ASSOCIATIVE STORE MODEL IN DETAIL in Chapter 8) is the most comprehensive of the indirect realist models since it explicitly allows for cyclical interpretation and *repair*. In principle, prosody has to be interpreted from the waveform, and is heavily dependent on stored knowledge of the language's prosodic system.

Acoustic correlates of prosodic features

Abstract prosodic feature	Correlating properties of the acoustic signal
Intonation	Relatively slow change of fundamental frequency spanning several syllables, and up to a sentence-length utterance
Stress	a. Abrupt change of fundamental frequency from one syllable to the next draws attention by potentially leading to a disjoint perception of the intonation contour b. High amplitude on a syllable to signal that it is stressed, low amplitude to signal an unstressed syllable c. Abrupt change in temporal patterning, particularly the use of pause to give prominence to the following word
Rhythm	Temporal patterning in the sequencing of stressed and unstressed syllables.

All the acoustic features are subject to a thresholding effect: it is always some *change* in the signal that is being detected, but our ability to do this is constrained by the minimal size of change that the system *can* detect. If the change is less than this it cannot be taken into account. This is the same kind of constraint as the perception of detail in the acoustic signal: the data is *thresholded* by the design of the hearing mechanism. However, the design of the system is complex and not fully understood: it may well be that detail we thought could *not* be handled can in fact be used under circumstances we do not understand yet. This will be true for all direct realist theories, including the detail classifier theories described in Chapter 8.

We need to have some idea of the units of prosody perception. The above table describes the prosodic features as changes of intonation, stress and rhythm patterning, though these are rarely kept completely separate. More often than not there are simultaneous changes occurring in different parameters.

So the acoustic correlates do not stand in a linear relationship with their abstract phonological features. Because, in *production* the relationship between prosodic features and their acoustic correlates is non-linear, it becomes hard to develop a formula for the reverse; that is, direct mapping of the acoustic signal onto abstract prosodic features in the listener. Instead, we invoke once again the idea that in perception the acoustic signal triggers an *indirect* realist assignment of stored labels, rather than follows a single path of cascaded transformation from acoustic detail to prosodic label. In the following diagrams we set out the two competing approaches: model 1 is a direct realist or detail classifier approach, and model 2 is an indirect realist approach, relying much more on STORED KNOWLEDGE.

STORED KNOWLEDGE

Knowledge of the phonological and phonetic properties of languages is acquired and stored in memory. Even direct realist models need some minimum of stored knowledge – often just a set of phonological labels to assign to the data detected in the incoming signal. The question usually is how much knowledge is needed: direct realism requires less and indirect realism requires more. Models which rely heavily on stored knowledge to interpret the signal are classed as *top-down* models, whereas those relying more on direct data are classed as *bottom-up* models. Top-down information consists of units and processes which operate on them; this knowledge is called upon to assist in assigning labels to the data.

In *model 1*, shown below, detection and transformation of the signal will enable assignment of prosodic stored labels. The transformations applied in the model are passive translations of the discovered correlates in the data which enable passive assignment of labels. The reason for including these transformations is to overcome the non-linearity of the representation of intonation, stress and rhythm in the data.

Correlates   *Labels*
↓

	Intonation	If yes, apply	Assign appropriate
↗	correlates? →	intonation	intonation label
		transformations →	
Acoustic →	Stress	If yes, apply stress	Assign appropriate
signal	correlates? →	transformations →	stress label
↘	Rhythm	If yes, apply rhythm	Assign appropriate
	correlates? →	transformations →	rhythm label

In *model* 2, shown below, detection, with appropriate application of stored knowledge of labels and *prosodic processes*, leads to interpretation and then assignment of the correct prosodic labels.

		Correlates	*Knowledge base (KB) of prosodic processes →*	*Labels*	
			$\updownarrow$	$\downarrow$	
	↗	Intonation correlates? →	Consult KB for active interpretation↑	Retrieve label →	Assign found intonation label
Acoustic signal	→	Stress correlates? →	Consult KB for active interpretation↑	Retrieve label →	Assign found stress label
	↘	Rhythm correlates?→	Consult KB for active interpretation↑	Retrieve label →	Assign found rhythm label

Units of prosody perception

The current descriptive model in phonetics sees prosodic features as changes in intonation, stress and rhythm (Carmichael 2003); some phoneticians also think of TONE as a prosodic feature. The acoustic correlates (based on observations of what speakers actually *produce* when rendering the prosodic plan) are said to be changes in fundamental frequency, intensity and rhythmic unit timing – though not in a linear relationship with the abstractions of the phonological tier (or component) represented in the utterance plan. But how accurate are these mappings for *perception*? Are there other characterisations that might be more appropriate?

TONE

Tone is sometimes said to be a prosodic feature because it involves the manipulation of fundamental frequency rather than other acoustic features. The fundamental frequency changes associated with tone occur *during* a single syllable rather than between syllables. For this reason, in the theoretical approach taken in this book, tone is a feature of segments; it is not a prosodic feature. As with other units, tone is a phonological feature which is rendered acoustically, and its acoustic correlate is fundamental frequency change. The usual examples of tone are taken from Mandarin Chinese, which has four systematically different changes of fundamental frequency which can be applied to a syllable. So /ma/ with (a) a high level tone, (b) a high rising tone, (c) a low falling-rising tone or (d)a high falling tone are all different words.

Our main theoretical reason for taking tone to be a segmental feature is that it never plays an intonational role; it is always independent of the current intonation pattern, and is fitted into whatever pattern is in play. Thus, for example, a falling tone can be inserted into a rising intonation pattern (using XML notation):

```
<intonation.rising>
    <tone.falling>
        <syllable/>
    </tone.falling>
</intonation.rising>
```

We say that prosodic features *span* a number of consecutive syllables – unless, of course, the entire syntactic group consists of just one syllable, such as *Go!* – but that segmental features are in principle attached to only one.

The perception of prosody – before or after segmental structure?

Classical phoneticians would probably assume here that either (a) prosody and segments were interpreted simultaneously, or (b) the interpretation of the prosodic structure of an utterance follows the working out of its segmental structure. Remember: the classical phonetics view of prosody in speech *production* is that prosodic contours are fitted to the planned segmental structure of an utterance. In this model, both speech production and perception of the prosodic features of an utterance seem subordinate to the segmental structure.

A more modern approach in speech *production* theory is to hypothesise that the prosodic framework for an utterance is worked out first, and then the segmental structure of the utterance is fitted to it: prosody comes before segments. We say that prosody *wraps* the segmental structure of an utterance, and that, in turn, expression wraps the prosody. This view of speech production is carried through to *perception,* and assumes that the wrapper would be interpreted first, followed by the segments it contains. So, if the model is reliable, the listener would first become aware of those aspects of the speaker's expression or mood, followed by its general prosodic properties (statement, question, etc.), followed by the actual message content conveyed by the segments. The listener could set up an *expectation* of the prosody after the first few segments.

If speech production is indeed organised in this hierarchical way, with prosody wrapping segmental rendering, it can be hypothesised that the nature of the PROSODIC CONTOUR (the prosodic features unfolding in time) will constrain the articulation of the segmental string. An example of this would be the way in which prosody influences segment duration, as when the slowing-down effect at the end of a sentence in English progressively prolongs the time spent on each syllable – which in turn changes the proportion of each syllable used in coarticulatory overlap. Thus, changes in segmental rendering cue the listener to assign a prosodic structure to the signal. This principle is much the same as the findings that coarticulatory effects such as formant bending cue detail of the underlying segmental plan (see 'Information from Spectrograms', Chapter 11). At the prosodic level the units are more likely to be syllables than individual segments **(EVALUATION – PROSODY AND SEGMENTS IN SPEECH PRODUCTION).**

PROSODIC CONTOUR

The prosodic contour is the shape or direction of the prosodic features as they unfold over time. Generally, this is abstract, and involves the phonological terms 'intonation', 'stress' and 'rhythm', but it can sometimes refer literally to the graphed shape of physical measurements of fundamental frequency, amplitude and temporal patterning.

PRODUCTION FOR PERCEPTION

Speaker and listener collaboration

We assume that speech is designed to be perceived. To make this idea more formal, a reasonable starting hypothesis would be that speaker and listener both know this, and work together. It may be possible to find examples where they are working to defeat, interrupt or deceive the perceptual process – but this too assumes that both know that speech is designed to be perceived. An early informal proposal was made tentatively by Nooteboom (1983), but contemporary theory (for example, cognitive phonetics; see Chapter 4) makes the idea quite central to speech production/perception.

Building on the ideas expressed above, a simple model along the lines shown below can be set up. In this model, part of the process of speech production involves consultation of the speaker's knowledge of speech perception, and part of the perceptual process involves consulting the listener's knowledge of speech production. We say that the speaker has *access to a model* of speech perception and that a listener has access to a model of speech perception. We can go a little further: these models are fully *predictive*. So, for example, a speaker is able to predict by consulting their perception model how a listener will react to what they hear, in terms of perceptual difficulty or accuracy. And even further: the producer can then modify the speech plan and the precision of its rendering in order to complement what is predicted to happen during the subsequent perceptual process.

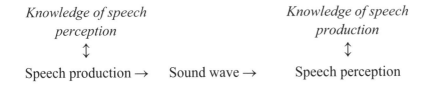

We can expand the production model as shown below. Here speech production hypothesises how the output will sound if nothing further is done. This hypothesised output is then passed through the perception model. Success *ratings* cause the rendering to be revised, thus producing a revised output more likely to score success during actual perception. The process could well be iterative until the speaker is satisfied that perception will be perfect, satisfactory or adequate.

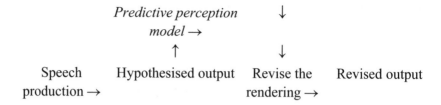

A similar expansion of the perceptual side of the overall process can be made (shown below). After an initial shot at perception, the process is repeated by consulting a predictive production model and making adjustments; the result is a revised and more accurate perception which has taken into account something of how the speech might have been produced initially.

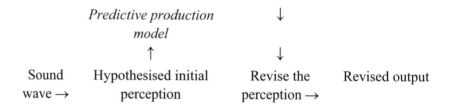

Below are examples of how production and perception might be adjusted for better performance consequent upon trialling, and then repeating, the process.

Required sentence	*I prefer the paper to the TV.*	
First-shot utterance plan in Cockney accent	/ai prɪfɜ ðə peiʔə tə ðə tivi/	
Revised 'clearer' utterance plan	/ai **prɪfɜ** ðə **peipə** tə ðə tivi/	/..ɪ ../ → /.. i ../ in *prefer,* /.. ʔ ../ → /.. p ../ in *paper*
Required sentence	*As a writer, I can't say.*	
First-short utterance plan in General American	/əz ə raiɾɚ ai kænt sei/	
Revised 'clearer' utterance plan	/əz ə **raitɚ** ai kænt sei/	/. . . ɾ . . ./ → /. . . t . . ./ in *writer*

There are many factors which could influence a speaker to come up with a revised utterance plan. One might be simply the desire to speak more clearly to the listener, or perhaps to speak with what the speaker judges to be a 'better' accent. There might be high background noise, and this might require a more careful plan; perhaps the speaker has a cold and knows that speech will be a little rough.

We have kept this discussion to phonological and utterance plan revisions. But it can also be the case the listeners have difficulty with some aspects of how the plan is rendered. In this case, revision of the plan may work, but there is also scope for more careful supervision of the rendering process itself (see 'Cognitive Phonetics' in Chapter 4).

EXPRESSIVE CONTENT

We have looked at some features of the speech sound wave that can trigger perceptual processes. Although there are difficulties in assigning static phonetic labels to acoustic features, the procedures work reasonably well for non-emphatic plain speech – often referred to as *neutral* speech, that is, speech which is considered to have little or no significant expressive or emotive content.

The procedures fall down when dealing with speech as it is actually spoken; that is, in speech styles such as general conversation, teaching, news reading, for example, or at any time when speech with expression and/or emotion is being described. For example, it is not yet part of any standard phonetic description to label speech which is detected by the listener as happy, angry, sad, etc. – that is, *expressive* or *emotive* speech (Tatham and Morton 2004).

Some researchers differentiate between expressive and emotive speech. Others use the terms as equivalents. We use them as follows:

- *Expressive speech*: used by the speaker to give *intended* information.

For example, expressive speech can refer to emphasis on a particular word or phrase – not necessarily because it is felt to be emotional, but, say, in reply to a query asking for information. The focus words may be emphasised, drawing attention to the information. The utterance may be slightly louder than usual or bounded by silence before and after the focus words; the duration of the word can be changed, the rhythm of the sentence can be changed, or there can be a slightly increased f0 change. For example, in the utterance *I said Jack, not Mack,* Jack is emphasised by raised f0.

- *Emotive speech:* arises from a general emotive stance by the speaker (Panksepp 2000).

For example, when the speaker is angry, researchers report many physiological effects such as increased heart rate, raised blood pressure (although these may be slight), and a general increase across the body in muscle tension. The speech apparatus is part of the biological system, and will also be slightly tense. In relation to most of the muscles in the body, the articulators are small muscle systems; so a small increase (or decrease) in tension will occur. This affects the configuration of the vocal tract, which affects the sound produced. And the listener can detect these changes, which correlate with the biological changes.

It seems that these acoustic features in the waveform can be interpreted by the listener as revealing feelings, attitudes or beliefs. Although the sound produced may be modified minimally, listeners usually report that they can even identify and label a speaker's subtle emotion as, for example, *slightly irritated*, or *calm*. Sometimes the listener uses the phrase *I don't like your tone,* but might not be able to say exactly what prompts that impression.

The basis for emotive content

Emotion has proved to be a difficult concept to define (Ortony *et al.* 1988). Current approaches are based on the division into two modelling types, cognitive and biological, which we discuss throughout. Emotion can be looked at from several points of view: biological, biological with cognitive elements, cognitive, or cognitive with biological bases (see Tatham and Morton 2004: ch.9 for a discussion of different approaches). In addition, whatever feelings, attitudes and beliefs we convey, we can generally use words to express them, but we can also convey the same information by using expressive or emotive tone of voice. In other words, a speaker can say: *I'm angry because my car's been stolen,* or simply say *My car's been stolen* with added anger emotive content. To discuss emotive content of speech we need to look at three modelling areas: biological, cognitive and linguistic/phonetic.

We suggest looking at emotion as biologically based, accompanied by both cognitive control and awareness. Four basic neurobiological systems have been identified as associated with four emotion reactions, accompanied by fairly predictable responses (Panksepp 1998). The words we use to characterise these are: angry, sad, happy, and neutral/nurturing. However, our lives do not centre on easily identifiable basic emotions but on their varying *intensity* or the *interaction* between them.

Secondary emotion

The term 'secondary emotion' is used to refer to variations in intensity of a particular category of basic emotions. It is also sometimes used to refer to *blends* (see below). For example, within the broad category *anger,* a range of emotion can be identified and labelled: irritation – annoyance – anger – rage. These words label an increasing amount of what we can basically identify as anger. This range can be represented by an anger-*line*, ranging

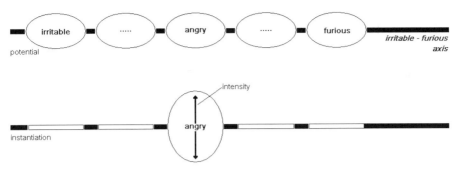

Figure 7.1 Potential anger-line or axis ranging from irritable through to furious. Below this we see a graphic of an actual instantiation in which anger and its intensity defocus the other possibilities.

from low to high intensity. Similarly, *happy* can range through: *content – pleased – happy – joyful – ecstatic*. Figure 7.1 illustrates a potential anger-line, together with how the particular emotion of anger on that line becomes instantiated – in this case with focus on its intensity.

We also seem to employ the cognitive function of *appraisal* to both our own emotions and to the identification of the speaker's emotive content. The system of appraisal involves assessing the significance of the emotion we feel (*not* a reaction to the emotion itself), the importance of the information it is giving us, and the importance to us of both *our* feelings and the *inferred* feelings and attitudes of the speaker (Scherer 2001).

Words

We use words to describe thoughts, ideas and observations, but also to refer to our internal emotive state. So, we ask what feelings words can convey. Here are some examples: *I am upset, I am overjoyed*, or *I feel disappointed*. Along with this verbal expression of feeling we can see physical manifestations of the emotion: *upset* and red face, *overjoyed* and smiles, *I am disappointed* accompanied by a gloomy face, and so on. LeDoux (1996) points out that there may be some confusion arising from the concept associated with the word(s) used and the feeling experienced. *I'm shocked* may refer to fear, surprise, fear and anger mixed, or laughter. In fact, speaker and listener may report quite different feelings or attitudes associated with the same phrase.

Blends

More subtle types of emotion can be identified, such as feeling both happy and sad at the same time, or angry and frightened with disgust (arguably a basic emotion, but the neurobiological evidence is not clear). Thus, in addition to varying intensity, we can also have blends and varying *intensity of blend*. Emotive states and words associated with them can be represented in a table (see below).

Word	Basic emotion	Range	Blended with
Irritation	Anger	Low	Calm (high)
Annoyance	Anger	Low–mid	Calm (mid)
Anger	Anger	Mid	Calm (low–mid) + fear (low)
Fury	Anger	Mid–high	Fear (low)
Rage	Anger	High	Fear (mid)

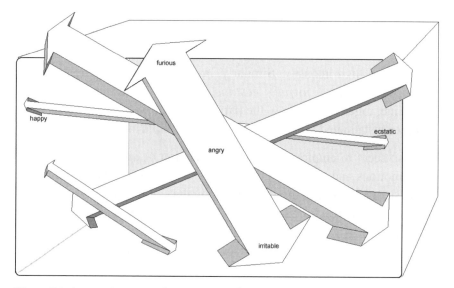

Figure 7.2 An emotion space, showing various lines or vectors of emotions (see also Figure 7.1). Notice how the vectors seem to deploy within the three-dimensional space in terms of their intersection and overlap.

Such a descriptive chart will soon become quite complicated, since adding more emotion words as blends will rapidly require a greater specification when dozens or hundreds of words and ranges are added. The cognitive phonetics model suggests a different representation, as shown in Figure 7.2.

We can show interaction as an 'emotion space', and assign words to this interaction. Ranges and blends can be clearly represented within this space, although the more are displayed, the more crowded the space becomes. This is an abstract model designed to show relationships among basic emotions, potential blends, and words describing the units and their interrelationships. Whether or not an individual's behaviour can be modelled fully in this way is another question; however, this type of model is predictive, characterising the data and generating hypotheses that can be tested within the model framework.

Each of the vectors in the diagram represents the range of its basic emotion. The intersection of the vectors characterises the intensity at that point, as well as the type(s) at that point. Referring to the chart above, we can immediately see that the word *furious* can express quite a high feeling of anger, but also may be accompanied by some fear. What we need to know is

- How do fear and anger interact at the biological level?
- How can the various intensities of emotion felt be related to relative amounts of activation of two basic systems?
- How reliable is the reporting of the feeling (for example, is it possible to suppress feeling, and thus the reporting of it)?
- At what point does the feeling assume significance for the person?
- What words and phrases are used to express the feeling?

This model can also characterise the changing emotions revealed or concealed in a conversation as it unfolds. Movement in the vector space can reflect change, such as going from mild anger to calm, when the listener has new information that activates a different neural mechanism. Appraisal is thought to provide internal information, such that the listener can modify basic reactions before making a response.

The acoustic signal

What concerns us in dealing with speech production and perception is the nature of the acoustic signal which forms the basis of the listener's assessment of expressive and/or emotive content. However, the nature of the correlating detail in the acoustic signal is not at all clear, although a great deal of research has addressed this question. Currently, acoustic features have not been reliably associated with the perception of emotive content of speech (see also 'Speech Technology' in Chapter 9).

One approach as a preliminary step is the *wrapper model* (see 'Experiments with Emotive and Expressive Hypotheses' in Chapter 6), which makes the assumption that all speech output results from a biological stance based on muscle activity. All muscles have some tension (muscle tone) unless heavily sedated – and even then there remains some residual tonic activity. If the biological setting changes, as it does under emotive load, the speech will also be affected, as will facial muscles, back muscles, hands, etc. The cognitive phonetics model proposes an overall framework – the wrapper – within which emotive effects are contained. During conversation, the emotive wrapper changes or evolves, reflecting the change in biological reaction to the conversation environment. The resulting acoustic wave contains emotive information, the result of the stance and consequent appraisal processes.

Classical phonetics or its static derivatives can describe acoustic features, but do not as yet provide an explicit or reliable means of relating acoustic features to emotive content, other than in broad outline. For example, characterisations such as increased intonational range expressing anger, or altered rhythm expressing excitement, are of little or no formal use. Unfortunately, there is no overall model associated with classical phonetics that might be productive in understanding expressive and emotive content of speech. Detailing which acoustic events are critical for triggering perception of expressive and emotive content in speech is very much a challenge for future work.

TUTORIAL

HEARING

TRANSDUCE

To transduce is to change one form of energy into another. In a simple example, headphones connected to a mobile music player transduce the digital signals of the recording into an acoustic pressure wave we can hear. Round the other way, a microphone transduces an acoustic wave into electrical signals suitable for processing and recording.

Hearing is the *physical* process by which sound pressure changes are TRANSDUCED into electrochemical neural signals suitable for passing along the auditory nerve to the part of the brain responsible for their processing: the auditory cortex (Mather 2006).

In the outer ear the eardrum detects and responds to sound pressure changes by vibrating. It can do this over a range of some 20 Hz to 20 kHz – the higher figure declining in usability with age in many people, down to around 10 kHz. However, the fall-off in frequency with age is of little importance in speech because sounds in all languages are contained well within the 20 Hz to 10 kHz range.

Sound pressure in air, however, is too weak to be useful when it comes to setting up pressure waves within the cochlea, which forms the important part of the inner ear. For this reason, the vibrations of the eardrum are mechanically amplified in the middle ear by means of a tiny, bony arrangement of levers which transmit the amplified signal to a window, similar to the eardrum, at the wide end of the cochlea.

Within the cochlea we find the basilar membrane, to which are attached hundreds of groupings of hair cells. The function of these organs is to take up the vibrations occurring in the fluid filling the cochlea. The grouped hair cells are of different lengths, and the basilar membrane itself is tapered – the result is a differential vibration in sympathy with the cochlear vibrations. Different hair-cell groupings respond to different frequencies in the overall signal. At the base of each group of hair cells is a plate whose function when compressed by movement is to generate electrochemical nerve impulses for transmission along a composite nerve fibre to the auditory cortex. There are perhaps as many of these nerve fibres as there are groupings of hair cells – and they are bundled together to form the auditory nerve. We speak of neural sub-channels responsible for conveying information about the spectral content of the incoming sound wave to the auditory cortex.

It is important to remember that, in the way just described, the cochlea performs a mechanical analysis of the incoming acoustic signal. This analysis operates in the frequency domain, extracting component frequencies of the complex acoustic signal. Frequencies are associated with individual, or groupings of, nerve fibres: this is called *frequency-to-channel conversion*, the nerve fibre being the channel along which the information is to be conveyed to the auditory cortex of the brain. The extent of activation of a nerve fibre (the rate of firing of neural impulses propagating along the nerve fibre) signals or codes the amplitude of the associated frequencies: this is called *amplitude-to-frequency conversion* because the amplitude of the signal is coded as the frequency of neural impulses. The auditory nerve conveys this frequency and amplitude information to the brain, where it is *projected* onto the auditory cortex. This projection is remarkably similar to the phonetician's spectrogram.

		Cochlea		*Auditory nerve*	*Auditory cortex*
		Spectral analysis	Coding for transmission	Transmission	Projection
Acoustic signal	↗	Frequency →	Frequency-to-channel conversion →	Identified neural sub-channel is activated →	Full spectral information
	↘	Amplitude →	Amplitude-to-frequency conversion →	Frequency of neural impulses →	

THE MAIN PROBLEM IN SPEECH PERCEPTION

TUTORIAL

Arguably, one of the main problems in arriving at a satisfactory theory of speech perception is accounting for the fact that speech sound waves are not a one-to-one encoding of phonological segments. The latter are *abstract cognitive concepts* anyway, and we might expect their physical coding to be complex.

Some researchers suggest that when the sound wave is produced the various features of the segments are spread around, merging segment with segment at the physical acoustic level. If this idea is accepted, then in principle perception (or decoding) has simply to recover the features from the sound wave and reassemble them to identify the original phonological segments. The *passive* theories of perception try to devise an automatic filtering type of procedure to achieve this.

Unfortunately, hard work over several decades has failed to come up with any suitable passive decoding procedure which can account for our observations of perceptual behaviour. In other words, the hypothesis that the acoustic waveform is a direct encoding, however complex, of phonological segments is questionable. So the notion that those segments are consequently in principle recoverable by passive decoding has so far defeated empirical verification. This does not mean that it will not eventually be possible to find segments in sound waves, but for the moment alternative models are more viable – see 'Direct Perception' and TUTORIAL – REALISM AND IDEALISM, Chapter 8.

Passive theories of speech perception share the essential property that they require little or no supervision on the part of the listener. The labels identifying, say, speech segments are in some sense already present, and just need to be *extracted*. The alternative hypothesis is that the sound wave is *not* a direct encoding of phonological segments. The segments are *not* in the acoustic signal and are *not* therefore recoverable from it – how could they be if they are not there to begin with? Remember, the segments are *abstract* but the signal is *physical*. Phonological segments are simply an abstract *descriptive device* devised by phonologists.

In *active* theories of speech perception the incoming sound wave is used to enable the recovery of appropriate phonological segments not from the acoustic signal, but from *within the listener's mind*. In this way labels are *assigned* to the signal rather than extracted from it.

EVALUATION

PROSODY AND SEGMENTS IN SPEECH PRODUCTION

There are two possible models in speech *production* theory for the relationship between segments and prosodic features:

1. segments planned first, then prosody:

    Create segmental   Fit prosody to the   Motor
    utterance plan →   plan →   control

2. prosody planned first, then segmental structure:

    Create prosodic   Create segmental utterance plan   Motor control
    contour →   and fit to prosodic contour →

In the second model, we speak of the creation of a *prosodic wrapper* within which the segmental plan is fitted; the prosody *wraps* the segmental string and its existence is *logically prior* to the utterance plan.

In speech *perception* the two approaches produce:

1. segments assigned first, then prosody:

Assign segmental representation →	Fit an assigned prosody →	Evaluate the interaction, if any

2. prosody assigned first, then segmental structure:

Assign prosodic contour →	Assign segmental representation and fit to prosodic contour →	Evaluate the interaction, if any

In the second models, the prosodic wrapper is assigned logically first, and this wraps the assigned segmental representation.

FURTHER READING

Damasio, A. (1999), *The Feeling of What Happens: Body and Emotion in the Making of Consciousness,* New York: Harcourt Brace.

Lakoff, G. and M. Johnson (1999), *Philosophy in the Flesh: The Embodied Mind and its Challenge to Western Thought,* New York: Basic Books.

LeDoux, J. (1996), *The Emotional Brain,* New York: Simon and Schuster.

Mather, G. (2006), *Foundations of Perception*, Hove: Psychology Press.

Ortony, A., G. Clore, and A. Collins (1988), *The Cognitive Structure of Emotions,* Cambridge: Cambridge University Press.

Panksepp, J. (1998, reprinted 2005), *Affective Neuroscience: The Foundations of Human and Animal Emotions,* Oxford: Oxford University Press.

CHAPTER 8 – THEORIES OF SPEECH PERCEPTION

INTRODUCTION

This chapter is about speech perception, beginning with an early modern model which is still current – the Motor Theory. We continue by presenting more modern, computationally oriented approaches which have yet to be tested fully. Perception models can currently be regarded as active or passive, depending on the degree of active involvement of the listener. We include a critical review of current approaches, with emphasis on top-down and bottom-up models.

THE MOTOR THEORY OF SPEECH PERCEPTION – AN ACTIVE THEORY

- *Important*: Do not confuse the Motor Theory of speech *perception* with theories of motor control in speech *production*. In perception, the term *motor* is used because this theory invokes a listener's knowledge of motor control. In production, theories of motor control are about how speakers perform the articulatory part of rendering, and are not about perception.

BASIC UNITS

Basic units are the main or principal units involved in processes – in this case, the perceptual process. The Motor Theory, Analysis-by-Synthesis and Direct Perception models all take the basic unit of representation to be the speech segment of phonology, though it is also possible to assume that the phonological syllable, or other unit, may be a suitable basic unit.

MOTOR CONTROL

Motor control refers to the general overall process by which the brain controls movement in the body. Speech motor control includes the mechanisms and processes for controlling the production of speech.

The Motor Theory of speech perception (Liberman *et al.* 1967) is an active theory of speech perception, involving participation by the listener in interpreting the incoming sound wave in terms of BASIC UNITS – sound segments. Perceivers ask themselves what MOTOR CONTROL they would have to perform to make the particular sound. When the articulation is identified, the next question to ask is what phonological unit would underlie the attempt. It is then hypothesised that it is that same phonological unit that underlies the speaker's production.

The Motor Theory of speech perception focuses on the idea that speech sounds are RENDERINGS of underlying phonological units and that a perceiver is trying to identify what these underlying phonological units are. The theory sees speech production in terms of three levels: abstract phonological planning, physical articulation in terms of motor control, and the resultant acoustic signal due to aerodynamic effects. Perception reverses this chain of events as shown below.

Production

Abstract planning	*Physical articulation*	*Physical acoustics*
Phonological unit	→ Motor articulation	→ Waveform

Perception

Physical acoustics	*Physical articulation*	*Abstract planning*
Waveform	→ Reinterpret the waveform in terms of motor control	→ Reinterpret the motor control in terms of the underlying phonological unit

RENDERING

Articulations and their associated acoustic signals are renderings of the abstract underlying segments found in the plan produced by a speaker's phonology. Planned segments exist in the *abstract* world, and rendered segments exist in the *physical* world; planned and rendered segments are said to correlate. Correlation means that there is a demonstrable relationship between two objects or processes, but that the exact nature of the relationship is not necessarily known or well understood, and certainly must not be assumed to be one of direct cause and effect. This applies particularly when we are trying to relate abstract and physical objects or processes.

THE ANALYSIS-BY-SYNTHESIS THEORY OF SPEECH PERCEPTION – AN ACTIVE THEORY

Analysis-by-Synthesis (Stevens and Halle 1967) is an active theory of speech perception, involving participation by the listener in interpreting the heard sound wave. Perceivers ask themselves whether they can make the sound they hear, and if they can, go on to ask what phonological unit would underlie the attempt. It is then hypothesised that it is that same phonological unit which underlies the speaker's production, as shown below. The theory recognises that speech sounds are renderings of underlying phonological units, and that a perceiver is trying to identify these phonological units. The theory omits reference to articulation or motor control – a level prominent in the Motor Theory of speech perception, which was contemporary with the Analysis-by-Synthesis theory.

Production

Abstract planning	*Physical acoustics*
Phonological unit	→ Waveform

Perception

Physical acoustics	Abstract planning
Waveform	→ Reinterpret the waveform in terms of the underlying phonological unit

THE ASSOCIATIVE STORE THEORY OF SPEECH PERCEPTION – AN ACTIVE THEORY

The ASSOCIATIVE STORE Theory of speech perception (Levinson 2005; Tatham and Morton 2006) is a comprehensive, active theory which accounts for a number of observations about speech perception. These include the following:

- The continuous acoustic signal is interpreted in terms of an underlying sequence of abstract phonological units; abstract cognitive labels are *assigned* to the acoustic signal.

- A device is present which detects and traps errors of interpretation, and causes a reappraisal of that portion of the signal which has been wrongly interpreted – *interpretation error correction.*

- Mechanisms exist to repair signals damaged before the interpretation process – *production and transmission error correction.*

ASSOCIATIVE STORE

The term *associative store* derives from the name of a type of hardware memory available in computers in the 1970s – around the time when this perceptual theory was developed. It is memory which can input a signal which is not quite complete – that is, is defective in some way – and associate it with a *complete* pre-stored signal. Once identified, the stored signal is used in the interpretative process as though it had been the original signal. So, for example, in an 8-bit store the signal 01100?10 would be matched against the nearest stored complete signal, perhaps 01100110, and further processing would be on the *retrieved* object 01100110. Alternative matches can be identified at the same time, and perhaps given a probability rating: thus 01100110 may have a probability of 60 per cent, but 01100010 may have a probability of 40 per cent. The higher-rated match is kept through subsequent processes until the solution is reached or until it is decided that an error has been made. The introduction of alternative matches and of a probability score models a listener's uncertainty when the solution is unclear: *I think the word was* dog *– but it could just have been* dock.

The incoming signal is sampled for interpretation, but importantly not lost. It is placed in a first-in-first-out (FIFO) holding buffer for rescanning if a subsequent error occurs. The buffer is generally taken to be analogous to short-term memory, and has a capacity of around seven items. Using the contents of the buffer to *reassess* the signal is a way of going back in time to attempt to repair a detected error of interpretation. Thus:

1. Noisy signal leads to the decoding of the start of a sentence: *The cat* . . .

2. Remainder of sentence decoded as . . . *fitted him well.*

3. Realisation that *The cat fitted him well* is statistically improbable – has a low probability rating.

4. Check back in the buffer, and decode the start of sentence again, avoiding *cat*.

5. Sentence reinterpreted as *The cap fitted him well* – statistically more probable.

There is another possibility:

1. Noisy signal leads to two possible decodings at the start of a sentence – *The cat . . .* and *The cap . . .*

2. As a trial run, *The cat . . .* is selected; meanwhile *The cap . . .* is buffered; *cat* is a more probable isolated word than *cap*.

3. Remainder of the sentence decoded as *. . . fitted him well*.

4. Realisation that *The cat fitted him well* is overall semantically improbable despite the frequency of the individual words.

5. Go back and select the alternative to *cat*, namely: *cap*.

6. Try the new sentence: *The cap fitted him well*.

7. New sentence passes as OK.

Whichever one of these two alternative models is selected, the point is that the Associative Store Model (TUTORIAL – THE ASSOCIATIVE STORE MODEL IN DETAIL) focuses on the ability to become aware of error, and *repair* it. We have included here one possible mechanism for the repair process: the use of a short-term buffer to review material which would otherwise have been discarded.

FIFO buffers have the property of constantly fading: the first-in object always drops out if a new object is acquired. So when the original signal or alternative interpretations have vanished from the system the listener will have to ask the speaker to repeat what was said. This might occur, for example, if the error is realised only much later when the buffers have lost the original.

PERCEPTION AS A SIMPLE GENERIC ACOUSTIC DETAIL CLASSIFIER – A PASSIVE THEORY

It is possible to model perception as a simple CLASSIFIER device designed to use features present in the acoustic signal to identify what phonological object or segment a speaker intends to be perceived.

> **CLASSIFIER**
>
> A classifier is a device which is able to sort incoming information into classes or categories. In the case of speech, a classifier inputs the signal, and, using the answers to a series of diagnostic questions, determines to which class the signal belongs. The classifier needs to have prior knowledge of the set of final classes available. Different forms of classifier are available, ranging from a straightforward yes/no discrimination tree, through simple Bayesian classifiers which spot patterns in the data determined by the probability of hypothesised solutions, to highly sophisticated expert systems relying on complex and *changing* probabilities. Classifiers are widely used for sorting data, including things like the automatic evaluation of medical symptoms, but the field is too complex and specialised to discuss in detail here.

Using the general approach of classical phonetics and the classification system adopted in that theory, we might analyse the acoustic signal to answer a series of questions about various acoustic parameters known to be involved in uniquely identifying various segments. Such questions might include:

- Is there a periodic vocal cord vibration source?

- Is there an aperiodic source?

- If there is a formant pattern, what is it? And how does this compare with known formant patterns in this language?

- Is there acoustic evidence of lip rounding or lip spreading?

- Is there a nasal formant present?

Provided the listener has prior knowledge of the acoustic specifications of the various sounds in the language, it is easy to see that several answers could eventually lead to identifying the sound heard.

Classifiers are likely to fail for at least two reasons:

- Speech sounds do not occur with an ideal acoustic structure matching the target answers to such questions; they are more than likely blended with adjacent sounds because of coarticulatory pressures.

- The variability due to accent or even variation within the speech of a single individual may often take the responses to such questions outside the range of values recognised by the classifier.

One answer to these criticisms has been an attempt to provide ever-more detailed acoustic specifications for speech acoustics. If we assume that listeners *are* able to proceed using a mostly passive classifier for perception, then understanding how they do this involves careful modelling of the enormous range of detail in the signal. The reason for this is that the more complex the data because of, say, variability, the greater the chance that a simple classifier working on minimal information will fail. There is clearly a trade-off here between amount of detail and success: the more detail available, the more likely that a segment will be correctly identified, provided that the detail is from a range of different parameters – if the detail is about the same parameter (variability), then the more likely the classifier will fail. The goal of research into identifying ever greater detail in the acoustic signal is to find the optimum amount of detail necessary and sufficient for satisfactory perception. Thus detail classifiers, and their attendant databases, need to be able to sort relevant detail from irrelevant detail. To date, most fail on this point.

We have to bear in mind, though, that it is not just quantity of detail which is important; it is also its quality. By this we mean its degree of relevance to providing a solution to the particular perceptual task. Some details will be more relevant than others, and a single highly relevant detail may well outweigh several less relevant details. Although as yet not thoroughly investigated, there is also the difficulty of tracking how any one detail may *vary* in importance depending on its context. There is no reason to suppose that the importance ranking of a particular detail remains constant. Consider, for example, formant bending following a plosive release. It has been shown that formant bending is sufficient to identify the previous plosive *in the absence of the release*. In no way should this be taken to mean that the importance of FORMANT BENDING (see 'Information from Spectrograms', Chapter 11) is equally high when the plosive release *is* present.

> **FORMANT BENDING**
> Formants are said to bend when they change their centre frequency values over time, and in particular when these depart from the 'steady-state' values associated with the pronunciation of sounds in isolation. The detail of formant bending is dependent on the surrounding sounds.

	Detail analyser	*Classifier*
Acoustic signal →	Identify detail →	Recognition of the correct segment
	↕	↕
	Knowledge base of all possible acoustic details	Knowledge base of segment labels

The diagram above shows how a perceptual model based on a classifier works. The acoustic signal – or a pre-analysed version of it – is input to analysis procedures whose job it is to identify and extract acoustic detail relevant to how the classifier proceeds. Next, the classifier itself uses this detail to consult a knowledge base of known segments in the language and their details. It is clear that success depends on:

- ability to identify relevant detail in the acoustic signal;
- knowledge of how particular detail matches particular segment labels.

Notice that the analysis and classifier procedures become more and more abstract – or distant from the original physical signal – as the identification proceeds. The way in which the knowledge base contains a list of segment labels (completely abstract) and matches these with appropriate acoustic details (an abstract version of something physical) is the key to the way in which this model solves the problem of associating abstract and physical descriptions.

In practice, because we can never be sure of how much detail needs to be modelled, this form of passive model is unlikely to succeed better than, or even as well as, models which allow a greater degree of active cognitive processing. Detail classifiers are almost certain to fail when trying to deal with damaged data (all detail of potentially damaged data would have to be known to a database of sorts), or when trying to reduce what is actually an infinite amount of variability in speech – even the speech of a single speaker.

Evidence from research on modalities other than hearing and associated perception suggest that knowledge which enables interpretation is important. Information from the external world, detected by the sensory systems, is usually somewhat ambiguous and needs prior experience and knowledge to interpret which of the multiple meanings is important to us (Frith 2007). The logic suggests that given enough fine detail, anything can be uniquely identified – an infinite number of objects could be perceived, resulting in cognitive overload and probably insufficient time to process the data.

Evidence from neurobiology suggests that processing time from receipt of a signal to production of a response to that signal varies considerably. When classifying speech information, the acoustic phonetic detail must be of a significant duration and amplitude to enable unambiguous processing (Posner 2005).

A theory which focuses mainly on a passive approach is said to involve bottom-up processing, whereas one focusing mainly on active interpretation is said to involve top-down processing (TUTORIAL–TOP-DOWN AND BOTTOM-UP PROCESSING).

CATEGORICAL PERCEPTION THEORY – AN ACTIVE THEORY

Categorical perception (Repp 1984) is the recognition, along a continuum of data, of categories meriting individual labels. Thus, for example, a rainbow is a continuous or linear spread of colour (frequencies) within which certain colours *appear* to stand out or can be recognised by the viewer. In fact these colours, it is hypothesised, are *not* intrinsically isolated or special in the signal; their identification is a property of the *way the viewer is cognitively treating the data*. Categorical Perception Theory is an attempt to model this observation.

Two observations are relevant to understanding categories:

- Listeners often assign the *same* label to physically *different* signals. This occurs, for example, when two people utter the 'same' sound. In fact the sounds are always measurably different, but are perceived to belong to the same category. What is interesting is that the two speakers also believe they are making identical or very similar sounds, simply because they are both rendering the same underlying plan for a particular phonological extrinsic allophone. The identity of the planned utterance within the minds of the speakers matches the label assigned by the listener.

- Sounds can be made which are only minutely different and occur on the same production CLINE. Take the example of vowel height, where there is a cline, say, between high front vowels and low front vowels. Acoustically this will show up as a cline in the frequency of formant 2 (F2) and also formant 1 (F1). Listeners will segment the cline into different zones, and assign a distinct label to each. Here we have the situation where, because phonologically there are two different segments to be rendered, both speakers and listeners will believe that the difference has carried over into the physical signal.

> **CLINE**
>
> A cline is a continuous range or slope between values associated with a particular phenomenon. For example, in English the series of vowels [u, ʊ, ɔ, ɑ] stand on a cline of back vowels ranging from highest to lowest.

Each of these two observations is the reverse of the other. On the one hand different signals prompt a belief of similarity, and on the other similar signals prompt a belief of difference. Categorical Perception Theory – and other active or top-down theories – propose that the explanation for these observations lies in the strength of the contribution made to the perceptual process by the speaker/listener's prior knowledge of the structure and workings of the language. Within certain limits, whatever the nature of the physical signal the predictive nature of the speaker's/listener's model of how the language works will *push* the data into the relevant category. We speak of such active top-down approaches as being *theory-driven*, as opposed to passive, *data-driven,* bottom-up theories.

So the categories in the minds of both speaker and listener are language-dependent. That is, they vary from language to language, depending on the distribution of sounds within the available acoustic or articulatory space. Imagine a vector running from just below the alveolar ridge to the lowest, most forward point the front of the tongue can reach for making vowels. Along this vector the tongue can move to an infinite number of positions – and we could, in theory at any rate, instruct a speaker to make all these sounds, or, at least, a large number of sounds along this vector. If these sounds are recorded, randomised and played to listeners, they will subdivide the sounds according to tongue positions along the vector which represent sounds in their own language (Rosner and Pickering 1994).

Examining TONGUE POSITIONING along a vector ranging from high front, to low front, we can identify categories by their position, as in the example below of French and English front vowel sounds.

	front			examples
high	i_{Fr}			qui $[ki]_{Fr}$
	i_{Eng}			key $[ki]_{Eng}$
		$ɪ_{Eng}$		kit $[kɪt]_{Eng}$
mid	e_{Fr}			quai $[ke]_{Fr}$
	$ɛ_{Eng/Fr}$			pet $[pɛt]_{Eng}$, tête $[tɛt]_{Fr}$
low	$æ_{Eng}$			pat $[pæt]_{Eng}$
	a_{Fr}			patte $[pat]_{Fr}$

TONGUE POSITIONING

Proponents of classical phonetic theory often refer to the tongue's position. However, any diagram of the oral cavity, or profile x-ray picture, shows that the tongue can occupy quite a large volume of the oral cavity, and stating its exact position in physical terms will be difficult; are we to describe the entire shape, for example? The classical phonetic solution is technically elegant: imagine point-positions in an abstract space, and relate the sounds and labels of vowels to these point-positions. The system has served well for over a hundred years, and is supported by the observation that listeners set up a perceptual space in their minds in which they can 'locate' vowels; these can be shown to be remarkably like the area within which the point-positions of classical phonetics are deployed (see the TUTORIAL – CARDINAL VOWELS, Chapter 3).

The table above (and the corresponding International Phonetic Alphabet (IPA) vowel chart) are abstract, and do not reveal the relative distance of the tongue between the different positions – categories *mean* positions. The English [ɪ] is usually positioned as slightly retracted from the vector, but this is of no importance here. Vertically, the differences between pairs $[i]_{Fr}$ and $[i]_{Eng}$, $[ɪ]_{Eng}$ and $[e]_{Fr}$, and $[æ]_{Eng}$ and $[a]_{Fr}$ are small – so small, in fact, that if we were to take a look at the spread of measurements which might be obtained by actually detecting the real physical positioning, we would find much more overlap than we find between other pairs. The existence of the overlap in the measurements leads to two conclusions:

- Positioning of the tongue is not exact, and can lead to overlap of zones, prompting us to ask which category the speaker intends.

- Such overlaps could potentially cause perceptual confusion, prompting us to ask which category the sound belongs to.

These observations hold whether we're talking about tongue positioning in the traditional classical phonetics way, or whether we're talking about acoustic parameters like the positioning of F2 on the frequency spectrum. We are focusing on the speaker's ability to *replicate* action and control *precision* of articulatory positioning. Human beings are not machines, and both replication and precision have their limitations. The exact extent of these limitations has not been exhaustively measured or calculated, but we are aware from X-ray video and acoustic analyses that they constrain us to produce sounds in *zones* rather than with pinpoint precision. Systematic phonological detail is, of course, carefully controlled, and systematic phonetic detail, because of, say, coarticulation, is well understood. What is less well understood is the way in which detail is able to be *controlled* – hence the SUPERVISORY notion introduced a few years back (Tatham 1995).

> **REMINDER: SUPERVISION**
>
> The special purpose of supervision when applied systematically is to enable control of details of the articulatory or acoustic signal
>
> - in the short term, to improve a listener's chances of successful perception;
> - in the longer term, to form the basis for the expansion of a language's phonological inventory.

Here is an important production principle:

- To make the acoustic code work 100 per cent effectively, languages must not try to set up a phonological contrast between sounds with overlapping zones. So no language can have the two [i] sounds we find in French and English in an attempt to code two different words: we could not have two words [ki$_{Fr}$] and [ki$_{Eng}$] in the same language because speakers could not keep them sufficiently distinct.

Another important principle for perception:

- Sounds must be sufficiently distinct to belong recognisably to different categories for the purpose of contrasting different words. So you cannot have [ki$_{Fr}$] and [ki$_{Eng}$] in the same language, but you can have [ki$_{Fr}$] and [ke$_{Fr}$], and you can have [ki$_{Eng}$] and [kɪ$_{Eng}$].

DIRECT PERCEPTION – A PASSIVE THEORY

Direct Perception Theory (Gibson 1950) proposes that the SIGNAL PROPERTIES (auditory or visual) as perceived are present in the physical signal, and are open to perception without cognitive mediation or interpretation. The task of perception is to detect and extract these properties from the signal. We say that the signal is recognised when the task is complete.

> **SIGNAL PROPERTIES**
>
> We speak of signals as having properties or features. In direct perception these are to be discovered in the signal; in the other theories presented here they are to be assigned to the signal and derive from the memory of previous encounters with this or similar signals.

Opposing theories regard the speech signal as a (rather defective) trigger for associating with the sound wave a cognitive representation which has already been stored in the listener's memory. It is this cognitively active element which basic direct perception theory lacks, though sometimes the theory includes an element of active participation by the listener to try to make up for some of the data which it cannot explain; for example, our ability to repair defective signals, even when the errors they contain make them ambiguous. The same problem is shared by the extensions of simple classifier perception discussed above – how to make the data sufficiently rich in detail not to need cognitive mediation but to be perceived or classified directly. The proponents of both ideas have yet to stipulate the extent of the required detail, or even to define how it is constrained. For example, what is the role of detail in the signal which has not been shown to be detectable by the peripheral hearing mechanism? Such theories fall within the scope of direct realism (Fowler 1986) (TUTORIAL – REALISM AND IDEALISM).

AUDITORY SCENE ANALYSIS – AN ACTIVE THEORY

Auditory Scene Analysis – a theory originating with Bregman (1994) – attempts to explain the observation that we seem to be able to perceive complex sounds sometimes as single *integrated* sounds and sometimes as a grouping of *segregated* sounds. When listening to segregated sound groups we can track individual components apparently without cross-interference from other components in the overall complex sound, whereas with integrated sounds all components contribute to the perception together. The process is cognitively based; that is, the integration or segregation appears not be a function of the peripheral analysis system or hearing. One example in speech perception is the so-called *cocktail party effect*, in which listeners are able to track or focus on a single speaker even when their speech is apparently mixed with the simultaneous speech of nearby speakers.

We have examined a mix of passive and active theories of speech perception. Although these date from different periods in the development of our ideas about perception, each still has its adherents. We have described some passive theories relying on direct realism (direct perception and the more recent approach of direct realism theory of speech perception), and some active or semi-active theories (Motor Theory (including the Motor Theory Revised), Analysis-by-Synthesis, Associative Store Theory, Categorical Perception). Classifiers represent perhaps the earliest approach within the field of perceptual phonetics, and ante-date ideas which explicitly discuss the role of cognition in the perceptual process (**EVALUATION – THEORIES OF SPEECH PERCEPTION**).

TUTORIAL

THE ASSOCIATIVE STORE MODEL IN DETAIL

The Associative Store Model proposes that speech is decoded in terms of an idealised or error-free internal representation held in the mind of the listener. This means that labels derived from the internal representation are *assigned* to the signal. The incoming signal is used simply as a trigger to enable the listener to access the internal representation.

This idea is invoked when characterising the ability of the perceptual system to repair a damaged or defective signal. Thus an English speaker may plan the word *cat* as a monosyllable consisting of a sequence of three phonological objects: /kæt/. In dialects such as Estuary English or General American the final voiceless plosive of the word is often unexploded, particularly if the word occurs in utterance or in phase-final position – that is, the final phonetic rendering that the listener will hear is without the release phase specified in the underlying phonology prior to the utterance plan. This means that there is potential ambiguity between the two words *cat* and *cap*. Phonemically, or in the underlying phonology, these are /kæt/ and /kæp/, and in the utterance plan, /kæt˺/ and /kæp˺/, respectively. The articulation rendered from these two utterance plans will produce, correctly, unreleased final plosives. But, of course, an unreleased plosive is *silent* – so to the listener both words appear identical, with an unhelpful silence at the end. In Cockney English the final voiceless plosive is often replaced by a glottal stop in the utterance plan: this too sounds silent to the listener – the same problem of ambiguity.

- In the above three dialects of English both voiceless and voiced plosives (six of them) can, under certain conditions, potentially collapse acoustically to a single phonetic form: silence. This is either as the result of failure to include the release phase in the articulation of the stop (Estuary English, General American), or because an unreleased glottal stop has been substituted (Cockney). The ambiguity is particularly apparent if the words are pronounced in isolation.

Nevertheless, a listener will correctly decode the underlying phonological specification of the word. How this is done is clearly an important question. The listener appears to use a number of cues in the signal (including the length of the vowel and the nature of the vowel's OFF-GLIDE) to assist in a database search for an ideal acoustic representation of the word. If asked to repeat the word the listener will usually do so on the basis of what was found in the database, and be quite unaware of the 'degraded' nature of the original signal. This latter point is so strong that a listener may even argue as to whether they actually heard the final [t] – they will usually assert that they *did* hear it, although it was in fact a period of silence in our example.

The model also includes the possibility of going back and reviewing data which in the previous models would have been regarded as lost. This is possible because the model emphasises the idea of incorporating a buffer (otherwise known as SHORT-TERM MEMORY in psychology) which can hold on to the data signal for a while to enable it to be reconsidered if the listener decides that an initial interpretation was in error.

OFF-GLIDE

Used mostly in classical phonetics, a segment's off-glide is the way in which its parameter values – for example, the centre frequency of formant 2 (F2) – change as it blends into the following segment. The off-glide, like the on-glide at the start of a segment, is associated with how it coarticulates with adjacent segments ('Information from Spectrograms', Chapter 11).

SHORT-TERM MEMORY

Short-term memory gives us the ability to hold limited amounts of information readily to hand in the memory for rapid accessing. The amount of information is quite small – a sequence of a few words just heard, for example – and fades rapidly as more information comes along to take its place. So long as the fading is not complete the information (up to around seven items or chunks of data) can be recalled on demand (Miller 1967).

TOP-DOWN AND BOTTOM-UP PROCESSING

TUTORIAL

All the perceptual models presented in this chapter involve decisions concerning the relative roles of top-down and bottom-up processing in the perception of speech.

THE TOP-DOWN APPROACH

Wholly top-down models of perception must proceed with an overview of what is being perceived and the system behind any data which may be presented for perception. From this is derived an expectation or hypothesis as to the label(s) available for assignment to the data.

Using the knowledge and the hypothesis, the model then proceeds to *evaluate* ever more detailed levels below the top overview level, in a cascaded or *mining* methodology. A solution is reached – perception is achieved – when no greater detail is required to refine the top-level hypothesis and declare it to be verified. The perceiver approaches the data with prior knowledge of what might be found; that is, the perceiver starts off with an internal representation which constitutes a hypothesis.

THE BOTTOM-UP APPROACH

Wholly bottom-up models begin by assembling as much low-level detailed data as possible. In extreme versions of the approach the assembly is not guided or based on any preconceived idea of what will be found; preconceived ideas are excluded because they would be part of a top-down approach.

The detailed data is organised, progressing through ever higher levels until no further refinement is necessary to declare recognition of the data – the solution has been reached and a label for the data has been found. Ideally it is not necessary for the perceiver to have prior knowledge of the label or any meaning that it may have because the data alone can provide this.

	Top-down models of perception	Bottom-up models of perception
Prior condition	Internal symbolic representations and knowledge	As much low-level detail as possible
Proceeds to ↓	Formulate a hypothesis about symbolically representing the current data	Organise the data in order to find patterns in it
And ↓	Drop to lower levels progressively to refine and test the hypothesis, starting with *gross* aspects of the data	Rise to higher levels progressively to refine patterns in the *detail* of the data
Finally ↓	Go down through levels just far enough to confirm the hypothesis	Work through levels of refinement until a stable pattern has been reached sufficient for a label to be assigned
Result	A symbolic label emerges, based on prior knowledge	A symbolic label emerges, based on patterning found in the detail of the data

In practice it has been found that no perceptual model escapes the requirement for either some prior knowledge or analysis of incoming data. And researchers have often asked how much of each is necessary for any one theory. We prefer to think of a cline of approach with top-down at one extreme and bottom-up at the other. This enables us to rank-order the models roughly in terms of how much they rely on either prior knowledge or detailed data to arrive at perceptual solutions. The table below gives an indication of this – though the actual ranking is still arguable.

Model	Top-down contribution	Bottom-up contribution
Acoustic or articulatory classifiers	*	****
Direct Perception (Gibson)	*	****
Direct Realism (Fowler)	**	***
Categorical Perception	**	***
Motor Theory	***	**
Analysis-by-Synthesis	***	**
Associative Store	****	*

VARIABLE PROCESSING DIRECTION

To make matters even more complex, it is almost certainly the case, we believe, that the ratio of top-down to bottom-up processing is *itself* a variable. That is, as an utterance unfolds, the listener changes the reliance on top-down and/ or bottom-up processing – sometimes more top-down processing is required, sometimes more bottom-up. The processing environment makes a difference to how much of each approach is needed.

Put simply, the amount of bottom-up data available will vary, depending on how damaged the data is. It is almost certainly the case that no speech data falling on a listener's ears is a perfect rendering of what the speaker intended. Furthermore it is almost certainly the case that the defect level in the speech will be varying. There could be a number of factors influencing this – but one comes from the speaker: if the speaker judges that perception will be easy, then the precision of the utterance rendering will be reduced, and vice versa. Varying precision during an utterance is the norm rather than the exception, and it is this evidence which leads us to the conclusion that production and perception are collaborative activities (see 'Production for Perception', in Chapter 7, and 'Cognitive Phonetics' in Chapter 4).

REALISM AND IDEALISM

TUTORIAL

We can identify three approaches to perception of any kind – visual, auditory, tactile, etc.

1. In the case of *direct realism* it is claimed that we can have awareness of the world outside ourselves directly through the senses.

2. On the other hand, *indirect realism* would claim that the awareness we experience is of representations we already have of the outside world. These representations are triggered by data from the senses, but it is not this data we are aware of, but the stored representation.

3. *Idealism* – an extreme approach – claims that there is no outside world, and that we are only aware of representations or ideas conjured in our own minds.

We are not aware of any theories of speech perception which take the idealist position. A few theories are *direct* realist in their approach, though most invoke the idea of mediation or interpretation of external stimuli by the mind to enable access to stored representations: that is, most theories of speech perception involve indirect realism to some degree. Even detail classifiers and direct perception require some stored knowledge of categories or events.

REALISM EXAMPLES

The Haskins Laboratories proposed the Motor Theory of speech perception we discussed earlier, and its later version, the Revised Motor Theory of speech perception (Liberman and Mattingly 1985). This is an example of an *indirect* realist theory, involving a knowledge base of motor and articulatory gestures and a mechanism for accessing the knowledge base. Essentially, the knowledge held in the database is a model of speech production: the model is compared with the incoming acoustic signal, traced back to the underlying articulatory and motor gestures by a comparison process. The signal is recognised when there is a match with plausible gestures generated by the production model.

The Haskins Laboratories also produced a perception theory within the *direct* realism framework: they called this the Direct Realist Theory of speech perception (Fowler 1986). Listeners still recognise or perceive gestures, but this time the perception relies on the actual structure of the heard acoustic signal: there is little or no cognitive interpretation of the signal in the way indirect realism theories call for. The Haskins theories are strictly within the domain of the psychology view of speech, rather than within the linguistics view – or the narrower domain of PERCEPTUAL PHONETICS.

PERCEPTUAL PHONETICS

The idea in classical phonetics that perception was direct and did not involve cognitive mediation is basically what drove 1930s perceptual phonetics. Units like *phone* – physical instantiations of what we now call phonological extrinsic allophones – were said to embody the necessary detail for the perception of their parent phonemes, though the extent of the required detail was never quite spelled out. The proponents of the more recent detail classifiers work within this long tradition.

We should also refer back here to the allied Haskins Laboratories' speech *production* theory of *articulatory phonology* (Browman and Goldstein 1986), in which articulatory gestures are produced largely through the task dynamics involved in production (see Chapter 3). Articulatory phonology, together with its supporting theory of task dynamics, complement Direct Realist Theory to form what is claimed to be a fully integrated theory of speech production and perception.

THEORIES OF SPEECH PERCEPTION

One way of evaluating these different approaches is to establish whether they are capable individually of meeting the general requirements of a theory of speech perception. The table below sums this up.

	Success with perfect signal input?	Success with defective signal input?	Cognitive processing needed?	Comments
Direct Perception (Gibson)	Yes – works best on individual segments	Very limited – cannot deal adequately with ambiguities in the signal	Little or none	Must be able to recognise the *intent* of the signal directly from the signal itself
Direct Realism (Fowler)	Yes – less good at connected speech	Limited – not good at dealing with ambiguous signals	Some	Must be able to recognise the *intent* of the signal directly from the signal itself
Categorical Perception	Yes, for individual segments	Limited – but can introduce serious errors because of ambiguities in the signal	Yes	Works best with parameterised acoustic input, best based on articulatory knowledge; knowledge of phonological categories needed
Motor Theory	Yes	Very limited	Yes	Requires both acoustic and articulatory knowledge, and limited cognitive recognition; knowledge of phonological categories needed
Analysis-by-synthesis (Stevens)	Yes	Very limited	Yes	Requires acoustic knowledge and limited cognitive processing; knowledge of phonological categories needed
Associa-tive Store (Tatham and Morton)	Yes	Yes – the theory deliberately focuses on defective inputs	Yes – complex	Knowledge of phonological categories needed and ability to consult an internal model of speech *production*
acoustic and articulatory classifiers	Yes – but work best on individual segments	Depends on how much cognitive processing is needed and how much detail is available to the listener	Minimal	Require optimised detail of either acoustic or articulatory parameters; knowledge of phonological categories needed

Different theories need different information from a top-down system. It is important to distinguish between the *knowledge* that a theory needs, and the *ability* to process the incoming signal. There might be a trade-off between what we as human beings need to know from the cognitive system above, and how much the signal from below is to be used. Remember that all acoustic signals will have passed through a pre-processing stage of spectral analysis as part of hearing, prior to the perceptual processes, and so the detail being supplied will not correspond exactly to stretches of the raw or unprocessed sound wave.

Theories can be combined. Thus supporters of Direct Realism might want to add a degree of cognitive processing for those obvious cases where the theory fails; for example, with a very defective input signal. The Associative Store Theory – now nearly thirty years old – benefits from the inclusion of a simple acoustic classifier as a front end to the system, thereby reducing the amount of cognitive processing needed and speeding up the perceptual process.

FURTHER READING

Bregman, A. (1994), *Auditory Scene Analysis: The Perceptual Organization of Sound*, Cambridge, MA: MIT Press.

Gibson, J. (1950), *The Perception of the Visual World*, Boston: Houghton Mifflin.

Levinson, S. (2005), *Mathematical Models for Speech Technology*, Chichester: John Wiley.

Miller, G. (1967), *The Psychology of Communication*, New York: Basic Books.

Rosner, B. and J. Pickering (1994), *Vowel Perception and Production*, Oxford: Oxford University Press.

CHAPTER 9 – APPLICATIONS

INTRODUCTION

The purpose of this chapter is to help acquaint you with some problems that may arise in applying linguistics models to specific real-world events. This section is not about *how* to apply knowledge and information, but to emphasise what *type* of knowledge might be found useful in carrying out applications work. We focus on two major areas: communications disorders, where the system is not functioning as expected, and speech synthesis, an aspect of speech technology which simulates or replicates speech production. For handling knowledge representation, we look at two current models: classical phonetics (see Chapters 1–3), a static model, and cognitive phonetics (see Chapter 4), a dynamic model.

We begin by summarising some of the major disorders, and then look from a linguistic modelling perspective at two in more detail: apraxia and aphasia. We then look at the role of models of speech production/ perception in speech synthesis in developing APPLICATIONS MODELS. The aim is to help you understand the usefulness of a coherent overall model, and the advantage of working within a model- or theory-driven framework is emphasised. CONDUCTING EXPERIMENTS within a model has provided the most reliable kind of data. Note that in applications of any type, rapid changes in attitudes, goals and techniques constantly occur; so these sections deal only with some of the current work.

APPLICATIONS MODELS

An applications model deals with a set of specific phenomena, for the purpose of applying knowledge to new events judged to be similar. Applications themselves can be based on theory, not explicitly theory-bound, or they can be atheoretical, meaning there is no theory to apply to the situation in hand (Tatham and Morton 2006: ch. 9).

Applications require an understanding of concepts and methods current in a supporting discipline, stated in such a way that they can be applied to a particular problem in the applied area. In speech synthesis systems, for example, the higher-level concepts are derived from speech production models and from perception experiments. In language disorders, applications models are based on several disciplines: for example, biology, psychology and linguistics/phonetics.

CONDUCTING EXPERIMENTS

There are two major ways of conducting experiments:

1. Observe, generalise and assemble a descriptive empirical model. Some predictive power can then be applied to a newly observed event – this technique is often used for getting scientific investigation under way.
2. Follow a more formal scientific methodology to build models which are designed explicitly to generate ideas and hypotheses for clarifying and revising earlier views; a focus of the technique is the generalisation and predictive powers of the model.

COMMUNICATION DISORDERS

Introduction

A basic understanding of speech production and perception models can be useful. Without taking a model-driven approach, it is certainly possible to make observations of surface phenomena, categorise these observations and seek to describe events. But the advantage of modelling underlying processes that could *account* for the observed events is that it leads to a better understanding of speech processes, suggesting novel ways of thinking about speech communication. Ideally, it should be possible to predict future, similar events. Careful recording of observations and test results made by practitioners also contributes to richer models of speech production and perception – in turn, helping gain a greater understanding of the underlying processes. Such an iterative procedural approach can be very productive.

Applications dealing with communication disorders call for models originating in several disciplines – linguistics, phonetics, acoustics, etc. – and reference to cognitive and biological modelling, experimental and perceptual psychology, etc. This kind of application is particularly difficult, because practitioners have to deal with both input and output system disorders, with no underlying integrated model yet developed.

> **COMMUNICATION DISORDERS**
>
> Communication disorders involve aspects of speech production and perception which are deemed to be outside the range of expected behaviour.

COMMUNICATION DISORDERS, broadly speaking, can be categorised as disabilities in speaking, perceiving, language, voice and hearing; there can be developmental and learning disorders (Kent 2004). Depending on severity and context, disorders can create problems in speech production (articulation and fluency) and perception (including deafness); but also can involve cognitive impairment (including comprehension, for example), learning difficulties, attention disorders, etc. Practitioners plan and implement programmes for improving communication by intervening as appropriate in speakers' and listeners' abilities to communicate. For example, with poor hearing – the detection of the acoustic signal – expert advice is offered on the specification of hearing aids to improve the listener's ability to interpret the signal. Exercises can be tailored to individual needs to improve, for example, stuttering. Procedures have been developed to improve reading difficulties, poor articulation, and language restoration from brain damage (Brady and Armstrong 2009).

Looking at communication disorders

Communication disorders can be looked at from several points of view. Three major ones are:

1. structural change in the biological system. If the physical and neurobiological systems are damaged, or altered in such a way that

the STRUCTURES cannot work normally, their FUNCTION will be affected. A difficulty is that apparently small biological changes can sometimes have a large effect, and large changes sometimes appear to have little effect.

2. functional problems resulting from biological change. Physiological functioning can also be affected by biochemical changes, neurotransmitter excess or insufficiency.

3. communication process problems. If structural and functional changes occur beyond some limit, the communications process will be affected. The speaker may report difficulties in producing speech, or the listener may report difficulties in understanding the waveform. There may be detection and reception problems associated with physical and neurobiological structures and resulting function in the listener. There may be biochemical changes that affect the ability to perceive the decoded waveform adequately. The listener might also have difficulty in reporting their understanding.

> **STRUCTURE AND FUNCTION**
> *Structure* means how something is put together; how it appears; how its components or units are related to each other.
> *Function* means how something works; what it does; how its components or units work together.

Underlying structural malformation

The causes of most communication disorders are not clearly known, so a comprehensive model of communication disorders linking probable causes with communication problems is not yet possible. However, some general major physical impairments *have* been implicated in communication failures, including the physical inability to hear sounds, malformations of the oral or nasal cavities which prevent the articulators moving smoothly, disorders of the neural system which prevent transmission of intended articulations, physical-based developmental problems, and acquired difficulties after normal development such as damage from injury, stroke or drug abuse. Some disorders are tentatively correlated with brain scans, with a view to establishing their neurobiological base. To this end, fMRI techniques are being investigated for their usefulness (Corr 2006: ch. 10) (TUTORIAL – FUNCTIONAL MAGNETIC RESONANCE IMAGING (fMRI) STUDIES).

> **fMRI**
> fMRI is an abbreviation of 'functional magnetic resonance imaging'. Images produced by this technique are interpreted as showing that a particular area of the brain is functioning at a particular moment in time. Many experts caution against drawing conclusions from these images without carrying out very carefully designed experiments.

Modelling the communication process

The first step in modelling speech communication for APPLICATIONS is to describe what is observable. The second step is to ask: what underlying processes produce what we observe? Underlying processes are not necessarily themselves observable. An exception is that we can measure end results from articulations using techniques such as electromyography, air-pressure and airflow detection, etc. (Chapter 10). The third step is to determine whether we are dealing with biological or cognitive phenomena, and what statements could be made about the relation between these two domains, considering the disorder being addressed. As mentioned earlier, it is more useful to derive MODEL-DRIVEN APPLICATIONS rather than empirical ones.

MODEL-DRIVEN APPLICATIONS

In developing model-driven applications, hypotheses can be based on empirical methods, and derived from observations of what speakers and listeners actually seem to do in real speech contexts. Models can also be based on generalisations characterising idealised communication.

Data is collected according to special *methodologies*. For example, a linguistic model might suggest a comprehension difficulty arising from an inability to access the semantic network with which the word *newspaper* is associated. Or it might lie in retrieving the word and its associated phonology (pronunciation pattern). Or the original storage process may be faulty. Or perhaps the speaker cannot pronounce the utterance plan /'njuzpeipə/, which would lead to querying a physical problem with moving the articulators, or possibly a comprehension, storage, access or retrieval error within the speaker's phonological processing.

Thus, a model gives rise to many ways of evaluating a disorder and provides a firmer basis for producing hypotheses. Of course, experience, intuition and empirical methods are useful, and can give good results. But adding *formal* models gives us a more powerful tool which can link more easily with other similar models. The practical result is a view and a set of formal statements that other researchers and staff working in the applications area can quickly understand without lengthy discussion of the usefulness of the initial observations.

Behaviour types

It is convenient to separate the study of behaviour into two areas: cognitive and biological. Cognitive refers to mental activity, and biological study is about physical behaviour. We cannot see or measure cognitive processing *directly*, but we can often observe and measure underlying biological activity. The *results* of cognitive activity are seen in behaviour change, and experiments can be conducted within limited conditions to measure these results. This division has been useful in discussing communication disorders and other applications such as speech synthesis. Core linguistics itself also makes this distinction when modelling spoken language: phonology describes the result of cognitive activity as the intention to produce sounds and prosodic patterns of the language, and phonetics describes as far as possible the physical action of the articulators correlated with features of the sound wave. Some current research effort is being directed to relating the cognitive and biological domains, mainly by seeking to identify brain areas that can be closely correlated with mental models of cognitive function using fMRI (see above). Other approaches are discussed in 'Future Areas of Application' below.

SIMPLE MODELS OF IMPAIRMENT

Production processes and errors

When dealing with speech, we have models of language that characterise or describe the structure (generative linguistics) and function (functional linguistics) of possible underlying systems.

The human being, producing spoken language, is a biological and cognitive creature; therefore we have three different models to associate with spoken language. We need to

- associate the underlying cognitive/biological models of the human speaker/listener, and then

- relate this to the linguistic model that is describing the language output.

The underlying cognitive-biological model must also

- account for other activity not directly connected with language such as intention to write, to use sign language, etc.

We must bear in mind that some of the coordinative structures active in speech activity may also be involved in other types of action.

The simple model shown below has two active parts:

1. COGNITIVE ACTIVITY (phonology), which begins with the intention to speak and outputs an appropriate utterance plan;

2. BIOLOGICAL ACTIVITY, which renders the plan: this activity consists of neuromuscular action and which finally, via aerodynamic and acoustic systems, results in the speech waveform.

COGNITIVE AND BIOLOGICAL ACTIVITY

Because the actual functioning of both cognitive and biological tasks is obscure to an observer, different models are often the product of different kinds of evidence or data, and are built up by inference based on these data (see Chapter 6).

Cognitive domain		*Interface*	*Biological domain*	
Intention to speak →	Phonological processes →	Utterance plan →	Phonetic processes →	Sound wave

Following on from this simple model, we can hypothesise that production errors may occur during either or both the cognitive and biological stages. Errors can be generated in the areas associated with forming the utterance plan (cognition) and while activating the pre-motor and motor areas associated with speaking. In the biological domain, there can be a malfunction in transmission or inadequate muscle function.

The nervous system and the muscular system are independent, unique systems which operate together to achieve a task or to carry out an intention (Corr 2006: ch. 5). The neuromuscular junction brings the two systems together. If the muscle is intrinsically weak the transmission will be ineffective. A malfunction at the neuromuscular junction will prevent activation of the muscle, even if the muscle is strong enough to complete its task. A failure to translate any cognitive intention into the appropriate motor program will stop peripheral activity. And with respect to spoken language, failure to formulate a proper phonological plan can easily result in no speech activity at all.

Perception processes and errors

Again, there are two parts to the perception system: biological and cognitive.

1. biological activity, which consists of detection of the speech waveform and transmission of the information to the brain;

2. cognitive activity, which consists of adequate decoding and interpretation of the hearing information, possibly by matching the incoming information with stored items (see Chapters 7 and 8).

Identifying and describing processing errors is somewhat less precise, because the evidence suggesting most detection and perception problems is gained by observing the result of the problem during speech production or from the report of the listener. The detection mechanism (hearing) may be damaged or poorly functioning (see Chapter 7). The hair cells involved decrease their sensitivity with constant high-amplitude sound (noise), and some deterioration occurs with age. There may be errors in transmission, and errors in decoding at some point in the brain where the signal is TRANSCODED from NEURAL PATTERNS to a cognitive representation. In a top-down system, further problems can arise with inability to access stored language representations, such as lexical, semantic and phonological, as well as other information such as memories in pattern matching, interpretation of context; the result is misinterpretation or confusion. The ability to access the production mechanism can also result in an inability to make a suitable response (see 'Production for Perception' in Chapter 7); thus it may be difficult to differentiate between a production, detection or perception error.

Relating ordered and disordered speech

There are currently no full and explicit models of either ordered or disordered speech, and consequently it is not possible to make full mappings from one to the other. This lays the ground for differing interpretations of the site of some major areas of disordered speech.

In general terms, a useful linguistically oriented model would need to deal with the relationship between underlying structural difficulties and functional problems such as comprehension, storage, access, and retrieval of linguistically described units: phonological units and their rules of

TRANSCODE

Transcoding involves changing one *set of codes* into another. The term is used with a similar meaning when transferring *data* from one format into another, including copying old analogue audio recordings to CD, or CD music to MP3 or some other compressed format.

NEURAL PATTERNS

The concept of neural patterning refers to activity in the nervous system which produces a specific bodily response, such as activity in the muscular system. In speech, unique patterns of neuromuscular activity may produce recognisable sounds.

REMINDER: COGNITIVE ACTIVITY

The term 'cognitive activity' refers to activity of the mind, in contradistinction to physical activity. Some cognitive activity can be associated or correlated with brain and other physical activity. Thus there may sometimes be some specific cognitive activity associated with certain neural patterns.

combination, syntactic units and rules of sequencing, meanings of words, and conventions of using the language (pragmatics). The list of speech production and perception errors noted by practitioners is lengthy (Kent 2006). They boil down into basically three types: cognitively based, biologically based and developmental. The third type, developmental error, is treated differently since there are special problems in *acquiring* language distinguished from *perceiving* language.

We have already seen that in speech production the *first stage* is the intention to speak, requiring the speaker to call on knowledge of the language characterised by the components: pragmatics, semantics, syntax, morphology and phonology. Note that the phonology includes extrinsic allophones for specifying the utterance plan, and for dialect specification (Chapter 6). The cortical areas most often referred to that may be correlated with language are Wernicke's and Broca's areas. There is some evidence that these areas may be implicated in loss of language ability, but the extent of involvement and how to account for inconsistencies in the data is unclear (Eysenck and Keane 2005).

Lateralisation of site and function is another claim that is being questioned; that is, the relationship between left and right hemispheres and activity associated with language. If we accept the linguistic descriptions, spoken language is analysed into segmental and prosodic representations. There is some evidence that most segmental activity occurs in the left hemisphere – and there are claims that prosody may be more closely associated with the right hemisphere. The question of how speech could be assembled with concurrent activity in two different areas is not yet comprehensively discussed – an obvious area needing elucidation.

- Accounting for some features in tone languages seems to contradict a two-area processing model. For example, although f0 changes (tones) are associated with morphemes in Mandarin Chinese, an overall utterance intonation pattern can also be described, and not all models in linguistics are clear about how this is done (but see 'Units of Prosody Perception' in Chapter 7 for an explanation of tone). The evidence is not convincing for lateralisation in this case. This suggests that the linguistic descriptive system might not adequately specify tone and intonation; or, if the descriptions are coherent and stable, linguistic tone is not directly and exclusively associated with activity in these separate biological areas.

The output of this first stage is an assembly of the appropriate words composed of the essential phonological units of the language. This string, called the utterance plan, is handed over to the *second stage*, currently thought to be a further stage of processing in the *supplementary motor area* (SMA), a pre-motor area of the brain (Corr 2006: 165). It is not yet known how the assemblage of the phonological units can be correlated with pre-motor brain activity. There is some evidence of timing activity for speech and other biological actions set up by the CEREBELLUM. Finer detail of timing is also a property of the coordinative structure production control model (see 'Action Theory' in Chapter 4). The output of this processing is handed to the *third stage*.

At this point, the motor area which organises neural signals for speaking is activated. (Note, however, that a strong correlation with linguistic components and specific brain areas is not yet definitively established, although there is *some* evidence, as already mentioned.) The result is activation of the appropriate coordinative structures, resulting in the articulations needed for speaking, as shown in the diagram below.

> **CEREBELLUM**
>
> The cerebellum is an area of the brain involved in rhythmic actions such as respiration. It is basic to muscle movement and motor control. It processes information from other parts of the brain such as the cerebral cortex, the visual cortex, and areas associated with cognitive processing including language and speech planning.

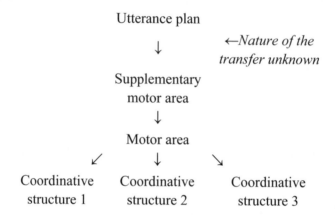

Utterance plan

↓   ←*Nature of the transfer unknown*

Supplementary
motor area

↓

Motor area

↙   ↓   ↘

Coordinative   Coordinative   Coordinative
structure 1   structure 2   structure 3

What needs to be done

Under comprehension and storage (perception), access and retrieval (production), the characterisations and classifications of phonological and phonetic units should be made explicit. Phonology is currently considered a cognitive event, and phonetics describes the physical rendering of phonological units. The distinction between these two types of description (cognitive and physical) can be blurred in some descriptions (see Chapters 3 and 4). This lack of full agreement among theorists, and a general lack of clarity, points towards our need for a strong and clear correlation to be set up between the *language descriptions* and the underlying processes associated with *communication disorders*. This will make available more precise intervention techniques for therapists, since the language-based indicators can point the way towards homing in on areas of the brain that are not functioning correctly, or suggest cognitive supervision procedures for non-productive ways of thinking.

Relating cognitive and biological models

At some point in modelling spoken language, the foundation of the models changes from biological-based to cognitive-based. Some researchers refer to this change in type as the mind–brain gap; but instead of a gap, others propose an explicit interface between brain and cognition (Hickok and Poeppel 2007). This approach may have some relevance to disorders of communication; disturbances in these areas may have observable external effects. Evidence identifying these areas could more precisely identify areas of disorder. We need to be careful, though, because even if two events or types of processing can be associated, it does *not* mean that one causes the other.

One way out of the difficulty of reconciling processes in cognitive and biological models is to ask whether some other underlying feature may affect both the brain area and the correlating behaviour. In other words, can a hierarchical approach provide a surer linkage between cognitive and correlating physical observations when there is a shared underlying process? In theory this approach might show promise, but, as an example of the difficulty, we can see that the pre-motor area responds to the phonological *utterance plan*, but that the signals underlying communication between the cognitive function and appropriate neurobiological areas have not yet been identified. What redeems the approach is that it generates hypotheses which enable us to direct our research towards specific areas of study. Hopefully, in the future clinicians will profit from advances here.

Similarly, lexical access and storage are currently being heavily researched, and we can expect changes of direction in applications work based on lexical-directed research (Finkbeiner *et al.* 2006). There are some important research questions that might be asked in this area, and which promise significant progress in our understanding of communication disorders. For example:

- Are linguistic features stored together, or as pointers to a range of features located in different brain areas associated with particular cognitive activity?

- Are storage, access and retrieval procedures common across speakers and listeners, or are there significant individual differences?

- If there are individual differences, are there implications for intervention and treatment when a speaker is judged to have disordered speech or when a listener reports that he or she cannot respond to speakers?

- For linguistically oriented models, how can language features be identified and described so that inferences can be made about the cause of the disorder?

Some dynamic models (not derivatives of transformational generative grammar) propose that phonology – units and sequencing of units – is essentially performed linearly. Others suggest that common words and phrases are not planned as sequences of sound to be assembled, but are stored in a gestalt (a collection of movements), directly related to a learned motor plan. However, it is not yet established whether

- speakers string segments in a linear fashion, or
- speakers store commonly used words and phrases as a unit, or
- a hierarchal storage representation enables identification of speech units, whatever they may be (segments, patterns, syllables).

The question most communication disorders practitioners would like answered in this respect is: would (a) pattern matching, (b) identification of acoustic phonetic detail or (c) a tree structure be most useful in characterising language representation at the phonological level (Ball *et al.* 2009)?

There is a large amount of evidence that speech comprehension is reduced after left-hemisphere damage, but there is evidence that some listeners can recruit systems in the right hemisphere to compensate for the left-hemisphere loss. Some imaging studies also show bilateral activity in the temporal lobes, but the specific activity shown by imaging techniques cannot as yet be firmly correlated with specific features in the acoustic waveform. For example, claims that prosody is processed in different areas from segmental aspects of speech must be regarded as tentative to date. Questions arise as to how prosodic features and segmental features interact, and if processed separately, how they might be perceived.

Can linguistic models really contribute to work in communication disorders?

The linguistic descriptive model is itself incomplete; there are a number of unanswered questions. For example:

1. Are utterances planned in syllables or segments, and what is the relation of either unit to prosody?
2. If syllable structure is damaged in that part on parts of the brain that are associated with their production, what happens to prosody?
3. Are there knock-on effects; for example, does the rhythm of the utterance fail?
4. Would there be similar effects in writing where prosody other than basic patterns (plain, question, exclamation) can be shown?

That is: what is the interrelation between syllable and prosody – rhythm, intonation, stress – all of which are essential to fluent speaking?

Models in linguistics can help with studies in communication disorders in two very simple ways:

- They can provide a means of labelling or annotating the waveform and the relation of disordered speech to ideal speech.

- They can characterise the underlying systems that produce spoken language, ideally in a dynamic way so that the processes can be understood.

The approach offered by linguists can be useful, simply because decisions made by practitioners are often based on linguistic or phonetic descriptions. The skill lies in making inferences from the observations available for *each sample* of disordered communication. We say *skill* because disorders specialists typically deal with small and inconsistent amounts of data, unlike the huge quantities of consistent data available to the linguist. However, because the linguistic/phonetic descriptions are fairly well formulated, they can be relied upon – once the basic model and point of view have been selected. The way in which the linguistics plays a supporting role needs to be formal, so that the support can be consistent and replicated. The major variable becomes the person making the descriptions – and then making decisions based on the descriptions (see Kent 2004 for a discussion of types of disorder, and the problems in drawing inferences).

The ideal model

Ideally a communication model will incorporate:

- *physiological and functional descriptions*, together with predictions about how speaking and perceptual features may be lost or changed following biological – mainly neurological – damage resulting in malfunction of the speaking systems;

- *hypotheses and test procedures* for alternative routes to performing different language tasks;

- *proposed cognitive structures* essential to language production and perception;

- *characterisations* of individual variability such as personal features, dialect and style;

- *predictions* about loss or change of features when the communication system fails.

Additionally, a worthwhile communication model should account for spoken language in context. Such contexts include social, emotional,

APPLICATIONS

teaching and other forms of behaviour that have a direct bearing on speech production and perception.

Speech communication is more than putting words together in the conventional sequence. While speaking we display emotive content, rely on social context to interpret what is being said, and include an assessment of other, non-verbal behaviour. We are aware of, among other things,

- special social circumstances such as speaking to a child or adult;

- gender, and known or apparent background of the listener;

- whether we want to provide or ask for information (communicative intention);

- whether if we want to follow the conversation and change our speech as it unfolds (discourse interactions);

- whether we're speaking to a computer and whether it expects a response.

Disorders in spoken language in such social contexts will disrupt communication. A model which would incorporate all the current circumstances of our daily speech might be possible at some future time, but does not yet seem imminent. It also would be quite useful and interesting to build a communication model which could be compared with motor-processing, perceptual and conceptual models of other biological/ cognitive activity such as music, art in other forms, dancing, sport, etc. That also appears to be somewhat distant.

TWO TYPES OF SPEECH MODEL – STATIC AND DYNAMIC

Here we summarise the main point of one or two approaches that are of use in dealing with communicative disorders. The models are presented elsewhere in the book, but the emphasis here is on how suitable they are for application in the pathological area. At this point, consider what the linguist has available for descriptive modelling (TUTORIAL – THE LINGUIST'S BASIC DESCRIPTIVE TOOLS).

Classical Phonetics

Classical phonetics (Chapter 3) is a static model which describes what phoneticians report they hear or have heard. Static models like classical phonetics provide a means for the observer to note and classify surface phenomenon. The anatomical structures used in speech are well defined in biological theory, and although classical phonetics deals with surface observations about movement and so on, it has not fully brought into its descriptive system much of the evidence now available from contemporary experimental phonetics. The result is that *underlying systems* are not part of the goal of its transcription system or theory. We can *speculate* about what might produce speech events, but within this model we cannot *associate* observed external observations with underlying biological structures and their associated functions.

Cognitive Phonetics

Cognitive phonetics (Chapter 4) is a dynamic model outlining a possible overall characterisation of processing. Contemporary cognitive phonetics is based on the earlier version presented in the 1980s, but today incorporates a supervisory agent responsible for managing the rendering process (Tatham and Morton 2006). The theory deals in broad terms with *types* of linguistic/ phonetics categories that might be useful in processing spoken language. The model is able to suggest hypotheses about classification of disordered language behaviour, and predicts areas of potentially difficult processing in speech production and perception. The model may well be quite incorrect, but it is *falsifiable* – built on data and interpreted according to standard scientific procedures. As with all well-formulated theories, it says: this is a coherent suggestion to help understand the phenomenon, and this is how we predict it will behave: change it where those predictions prove false.

Differences between Classical Phonetics and Cognitive Phonetics

The classical phonetics model abstracts away from variability, but in a non-transparent way. Variability might have been introduced by coarticulation or emotive information, be the result of noise in the system or of cognitive supervision, or have been caused by as yet 'random' caused, unexplained events which may or may not be significant. Any information which could prove helpful in understanding disordered speech is obscured by or lost in the abstraction procedure of classical phonetics. For example, transcription relies on auditory-perceptual methods (Kent 2006), and reduces variability even when performed by a 'trained' expert in communication disorders – the subjectivity of the transcriber is inescapable. The recorded symbols are the result of the transcriber's perception, training and experience. A disorder could be the result of, among other things:

- correct intention to speak and failed rendering;
- incorrect intention and correct rendering;
- incorrect intention and failed rendering.

The norm would involve correct intuition and correct rendering on the part of the speaker, but the source of the disorder is not revealed in the pathologist's transcription, and the underlying theory has nothing to say on the matter. This is extremely important for the specialist, because if variability is not accurately noted, it is not clear which of the above sources might be responsible. We cannot successfully work in a framework that does not distinguish levels of processing.

Cognitive phonetics seeks to provide a framework capable of drawing attention to failures to control rendering: their sources can be suggested, or, more formally, hypothesised. The transcriber/investigator can ask whether they are listening to:

- failed utterance *plan*;
- failed general *control*;
- failed *rendering* in specific areas;
- failure to establish the plan – *comprehension* failure.

This degree of investigation is possible because the theory makes transparent how the final signal is derived, thus pointing the way to the various stages the 'information' has passed through. At each point, what constitutes a potential failure is detailed.

The final acoustic signal contains information from which we can make inferences about the utterance plan, the control system and the rendering processes. Take voice onset time (VOT) as an example (Chapter 10): an error produced by a native speaker of English could be taken to be accent variation or perhaps a disorder; in a non-native speaker, the native language may be interfering, and the poor rendering in English is not a disorder. As another example, 'deaf speech' often displays poor rhythm control which in turn will have an effect on coarticulation. How can a potential diagnosis of deafness be based on the 'slurred' speech noted in an unhelpful, flat, linear transcription? But a model which focuses on the underlying hierarchical structure of speech can note all the possible candidates for explaining the problem.

Dynamic computational models

An important feature of computational models is their transparency – that is, all the hypothesised parts of the system are labelled, with rules or descriptions stating how the parts function together within the system, how the system responds to input (change in context) and what we can expect the output to be (response). If the model runs (that is, runs as a program), and especially if it is reasonably complete, structural sections of the computational model corresponding to biological structures can be deliberately damaged, and the effect noted. If the computer model is a good representation of a human system, then we can hypothesise that the human system might have suffered similar damage. As yet, however, although there is a great deal of information about the nature of the human speech system, there doesn't appear to be enough to build a full and useful working model.

We need to make a distinction between a computational model designed specifically and uniquely as a computer program, and the ability of other models to compute, simply because they are fully explicit. Ideally any model should compute if rewritten as a computer program; this is a technique sometimes used to spot gaps in the arguments of a theory (Tatham and Morton 2006: ch. 9).

Let us use one final example outside the speech area. If the main tendon in the heel is badly damaged we can see that the foot does not work, and describe what can be seen of its behaviour. The damage can be observed as part of the total structure. There is a great deal of knowledge about the structure of the foot, and about the function of this tendon within the total foot and leg structure. Intervention techniques backed by sound models might be called for and might involve surgical repair to the structure. Exercises can be used to improve function, or the body may adapt to recruit alternative muscle/tendon systems if the repair is inadequate. A similar type of model of structure and function, suggesting useful interventions, would be helpful in spoken language disorders. As yet the models in linguistics and phonetics do not themselves make these suggestions; for the moment, what is important is to recognise which core models could potentially assist in communicative disorders studies.

In summary, a model which does not specify underlying structures *cannot* make hypotheses about human performance which can be tested. In sharp contrast, a model detailing underlying structures associated with spoken language production *can* suggest hypotheses about human speech production, and these are open to extension into the field of disorders.

EXAMPLE SPEECH PRODUCTION DISORDER – APRAXIA

Apraxia is a syndrome expressed as a loss of skilled movements that are not based on physiological damage of the neuromuscular system other than motor deficit, but are thought to be associated with cortical motor dysfunction (Kent 2004). The effects are modelled as loss of the ability to plan the appropriate peripheral system movement. There is some evidence to suggest that in apraxia learned and planned movements have been stored but cannot be retrieved. In these disorders, movement plans may also not be accessible, either because the access route has been disrupted, or because the *representation* of the plan is damaged. To what extent the motor plan is completely stored, or stored as a gestalt, or whether the plan is simple, with on-going articulatory forces manipulating coordinative structures to change articulatory movement patterns, is not understood (Varley 2010).

The observable disordered speech behaviour includes variation in articulatory movements, resulting in segmental and associated coarticulation errors. Variability is noticeable in speech-rate change, resulting in increased or decreased segmental durations (especially in vowel production) and in disruptions to utterance rhythm. We outline in general terms what might happen in apraxia of speech.

In spoken language, apraxia refers to the inability to carry out a plan to speak because the MOTOR CONTROL system cannot be adequately planned or programmed. This is an example of cognitive/biological association at the point of moving from the cognitive planning stage to actually carrying out the plan. *Where* this might occur and *how* it might occur – that is, where the junction is and its features – are not as yet adequately modelled.

It is thought that potential movement patterns (praxis representations) are transcoded into innervatory patterns held in the pre-motor areas. This information moves to the motor cortex and, when actioned, the appropriate neuromuscular system is activated and the relevant muscles move. Damage to the pre-motor cortex or the supplementary motor area (SMA– part of the sensorimotor cortex) disrupts normal movement because of errors in transcoding the innervatory patterns for actioning by the motor cortex. The knowledge associated with the pre-motor area seems unaffected, unless by some other damage – it is thought that knowledge is present, but the ability to move correctly is absent. There is also some evidence that damage in the parietal lob may result in loss of the concept of knowing *when* to plan a movement. Thus, there are two possibilities for disruption in movement – loss of:

- the physical *ability to move*;
- the cognitive knowledge of *how to move*.

To summarise: some differences can be seen between the classical phonetics and cognitive phonetics models with respect to dealing with apraxia.

1. Cognitive processes produce an utterance plan. The plan's units are extrinsic allophones at the exit point of a dynamic phonology. The plan is linked with the concept of physical target (Chapters 2 and 4); cognitive phonetics requires a full specification at this level, and any error in the plan itself will have predictable effects as rendering proceeds. This kind of error may be added to by errors further down in the chain of processes culminating in the final acoustic signal.

2. The utterance plan transcodes into the motor plan where motor targets are specified; no information is added or deleted, unless

an error is detected in cross-checking. Any error may also effect processing further down in the rendering. Notice the target concept, which, in the model, functions as bridging the gap, or providing equivalence, between the cognitive and physical domains.

3. Targets (planned and motor) are parametrically specified.

4. At the motor control stage, muscle movement can be calculated – the accuracy relies on feedback acting as part of the input for supervision of the motor control processes (see 'The Abstract Theory of Articulator Control' in Chapter 4).

5. Gross physical instructions are sent to the appropriate COORDINATIVE STRUCTURES in the vocal tract. Actions are carried out under the management of the supervisory agent.

REMINDER: COORDINATIVE STRUCTURES AND SUPERVISION

Coordinative structures first appeared in the 1970s as a concept in speech production theory in Action Theory (Chapter 4); the idea was picked up in cognitive phonetics, developed in the 1980s. The introduction of the *cognitive* supervision or continuous management of *physical* motor control, and the agent responsible for this, came in the mid-1990s. Take an example from outside the field of speech:

- If a tendon in the leg is badly damaged, the person is said with rehabilitation to *relearn to walk*. In effect, this will involve retraining of the coordinative structures recruited for walking, or it might involve organising the brain to reprogram the system in extreme cases. If the leg is not so badly damaged, there can be local adaptation (under supervision) and local self-retraining. These processes are mediated by the coordinative structure system.

And from speech:

- Consider the bulk and structure of the tongue – anchored at the back, but very flexible at the blade/tip. Several muscles form the tongue's structure. In using the tongue for language, placement has to be very accurate (perhaps down to a single millimetre), and the timing of gestures has to be quite precise. Are such positional and timing gestures centrally controlled, and if so, would we need stored movement patterns and specifications for every possible extrinsic allophone in the language/accent inventory? A model relying entirely on central computation, recomputation and control of all parameters is barely plausible – the computational loading seems excessive. The coordinative structure model transfers much of this load to the periphery, where, *provided there is careful supervision*, complex and precise movements are more plausibly handled.

In this section comparing the usefulness of the classical phonetics and cognitive phonetics approaches, we have seen just how much a surface abstract model is limited. Although couched in comparatively general terms, the cognitive phonetics model attempts to capture the entire process as a coherent system. The advantage is a more powerful theory, which is able to account for more speech effects while forming a dynamic *total process* model going significantly and usefully beyond the simple observations and abstractions of the classical phonetics surface descriptive system.

- It is important to note that both models and approaches have very important roles to play, not only in general speech theory, but also in work in areas of application. We cite two specific models because we can talk about their specific properties, but what we have been saying applies generally to *all theories of speech production,* detailed in Chapters 3 and 4. We have used these two theories only as examples of classes of theory – static, surface, non-explanatory vs. dynamic, hierarchical, explanatory – and tried to show how more contemporary approaches are more relevant to applications.

SPEECH PERCEPTION DEFICITS OTHER THAN HEARING DEFICITS

Perception (as distinct from *peripheral* sensory processing – in speech, hearing; see Chapter 6) is the act of assigning labels to incoming stimuli from any of the five senses. But note what might happen between sensory input and brain activity. The external signal is detected by the peripheral sensory system, accessing channels through which the relevant input information must travel. In the case of speech the pathway followed is shown in the diagram below.

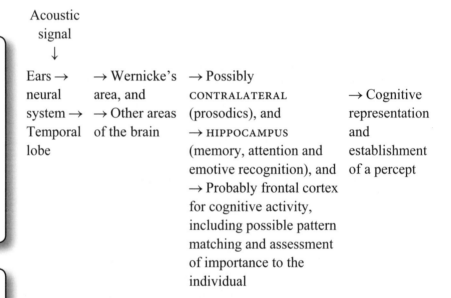

Acoustic
signal
↓

Ears → neural system → Temporal lobe

→ Wernicke's area, and
→ Other areas of the brain

→ Possibly CONTRALATERAL (prosodics), and
→ HIPPOCAMPUS (memory, attention and emotive recognition), and
→ Probably frontal cortex for cognitive activity, including possible pattern matching and assessment of importance to the individual

→ Cognitive representation and establishment of a percept

CONTRALATERAL

This means literally 'opposite side'. Thus, information coming into one side of the brain is processed in the opposite hemisphere, and a signal originating in one side of the brain results in activity in the opposite side of the body. For example, a serious lesion in the right side of the motor area results in difficulty in moving some part of the left side of the body.

HIPPOCAMPUS

This is a structure in the mid-area of the brain. It is active in learning, memory storage, recall and language processing.

There are several models of speech perception; importantly, they are distinguished by the extent to which they rely on cognitive processing of the incoming signal to reach its recognition, or the establishing of an appropriate matching percept. Chapter 8 gives details of these, comparing them with respect to where each stands on the direct realism/indirect realism vector. Here we need to look at one or two properties of such theories, since they are relevant to dealing with perception deficits.

One old, yet pervading idea, the belief that acoustic phonetic detail might contain phonetic and linguistic information, is tenable only in a direct realist approach (see Chapter 8). For example, many researchers have felt that phonetic details of speech inform listeners about the message, about speaker identification including some characteristics of their social status, their mood or their emotive stance, and about their current attitude towards the listener as the dialogue unfolds. However, only in extreme direct realist models could acoustic features *of themselves* convey or inform. It is more probably the case that these features trigger recognition and identification of the message and speaker characteristics within the mind of the listener, based on their experience and prior knowledge.

Despite these direct realist ideas, the general view among researchers in the area of perception is that basically, the waveform is largely unstructured, but that any patterns which do exist are detected, transmitted through the chain detailed above, and interpreted by the listener. If the listener does not have some experience of the language, the message itself is not conveyed; if the speaker uses unfamiliar or unconventional means for expressing information about social status, then this part of the communication will also fail. *Some* information about gender and age may be conveyed, because the listener has had experience in their own language, and the particular phenomena involved may not be under the control of the speaker – that is, may have universal content. But all information conveyed by the waveform needs detection and interpretation by the listener. Segments and prosodic features do not and *cannot* exist in the waveform – simply because they are abstract concepts. At best there are traces of some acoustic correlates of these concepts (Chapter 7).

Modelling speech perception processes is uneven because data is difficult to obtain and sometimes inconsistent. The problem is even greater with perception disorders – there is a very considerable amount of variation. Possible component processes have been described, but it is not clear how they may be related. For example, a great deal of work has been done on hearing (see TUTORIAL – HEARING in Chapter 7), but what happens after detecting the speech signal has been inferred mainly from observing output – written, spoken (expressive linguistic skills), and responses from a number of testing procedures.

Perception disorders

Cognitive representations are not well defined. What researchers have to assume is that some event has occurred, resulting in the beginning of a further series of events or processes, the outcome of which we can call a *percept* or cognitive unit. Biological systems with cognitive capacity (that is, excluding plants, for example) are hypothesised to establish concepts when functioning normally.

Spoken language models usually take into account the linking of this cognitive capacity with a biological underpinning. When errors occur, researchers do look for the source of the disorder by focusing on particular sites in the brain, but in general, the data available for defining perception disorders is mainly based on an analysis of the subject's speech output, *after* the concept has been formed. It is therefore difficult to say whether an error is due to perceptual processing or to an inability to produce the response.

Possible error sources

Biological underpinning
↕

Cognitive processing →   Subject's
reporting   Subject's output *with error*
process →
↕

Therapist/researcher observes
the error

The diagram above shows the relationship. There are three major areas in the subject where error can occur: the biological underpinning, the cognitive processing and the subject's reporting process. The error detected by the therapist or researcher could arise from any of these areas. Diagnostics to clarify the source of error are not too reliable at the moment.

Aphasia

APHASIA (Varley *et al.* 2004) can be viewed as a disorder in either perception or production of language – or both. It is distinct from hearing disorders in so far as this distinction can be made. Disordered perception is thought to be involved in comprehension and in the ability to repeat words and phrases. Recognition or comprehension assumes components of perceptual processing which recognise language input as characterised by linguistics: thus there may be a component in the listener which recognises stored phonological units of the language and can separate them in the stream of speech. Adopting an indirect realist position, we are assuming this is how the listener performs the recognition task.

APHASIA

Aphasia is an acquired language disorder arising from brain-based impairment. Cognitive function is impaired in areas of language communication such as speaking, writing, reading and understanding. There are many subclassifications of the disorder, depending on whether motor functions or cognitive functions are affected.

Similarly, stored areas of the lexicon will be triggered by the incoming decoded acoustic waveform, and recognised by an intact perceptual/ interpretatative component. Disorders in comprehension can involve failure of these processes. However, they may also involve difficulties with self-monitoring, decision-making, thinking logically, planning activity, problem-solving and so on. Memory and attention disruptions probably also contribute to poor comprehension. The subtype 'receptive aphasia' refers to such areas of disorder. The term aphasia is *also* applied to a range of observations such as distortions in normal language (Ball *et al.* 2009).

To remind ourselves, features of *normal speech* include:

- speaking spontaneously in conversation without special prompts;
- forming words morphemically and phonemically with acceptable structure;
- using appropriate grammatical and prosodic patterns;
- naming objects without substituting non-standard words;
- selecting appropriate words without creating neologisms.

Using this list, we can identify five types of disorder which may also involve production problems at the point where the speaker accesses the stored lexicon. Whether these disorders are ascribed to perception or production disorders is a matter for the practitioner and researcher. What appears to be a production disorder may in fact be a perception difficulty: for example an inappropriate lexical item may have been stored, retrieved and produced acceptably, but some deficit in perception has changed the expected set of features. Naming of objects may seem to the speaker to be correct, but an inadequate function in the comprehension process may result in incorrect storage and the production of disrupted communication. Receptive aphasia usually refers to difficulties in comprehension, but is difficult to pin down since the evidence is primarily based on production, and, as we have seen, the syndrome is inferred from production evidence.

The research problem of separating perception and production processes is currently being addressed in the research field. The hypothesis is that perceptual problems might underlie production disorders. Distinguishing one from the other began with suggesting that a lower-order production disorder was preceded by lower-order perception disorders. Similarly higher-order production was linked to higher-order perception deficits. A series of experiments (Nijland 2009) suggests a strong correlation between production and perception scores at these different levels.

Questions to ask about perception

The list of questions to ask about normal and disordered perception is long. Some have answers, others are vague, many are being investigated currently, and others await investigation. The problem for the pathologist should not be underestimated, and is not helped by lack of clarity in some of the models which have been developed for normal language. We set out some of these questions here, involving speech production where appropriate.

- Remember again that the linguistic units used here are terms from a *model*, attempting to make analysis simpler. There is no scientific implication that there is a 'prosodic component' – or any other – stored in brain tissue and able to be revealed. It is not possible to stress this point too much.

How these questions are ordered will depend on the reader's perspective, but we have tried to be logical in their presentation.

1. How does a listener decode? Is it:

    (a) as a sequence of perceived and recognised sounds, or
    (b) as a familiar unit?

2. How does a listener predict segmentation of utterance sections or words?

3. Where does this information come from?

    (a) How has it been triggered, and recognised?
    (b) What are the access and retrieval routes?

4. Do speakers/listeners have separate internal representations of segments and prosodic features?

5. Do speakers produce segmental and prosodic structures simultaneously – requiring simultaneous perception?

6. If it is useful to recognise two different types of speech structures – segmental and prosodic – what is the nature of the speaker's utterance plan which the listener has to recover?

    (a) Do we put a string of phonological units together, and then add the appropriate prosodic features?
    (b) Do we have a prosodic *wrapper* assembled before the segments are sequenced?
    (c) Do we have a prosodic framework before a learned motor target plan for a word or phrase?

7. What is the *cognitive* evidence for listeners' or speakers' impaired prosody?

8. What is the *physical* evidence for impairment of prosodic features?

9. Can pathological data help in building models of normal speech, or in filling in gaps in existing ones?

10. Can pathological data contradict known normal models? Distinguish between EMPIRICAL AND THEORY-DRIVEN MODELLING.

11. How does data from disordered speakers differ from that from normal speakers; and where is the line to be drawn?

12. Do judgement and labelling strategies differ between normal and pathological studies?

13. How does the role of perception in the listener differ from that in the practitioner, and what bias might enter into practitioner judgement if there is a difference?

EMPIRICAL AND THEORY-DRIVEN MODELLING

Empirical models, broadly defined, comprise sets of statements based on observation of data and experience; assembling these is sometimes called data-driven modelling. Narrowly defined, they are hypothesis-driven models based on observations; that is, the hypotheses are derived from the observations. These models are not as powerful as theory-based models, where the modelling process is driven by hypotheses thrown up by the theory, not by new data.

SUCCESSFUL MODELS IN PRACTICE

We are able to characterise the general features of any speech production/ perception model, whatever its point of view. But the practitioner might find it useful to understand what, from a model point of view, is basic and what is desirable. This list has been compiled from a number of course descriptions published by various institutions.

What is needed *as basic* is an understanding of:

1. the difference between articulatory and phonological disorders;

2. how different assessment techniques are required with differing underlying models, and why they *are* different and useful;

3. how to make a reasoned decision about intervention and rehabilitation techniques suitable for the assessed disorder – different underlying models call for different techniques;

4. the scope and limitations of the descriptive systems available; for example, the International Phonetic Alphabet (IPA) for phonological/ phonetic transcription, word categories, rules at all levels, and suitable descriptions for semantic- and pragmatic-based disorders.

Future areas of application

One of the current areas of research impinging on studies in communication disorders is work in lexical access. We currently use the labels 'words' and 'morphemes' to specify basic units which carry semantic and phonological information. Some current research is directed towards understanding what brain structures might be associated with these units. Questions arise such as:

1. If a word is stored with relevant features closely associated in a type of dictionary store, is there evidence from studies of disorders to suggest an entire complex unit is removed, or are selected features only not accessible?

2. What is the relationship between morpheme storage and memory? What function does IMPLICIT MEMORY have in speech processing; and what weighting can be put on explicit memory in communication?

There is great interest currently in characterising the lexicon. For example, if a word can be modelled as a pointer to a networked system, and if a part of the associated brain structure is not functioning, then would some features associated with that word be removed? Or would they be changed or accessed according to remaining features, resulting in production of a synonym, or neologism?

IMPLICIT MEMORY

The term *implicit memory* is used when a change is noted in behaviour (specifically, performance of a task) and when that change can be attributed to an earlier experience, even if no particular experience can be explicitly recalled. The memory is thought to be formed as a result of an interaction between perception categories, concept formation and, in the case of action, those motor systems that are involved in carrying out the task.

Contrast *implicit memory* with *explicit memory*. Here the term refers to an event that can be recalled and of which the person is aware. The event is able to be described in varying amounts of detail.

Developing models *outside* the fields of linguistics and phonetics may provide good and productive bases for enlarging the areas that linguistics and phonetics currently address. These other research areas can help provide explanation, enable more reliable prediction, and change the way we regard speech processing – and perhaps prove helpful in the study of communication disorders. By researching in areas *underlying* speech production and perception, we are developing

- more knowledge of how the psychobiological system works (Corr 2006; Poeppel *et al*. 2008; Ziegler 2010);

- improved cognitive-based speech modelling (Varley *et al*. 2004);

- reliable and useful models integrating production and perception (Nijland 2009), cognitive psychology and perception (Eysenck and Keane 2005), cognitive linguistics (Lakoff and Johnson 1999) and lexical representation (Evans 2009).

Separately, work on mirror neurons and the debate surrounding this representation contrasted with sensorimotor models (Haggard *et al*. 2008) is looking promising. Okada and Hickok (2006) and Poeppel (Poeppel *et al*. 2007) are investigating whether the same neural regions seem likely to support both perception and production – relevant to the basic theory of language. Mattys *et al*. (2009) are breaking down a general model of speech processing into subunits as seen from an experimental psychology perspective, and incorporating methods from visual processing models. The aim is to build up a larger model from reasonably well-established smaller units. Importantly, researchers are now achieving more reliable and comprehensive statements of the state of the art in practice (Kent 2006; Ball *et al.* 2009).

SPEECH TECHNOLOGY

The phonetician's skills and speech technology

Attempts at synthesising speech and at automatic speech recognition have often tried to assemble a knowledge base of phonetic information from phoneticians' observations about speech and its perception. But there has always been something unsatisfactory about the idea, and the results are never as good as might be predicted. The idea is simple: take an expert on speech – the phonetician – and capture all that they know about its production and perception. This would be at least, goes the hypothesis, a good start to a computationally based simulation of these processes. So why is it that

- the phoneticians' skills do not translate directly into speech technology?

- the descriptions phoneticians have of speech, when applied in speech recognition and speech synthesis, do not appear to be adequate to enable the technology to work satisfactorily?

An example illustrates the problem: take the contrast between /t/ and /d/. For phoneticians this lies in the voicing parameter ([t] is voiceless and [d] is voiced) and in the tensing parameter ([t] is tense and [d] is lax). The distinction made by phonologists in distinctive feature theory is the same: /t/ is [−voice, +tense] and /d/ is [+voice, −tense] (see TUTORIAL – DISTINCTIVE FEATURE THEORY in Chapter 4). If we program a speech synthesiser according to these descriptions to say words like *sat* and *sad*, we can hear immediately that something is wrong towards the end of *sad*. Comparing the waveforms of a synthesised word *sad* and the same word pronounced by a human being, what we see is that although the phonetician describes the final [d] of *sad* as voiced, the commonly accepted correlate of that feature – vocal cord vibration – is in fact absent.

So why does the phonetician or phonologist use [+voice] when there is no vocal cord vibration in the actual signal? In phonology the answer is easy: phonological descriptions are about the mental image speaker/listeners have of speech, rather than of the actual sound wave, and for speakers of English it is felt by speaker/listeners that this is how they hear the sounds to be distinguished. We saw in Chapters 7 and 8 that this apparent anomaly is a function of the way the perceptual system works: speaker/listeners fit what they hear into pre-established mental or cognitive representations they hold in their memories. This happens even if there is an apparent mismatch between the physical facts and the mental representation, so long as the system actually works to distinguish between otherwise ambiguous sound objects.

Phonological and phonetic descriptions

The table below sums up the chain of events in the above examples of *sat* and *sad*.

Phonology	Phonology	Phonetics
underlying word- or morpheme-distinguishing representation	surface speech plan representation	post-rendering articulatory or acoustic representation
$/sæt_{[-voice]}/ - /sæd_{[+voice]}/$	$/sæt_{[-voice]}/ - /sæd_{[+voice]}/$	$[sæt_{[-vocal\ cord\ vibration]}] - [sæd̥_{[-vocal\ cord\ vibration]}]$

- Reminder: in the transcriptions in the table we have used / . . . / to enclose both underlying (phonemic) and derived (extrinsic allophonic, or plan) representations, and [. . .] to enclose phonetic (intrinsic allophonic) REPRESENTATIONS.

The abstract feature [voice] is used in the PHONOLOGICAL representations, but the physical feature [vocal cord vibration] is used in the PHONETIC representations. Vocal cord vibration is a physical correlate of abstract voicing, though there might be others such as absence of tensing, or even a change in an adjacent feature (see Chapter 3).

REMINDER: PHONOLOGY AND PHONETICS

Remember that phonology is cognitive and its representations and categories are abstract, but that phonetics is physical and its representations are of the physical world and therefore, though abstract, are less so than those of phonology. Phonology is said to underlie phonetics in the sense that in the human being (and in the description produced by a linguist) it characterises those cognitive processes which go towards establishing the plan for speaking utterances. The model assumes that speech production involves the formulation of an abstract speaking plan which is then rendered physically. This is rather like taking an architect's drawings (which are abstract and stylised) and using them to build an actual building; this, of course, involves much more physical detail than what is conveyed in the drawings.

- In terms of perception, the analogy might be a relatively objective photograph which records in a mechanical way the light falling on the camera's photosensitive chip, and an artist's relatively subjective drawing which is an interpretation of the same light. The artist, while putting something of themself into the drawing, is also attempting to capture something of the subject which is not conveyed, it is felt, by the photograph. The analogy is complex because a photograph can also convey an art beyond the simple recording of a scene – the photographer can choose camera angles and other effects designed to add to the scene.

REPRESENTATIONS

The representations designed to show the distinguishing characteristics of different words or morphemes are symbols representing phonemes or underlying phonological units (sometimes called *descriptive units*). Those which figure in the utterance plan are symbols representing cognitively derived allophones, called *extrinsic allophones*. The symbols used in phonetics for showing acoustic or articulatory detail in the output are called *intrinsic allophones* because the detail has been derived intrinsically to the speech production system itself.

Synthesis systems

There are many engineering-based systems that produce computer speech. Contemporary systems all work with more or less success, but at the same time they all lack a really satisfactory language model to drive them. It is unarguable that models of speech production/perception have an important role in delivering good computer speech, but the question is always: how can the models appropriately describe the most useful features of speech for delivering improved synthesis (Tatham and Morton 2006: ch. 10)?

- Remember, this section of the book is about applications of speech production and perception theory: it is not really about trying to create speech technology systems which explicitly deny the theory – such as statistically based systems.

Computer speech

Acceptable and appropriate speech output is still not available for general use. Good speech is important, since without a convincing, truly human-like output the result is an impression that the information conveyed to the listener and the system *behind* the speech are probably not going to be very reliable. This is not, of courses the impression the system or its designers want to evoke.

Synthesis systems are now fairly intelligible, but still lack what is often termed *naturalness*; that is, the speech does not fully have qualities we associate with human speech. Put another way, other than in short bursts, the speech is highly unlikely to be confused with real human speech. The features which need to be improved are:

- *prosodics*, including good intonation patterns;
- clear and consistent rendering of *segments* and their combinations into words;
- acceptable *timing features*;
- appropriate *emotive content* for the dialogue.

Improving these features is particularly important in systems that require human–machine interaction. The acoustic parameters must dynamically respond to changes in the dialogue, just as human speakers/listeners do (Tatham and Morton 2005). The lack of expressive content and appropriate variability continue to make synthesis systems unacceptable for general use among the lay public.

The need for these qualities is seen particularly in special machine-driven interactions with humans. For example, when seeking telephone advice about our bank accounts, we need to interact with a voice which sounds firm but reassuring. But when asking about train timetables, a more direct and fairly neutral presentation of facts is enough. Speech-based medical advice – which may occur in the future, replacing the text-based versions currently available – will probably require a reassuring, factual, authoritative but friendly tone of voice. Call centres, e-learning and various voice-based media are predicted to rely on computer speech for communication shortly; indeed, some already do. But today, these applications are not realistic except in special circumstances where low quality is better than nothing. As the public tires of the novelty it will become necessary to improve the quality before the user decides to abandon the system because of frustration.

Building synthesis systems

Two philosophies are possible in building synthesis systems:

- They can be built as simulations of the human *process* of production, including some idea of the listener's perceptual process.

- They can be built recreating just the *output* of the human process, paying attention to what acoustic cues appear to trigger listeners' perception best.

The first approach requires a full and adequate description of speaker/listener communication systems; the second requires an adequate understanding of *what* produces the required effect in the listener, but not *how* it produces the effect. So far, neither production nor perception models have provided adequate information for building good speech systems.

- Note that automatic speech recognition (ASR) requirements are different from those of synthesis. ASR needs an adequate description of the waveform which can be matched up, or associated with, stored information in the system about the world and the speaker's likely interests. In addition, successful ASR requires a module for speech understanding, after it decodes and assigns a representation to the signal. These systems also need adequate descriptions of sound waves and correlating language units, adequate knowledge representation of the world the ASR and the speaker are in, and a method of letting the speaker know they have understood the message (Holmes and Holmes 2001).

It is clear that we need to know what has held up this obviously useful application of speech production/perception theory. A number of difficulties have arisen:

- *determining relevant features within the variable waveform.* The speaker's phonological utterance plan is rendered slightly differently with each utterance repetition, producing differing acoustic waveforms and introducing largely unmodelled variability. We are thinking here not just of the variability in segmental and prosodic specification and rendering, but also of wide-ranging signal variations due to expressive content. These variations happen even though the underlying abstract intention of the speaker may be invariant. Even syntactic structures vary with repetition. Making meaningful generalisations from the variable waveform has not been successful.

- *prosodics*. A major property of speech is its prosodics, or suprasegmental features. The perceived intonation contour is a representation triggered by changes of fundamental frequency produced by the speaker. In machine systems, this contour is often implemented by rule, relying on a simple parse of the utterance or sentence. However, typically only a limited number of utterance prosodic patterns among the many possible ones can actually be produced by a synthesiser in this way. This small number has not proved useful over many wider ranges of application, because users tend to notice the prosodic monotony which results.

- *emotive content*. For successful rendering, emotive content needs an overarching algorithm for changing fundamental frequency for assigned intonation patterns, adjusting durations on some words, and occasionally, with great care, changing amplitude values on stressed words. Parameters such as rate of speaking, change of fundamental frequency (perceived as pitch changes), and range of fundamental frequency used, voice-quality changes, and amplitude changes on segments have all been measured or assessed in human beings in experiments designed to discover the acoustic correlates of emotive content in speech. But attempts to establish the relationship among these parameters and the identification of others have not been entirely successful. Since the emotive content cannot yet be fully modelled for human speech, programming a computer system adequately is not yet possible (Tatham and Morton 2004).

A major problem has been establishing exactly what acoustic characteristics in the varying waveform can trigger recognition of emotive content. At present, some progress has been made which identifies basic emotive content such as anger, happiness, sadness, and neutrality to the subject matter of the utterance. But how useful are these four basic emotions in an interactive computer system, or when simply giving information? Models of subtle characteristics which can evoke, in the listener, feelings of friendliness, understanding, firmness, authority, etc. on the part of the machine would be useful.

There are problems of definition in the research. Exactly what *is* happiness or what is anger? But also, what is mild irritation, and how do we characterise moving through anger to rage? Nonetheless, in use emotive language itself is fairly clear, and speakers and listeners seem to share a common intuition; the problem is capturing this intuition in a model of emotive content, in a way which quantifies it for simulation in a synthesis system. The task is to find a method for varying the waveform according to principles that will trigger the perception of expressive speech within listeners, and be responsive within the dialogue to the listener's speech back – this is a two-way exchange of information in the natural situation. Not only are we a long way from a full characterisation of the intuitions shared between speaker and listener, and their correlating acoustic signals, but the *variability* in this area is as great as it is in segmental and prosodic areas of speech.

Variability

It is convenient to distinguish between types of acoustic variability detectable in the speech waveform.

1. intended variability:

    a. arising from choice of phonological unit – for example, choosing to say /bɪt/ rather than /pɪt/ to contrast *bit* and *pit*;
    b. from accent or dialectal variants – for example, planning /bɪʔ/ or /bɪʔ/ rather than /bɪt/ for *bit*;
    c. introduced by expressive content, such as the intention to emphasise certain words contrastively – for example, *I said dog, not cat* – needing special treatment of fundamental frequency.

2. Unintended variability:

    a. as part of the biological stance of the speaker, giving rise to perceived emotive effects – for example, changing speech rate when excited;
    b. from varying articulations – for example, timing changes when out of breath.

3. Supervised variability:

    a. under cognitive control because of demands (like coarticulation) on the speaker or listener – for example, speaking louder and with more precision in a noisy environment.

Simulating these effects in synthesis also requires a pragmatic knowledge base in order to associate social context changes with changes in the acoustic waveform which will trigger the perception of the *machine's* putative feelings and attitude.

Current solutions

As a temporary measure, it has been shown that introducing words and phrases beyond the plain text can be helpful in conveying more human-like messages. Adding *thank you, please, one moment*, etc. can improve human–computer speech interaction. These phrases stand in for the tone of voice that we might expect in human speech – we are trying to transfer expressive or emotive content to an *augmented* message, to end up with the same result in the listener.

Associating such phrases requires matching the phrase with the appropriate pragmatic and social contexts. For example, a phone caller, asking for information about cost of an article, might have a different emotive attitude from someone calling to complain. Many systems are now matching phrase with context with some success. However, human speech variability, pragmatic features and current social context themselves all vary considerably, simply compounding the problem. It seems that adding emotive content and expression appropriately to synthetic speech is someway in the future.

Usefulness of the classical phonetics and cognitive phonetics models

The classical phonetics approach enables users to devise a linear string of symbols representing speech output as it is heard by the listener, rather than as it is in physical reality. The transcription system does not enable a specification of every significant articulatory or acoustic variation necessary for all instances of synthetic speech. The phonetician is also limited in what can be explicitly written down – simply because their hearing and perception are constrained physically and cognitively. But importantly, much of the detection of dialect and of expressive and emotive content appears to be implicit; the listener *knows* what is significant, but the phonetician cannot make all this knowledge explicit. At the very least, though, the phonetic linear representations available to classical phonetics can be roughly correlated with the speaker's intended phonological units.

The cognitive phonetics model, or others of this type (Action Theory, articulatory phonology, etc.; see Chapter 4), can *formally* relate the specification of the final waveform to phonology, and, in addition, to other sources of variability as well. The ability to manipulate articulation by the cognitive phonetics supervisory agent, according to the demands of an *on-going* conversation, is a way of specifying very important variability in the waveform (Tatham and Morton 2006). There is no possibility for classical phonetics or detail knowledge bases to capture the system underlying this kind of variability. Distinguishing between extrinsic and intrinsic allophonic representations (utterance plan and its rendering) both establishes invariance at a useful level, and makes explicit where unintended variability occurs. The overall wrapper containing information about emotive content of speech characterises potential variable excursions in the waveform.

SUMMARY

Disordered communication and synthetic spoken language have some features in common:

- Both require a specification for the sound system of the language – characterised by phonology.

- Both focus on the acoustic waveform produced by the speaker.

- Both concentrate on the requirement to produce a waveform that listeners can decode and recognise as speech.

- Both benefit from labelling the waveform with linguistic/phonetic units. The standard practice is to draw on symbols in the IPA system or sometimes, in synthetic speech, labels from other systems that software engineers find useful.

In a model-driven approach both practitioners and technologists would benefit from:

1. some understanding of variation in styles of speaking – for example, across the age range;

2. an awareness of regional speech patterns and varieties of language;

3. some understanding of the role of spoken language in the individual's social life;

4. an awareness of special minority groups and their vernacular language, as well as stereotypes in spoken language (especially in perception).

Until there are comprehensive descriptions of the human communication systems, productive models of perception, and a way of relating production and perception models to disordered speech, establish acoustic cues that trigger percepts in the listener, and coherent modelling, there will be frustration in clinical applications and disappointing synthesis applications.

FUNCTIONAL MAGNETIC RESONANCE IMAGING (fMRI) STUDIES

TUTORIAL

fMRI studies are used frequently in diagnostic procedures, and as a research tool for developing brain function models. The images produced reflect some aspect of the mechanism of brain function but not the function itself. The description tells us that brain cells are working, and that they have worked, but not *how* they work. Just as we have surface descriptions of speaking – a transcript of the output of speech and observations about lip movement etc. – so we can refer to surface descriptions of the result of groups of cells having worked together to produce a change in the chemistry of the brain. The result of this activity is displayed using fMRI techniques to give a static representation.

The image does not give information about how it is structured, why is it this way, or how we might correlate such activity with what's going on at the surface during speech, for example. The image represents data at a *pre-model* stage – it tells researchers which part of the brain might contribute to building a model, but the image is *not* itself a model. There is also the problem that apparently active areas of the brain do not show up in exactly identical ways with different subjects. Additionally, there are difficulties in using the technique, including the subject's anxiety. Researchers also have some uncertainty in interpreting the images (Raichle 2003).

Even if we were able to model brain function, from fMRI or other studies, more fully than is now possible, correlating this with cognition is a totally different matter. It is possible to discuss and research cognition with no reference to the brain. Diverse cognitive behaviour, such as reasoning ability, writing fiction, painting landscapes and so on, can be discussed and researched simply as activities we humans engage in, without looking for explanation outside cognitive psychology, aesthetics or literary studies. This possibility of treating cognition independently simply means that biological explanation is important, but is not the *sole* contributor of explanations for what we observe.

THE LINGUIST'S BASIC DESCRIPTIVE TOOLS

TUTORIAL

Linguistics is an extremely complex and fluid area. But there are some basic descriptive tools without which it would be almost impossible to proceed in the study of communicative disorders. Among these is the simple concept of dividing the study into a number of fundamental areas or components, which, although clearly interactive, are usefully treated separately to begin with. The position here is almost simplistic, but essential.

- *Phonology* describes the significant sound units of the language, along with the phonotactic rules stating the way these units can combine in this language. For example, /ŋ/ occurs in English word-medially, as in *singer*, or word-finally, as in *song*, but never word-initially, as in /ŋat/. This sound can however, occur in other languages word-initially.

- *Morphology* describes the form of morphemes, their phonological structure, and rules of conjoining, such as plural formation – for example, *boat/boats*, but *child/children* and *goose/geese*, etc. Note that significant changes can be made to basic meanings by conjoining morphemes; for example, *swims/swimming/swam*.

- *Syntax* describes the patterns for combining morphemes within sentences and utterances. For example, in English, adjectives occur before nouns, such as *the large green house* (adj+adj+N), whereas in French adjectives most frequently come after nouns, as in *le livre bleu* (*the blue book*), though we can have *la grande maison verte* (adj+N+adj) (*the large green house*), and *l'ancien professeur* (*the former professor* – not the old one!). The descriptions are frequently formulated as rules, though there is *never* (or should not be) any implication that rules 'exist' in the brain or mind.

- *Semantics* characterises the meaning of words and sentences/utterances. If the word is known, it should be possible to paraphrase its meaning or define it in some way. For example, if asked *What is a tree?* we should be able to say *A plant with a woody bark and leaves*, or point to a tree. Meanings are not static, but change over time.

- *Pragmatics* describes the many contexts in which words, sentences and utterances may appear, together with their associated meanings, since meanings can change with usage.

FURTHER READING

Ball, M., M. Perkins, N. Muller, and S. Howard (eds) (2008), *The Handbook of Clinical Linguistics*, Oxford: Blackwell.

Ball, M., N. Muller, and B. Rutter (2009), *Phonology for Communication Disorders*, New York: Psychology Press.

Clark, J., C. Yallop and J. Fletcher (2007), *An Introduction to Phonetics and Phonology*, 3rd edn, Malden, MA and Oxford: Blackwell.

Evans, V. (2009), *How Words Mean: Lexical Concepts, Cognitive Models, and Meaning Construction*, Oxford: Oxford University Press.

Evans, V., B. Bergen, and J. Zinken (eds) (2007), *The Cognitive Linguistics Reader*, London: Equinox.

Guendouzi, J., F. Loncke, and M. Williams (eds) (2010), *The Handbook of Psycholinguistic and Cognitive Processes: Perspectives in Communication Disorders*. New York and London: Psychology Press.

Haggard, P., Y. Rossetti, and M. Kawato (eds) (2008), *Sensorimotor Foundations of Higher Cognition (Attention and Performance)*, Oxford: Oxford University Press.

Holmes, J. and W. Holmes (2001), *Speech Synthesis and Recognition,* Wokingham: Van Nostrand Reinhold.

Keller, E. (ed.) (1994), *Fundamentals of Speech Synthesis and Speech Recognition*, Chichester: John Wiley.

Kent, R. D. (ed.) (2004), *The MIT Encyclopedia of Communication Disorders*, Cambridge, MA: MIT Press.

Ladefoged, P. (2003), *Vowels and Consonants*, 3rd edn 2006, Oxford: Blackwell.

Levinson, S. (2005), *Mathematical Models for Speech Technology*, Chichester: John Wiley.

Minifie, F. D., T. J. Hixon, and F. Williams (1973), *Normal Aspects of Speech, Hearing and Language*, Englewood Cliffs, NJ: Prentice Hall.

Tatham, M. and K. Morton (2004), *Expression in Speech: Analysis and Synthesis*, 2nd edn 2006, Oxford: Oxford University Press.

Tatham, M. and K. Morton (2005), *Developments in Speech Synthesis*, Chichester: John Wiley.

CHAPTER 10 – EXPERIMENTAL WORK I – NON-ACOUSTICS

INTRODUCTION

This chapter outlines the types of non-acoustic experiments that have been performed while developing models of speech production, such as airflow and electromyography studies. Attention has been diverted from this type of work, since acoustics equipment and software are more readily available and easier to use – though experiments are not simpler to design. The relationship between results from physiological experiments and some acoustics correlates is introduced.

AIRFLOW

> **REMINDER: AERODYNAMICS**
>
> Aerodynamics is a branch of physics dealing with the movement of air. In speech production we use the term to cover anything involving airflow and air pressure. In particular we focus on how airflow and air pressure are used to create the sounds of speech.

Studies of the AERODYNAMICS of speech are about the airflow

- in, out and through the vocal tract;

- from and to the outside world;

- to and from the lungs

Airflow into the vocal tract system from the outside world is via the mouth and nose, and into the vocal tract system from the lungs via the trachea and through the larynx. During *egressive* sounds the air flows from the lungs to the outside world, and during *ingressive* sounds the air flows from the outside world in towards the lungs. There are a few sounds available in some languages which, strictly, are neither egressive nor ingressive and involve locally produced effects. For example, the clicks used in many African languages are made by placing the tongue against the palate and pulling down sharply either the blade or the back – the sudden filling of the resulting partial vacuum becomes audible; the opening motion is quite energetic and often there is a collaborating movement of the lower jaw.

Nasal Coarticulation

We have seen that coarticulation (Chapter 3) is often defined in terms of the influence of phonetic segments on their linearly placed neighbours. Using equipment able to detect and quantify airflow out of the mouth and nose while someone is speaking, researchers have set up experiments to investigate nasal coarticulation as a representative example of this influence.

Consider the word *Manchester* in most accents of UK English. Traditionally this is represented as a sequence of underlying phonological objects: /mæntʃɛstər/, and, for the purposes of its normal utterance plan, as a sequence of derived phonological objects (extrinsic allophones): /ˈmæntʃɪstə/ – including stress on the initial syllable.

We shall focus on the initial part of the word: /mæn/. It is important to notice that the utterance plan calls for a sequence of objects whose nasal feature or parameter is represented as: /[+nasal] [−nasal] [+nasal]/. The reason why this is important is that, because the utterance plan represents an abstract version of how the speaker expects the word to sound and how the speaker wants it perceived, the second segment is marked as [−nasal]. Remember there are *no* NASAL VOWELS in English, except in a few loan words coming mostly from French.

> **REMINDER: NASAL VOWELS**
>
> Unlike, say, French, Polish or Portuguese, English has *no* nasal vowels. What this means is that there are no nasal vowel phonemes or underlying phonological segments marked [+vowel, +nasal] available to distinguish words in English. What English *does* have is nasalisation, in which the oral vowel acquires nasality by coarticulation. This is one of the coarticulatory effects which can be limited or enhanced by cognitive supervision as part of the process of supervising motor control.

The utterance plan's representation is passed for phonetic rendering. That is, the speaker's intention is now to be rendered as an articulation which will produce an acoustic signal for listeners. We can now say that the utterance plan 'objects' are re-represented as a sequence of articulatory targets (see 'Target Theory' in Chapter 2), the appropriate parameter being [[lowered velum] [raised velum] [lowered velum]], which should generate an airflow pattern [[+ nasal air flow] [−nasal air flow] [+ nasal air flow]].

So here is the HYPOTHESIS the investigator has to work with:

- The desrived phonological sequence /[+nasal] [−nasal] [+nasal]/ at the start of the word *Manchester* produces, when rendered, an airflow pattern: [[+nasal] [−nasal] [+nasal]].

The hypothesis predicts that a [−nasal] utterance plan for a vowel segment will be rendered without a phonetic nasal correlate – that is, will be a faithful rendering of a non-nasal or oral vowel. If the hypothesis fails in the experiment then we can be confident in our rejection of it.

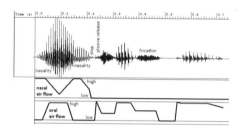

Figure 10.1 Waveform, nasal and oral airflow during *Manchester*. Notice the way in which the aerodynamic tracks do not synchronise entirely with the waveform.

The investigator collects sample data – many examples, often from different speakers, to make sure what is collected is a good representation of what normally happens. The reason for this is that human speech patterns vary enormously, and if just a single sample is taken it may not be truly representative. The wide range of data is processed statistically to make sure that what is typical in the data is drawn out and properly observed. Figure 10.1 shows one such typical example. In the diagram we see the waveform, a stylised nasal airflow track and a stylised oral airflow track. Remember the velum at the upper back of the oral cavity controls whether air flows out through the mouth, the nose or both. In the rendering of the first syllable, /mæn/, we see that nasal airflow is never quite stopped off. This means that there will be proportional nasality present in the oral vowel, despite its [−nasal] phonological plan. This is an example of coarticulatory nasalisation. You can trace through the aerodynamic tracks, matching them up with the waveform. Notice that the concept 'segment boundary' makes little sense here.

Performed in the early 1960s under the guidance of the classical phonetics model, this data would have been segmented into the sequence [consonant + vowel + consonant] with boundaries marked appropriately. Immediately we see that nasal airflow neither starts nor ends in alignment or synchrony with these boundaries. In fact, typically, nasal airflow is present throughout the initial syllable of *Manchester*, though it does have a minimum around the centre point of the [æ]. In some accents of English, particularly in slow speech, the nasal airflow reaches more of a minimum, and in others the airflow is almost the same in the [æ] segment as it is in the surrounding nasal consonants. Generally, therefore, the hypothesis is refuted: it is *not* the case that the planned [−nasal] is rendered without nasality.

This is an example of the phenomenon which Coarticulation Theory sought to explain, beginning in the early 1960s. In this case, the [open + close + open] sequence of MOTOR COMMANDS to the velar structure is unable to overcome completely the mechanical inertia in the structure itself. Put another way, it is impossible for the velum to close immediately – in zero time – at the boundary between the initial nasal consonant and the following *non*-nasal vowel. Remember, we say it is *non*-nasal because the utterance plan does not call for nasality in the vowel. The surface descriptions of classical phonetics would speak of the vowel as *becoming nasalised*, and would point out that this is something that happens to a vowel sandwiched between nasal consonants. The Coarticulation Model (Fowler and Saltzman 1993; Tatham and Morton 2006: ch 2 and 3), though, doesn't *just* say this – it attempts to *explain* what has happened in terms of two factors: the mechanical inertia of the velar structure and the timing of the sequence of segments. In general, the theory claims, the faster the utterance the more likely it is that serious coarticulation will occur, and conversely, the slower the utterance the less likely – though there will always be *some* coarticulation.

> **MOTOR COMMANDS**
>
> A motor command is a complex of innervating neural signals which control the contraction of muscles associated with a mechanical structure. Some of these signals will be quite gross and have their origin in the motor cortex of the brain, while others will be more detailed (certainly in their effects) and originate with the group of muscles itself (see 'Action Theory' in Chapter 4).

AIR PRESSURE

Understanding the aerodynamics of speech also involves studying the air pressure in the oral cavity, extending down to the vocal cords, that is, the oral or supraglottal air pressure and, in addition, the tracheal or subglottal air pressure. It is the difference between the sub- and supraglottal air pressures which sends the vocal cords, if they are appropriately tensed, into SPONTANEOUS VIBRATION.

> **SPONTANEOUS VIBRATION**
>
> Spontaneous vibration of the vocal cords occurs when the parameters of subglottal air pressure, supraglottal air pressure and vocal cord tension come together with values which are just right for the vocal cord system to go into vibration. The term 'spontaneous' is used because the vibration is an intrinsic *consequence* of the setting of the parameters, not of some motor command to the vocal cords (or their associated musculature) to instruct them to vibrate.

Vocal cord vibration

The difference between the sub- and supraglottal air pressures is critical if vocal cord vibration is to be initiated and then sustained. Also critical is the tension in the vocal cords. Vocal cord vibration occurs when the values of these three parameters are balanced within a fairly narrow range:

- subglottal air pressure;
- supraglottal air pressure;
- vocal cord tension.

Errors in any one or more of these will result in vibration failure of the intended vibration. Put another way, intention to vibrate the vocal cords involves setting the values of these three parameters within the correct range of balance; any change in the value of one parameter involves compensating changes in one or both of the other parameters to sustain vocal cord vibration.

We are quite good at getting the balance right, and can adapt to a wide range of variation. For example, shouting involves a large increase in subglottal air pressure, requiring a compensating increase in vocal cord tension. A simple equation describes the relationship:

$$V = T_{vocal\_cords} \cdot AP_{supraglottal} \cdot AP_{subglottal}$$

provided that:

$$AP_{supraglottal} < AP_{subglottal}$$

in which V is spontaneous vibration, T is tension and AP is air pressure. The equation simply says that vocal cord vibration results from an interaction between vocal cord tension, supraglottal air pressure and subglottal air pressure.

It is important to understand that V is a *constant* or goal, and that T, $AP_{supraglottal}$ and $AP_{subglottal}$ are variables which are made to interact in a compensatory way, with the object of maintaining the goal. Management of this compensatory interaction enables us to speak quietly, loudly, etc. – even to handle, within limits, situations like inflamed vocal cords, which we might have if we have a cold.

Sometimes the balance of one of the three parameters changes to a level where compensation by the other two is *not* possible, so vibration comes close to failure or fails altogether. An extreme example might be simply running out of air before a sentence is finished: the voicing goal will fail as $AP_{subglottal}$ approaches zero or goes too low to maintain the right subglottal– superglottal pressure balance. As another example, take what happens if someone hugs you hard while you're talking – subglottal air pressure will rise suddenly, and the rate of vocal cord vibration will become uncontrollable.

We can examine how change in the supraglottal air pressure parameter might bring about vocal cord vibration failure. Let us look at two different events which, among others, can do this.

Intervocalic voiced stops – vocal cord vibration failure

Sometimes supraglottal air pressure can build to an unacceptable level due to an obstruction or partial obstruction further up the system, for example somewhere in the oral cavity – thus reducing flow out of the mouth. Take oral stops like [b], [d] and [g] which phonologically are specified as voiced, or [+voice]. The phonological specification reflects the speaker's intention, and forms part of the cognitive plan for how the sound is intended once it is rendered phonetically. As we have noted before, the physical or phonetic correlate of this abstract phonological voicing intention is usually taken as vocal cord vibration – that is, ideally these sounds are to involve vocal cord vibration when rendered. The problem is that although the vibratory system is initially set up properly for spontaneous vocal cord vibration to occur during these stops, the system quickly breaks down and vibration fails. The breakdown occurs because as the air flows into the oral cavity, it is prevented from continuing out from the mouth, and so the intraoral pressure begins to rise. The supraglottal air pressure is no longer lower than the subglottal air pressure by the right amount, so transglottal flow (the flow through the larynx, between the vocal cords) slows and eventually stops. There may be some attempt to increase the subglottal pressure to compensate, but, because of inertia in the system, this is a long-term solution and probably cannot happen fast enough to affect individual segments.

Take, for example, the word *moody* /mudi/ (see Figure 10.2). During the rendering, vocal cord vibration is working just fine for the [u] – a heightened air pressure below the vocal cords promotes flow through the larynx, in which the vocal cords are tensed just right, on into the oral cavity and out through the mouth. But the rendering of the /d/ plosive obstructs the smooth flow of air out of the mouth, and the pressure starts to build

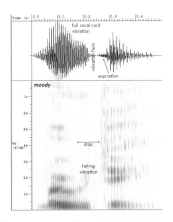

Figure 10.2 Waveform and spectrogram of *moody*. Notice how vocal cord vibration fails in the rendering of the [+voice] plosive /d/.

up in the oral cavity. Quite quickly the supraglottal air pressure rises to an unacceptable level compared with the subglottal pressure – the balance between the three parameters is destroyed, and progressively over a period of a few milliseconds the vibration fails and the vocal cords come to a halt. Note that the *rate* of vibration stays more or less correct; it is the *amplitude* or extent of the vibration which fails. Vibration resumes only when we move past the release phase of the [d] and on to the vowel, where, after a faltering start as the air escapes, pressure balance is restored and vibration gets going again.

Initial stops – vibration failure at the start of the vowel

Looking more closely at what happens surrounding the release of stops, take the word *pea* /pi/. /p/ is specified as requiring bilabial closure, which prevents airflow out of the mouth and consequent pressure build-up behind the stop (refer to Figure 6.1 above). Towards the end of the stop period, we are getting ready to release the built-up air pressure, and the vocal cord vibration system is being set up to enable vocal cord rendering of the phonological voicing requirement for the vowel /i/. The subglottal and vocal cord tension parameters are ready to give us vibration immediately the stop is released, but of course it takes time for the intraoral, or supraglottal, air pressure to fall to a level suitable for vibration to take place. Not until this level is reached and the pent-up air has been released will the system be in the right state to get the vocal cords vibrating. Meanwhile air is rushing out of the mouth with enough force to make it audible; we call this sound *aspiration*, and in languages like English, there is a period of aspiration following all phonologically [–VOICE] STOPS in initial position in stressed syllables. Note also that the reduction in air pressure is *elastic* in the sense that the pressure does not just drop to the required level and stay there; it actually falls too fast and overshoots the target or ideal level – it can go negative, and this is still not right for the vibratory system. The pressure bounces back from negative and again overshoots to positive, but less this time, and then repeats back and forth, negative and positive, until it settles at the right level. We call this back-and-forth occurrence an *oscillation*, and, because it gets progressively less in amplitude before finally settling, we call it a *damped oscillation*. In the case of an initial [p] the delay in restoring the correct balance can be around 25 ms; for [t] it can be around 45 ms; and for [k] it can be around 65 ms. There is quite a lot of variation in these numbers, but what is important is the ratio between them: the delay in vocal cord vibration onset is shortest following the release of [p], next shortest after [t] and longest after [k] (**EVALUATION – MODELLING ASPIRATION**). Perceptually, the important feature is whether or not there is a significant delay in vocal cord vibration onset, rather than its exact duration.

ELECTROMYOGRAPHY

Electromyography (EMG) is a method of accessing and recording the electrical signals produced when there is MUSCLE CONTRACTION. These signals can give us some information about the *timing* of muscle contraction – when it starts and stops – and the *extent* of muscle contraction – how hard the muscle is working. EMG has been used in speech research since the 1960s (Lubker and Parris 1970; Tatham and Morton 1972), though we should point out that the results should be taken as a record of what is probably happening, rather than what is actually happening during speech. The reason for saying this is that, in the techniques used, the exact correlation between the displayed signals and the behaviour of the musculature is not entirely understood. This has not prevented researchers from doing meaningful investigations.

MUSCLE CONTRACTION

When a muscle contracts there are two main effects:

- a *mechanical effect*. The overall muscle shortens, or if shortening is physically prevented, there will be a force equivalent to the shortening if it had been allowed to occur. The overall muscle shortening is the cumulative effect of the shortening of groups of muscle fibres within the muscle.
- an *electrochemical effect*. This occurs within the individual fibres making up the muscle, and results in the combined electrical signal from *firing* fibres being diffused into the surrounding tissue. The signal has a strength (its voltage) usually taken in EMG experiments in speech in the 1960s as approximately equivalent to, or correlating with, the force of the contraction.

As soon as the contraction has occurred in individual muscle fibres, there is an immediate *recovery period* during which the mechanical and electrochemical effects settle back to their state before the contraction was signalled by the original motor command. *Overall* continuous contraction of a muscle is achieved by asynchronous rapid contraction and recovery of the muscle fibres within it.

Tense and lax

An early use of EMG was to attempt to test the claimed difference between tense and lax consonants. Traditionally in classical phonetics theory, the tense (or [+tense]) plosives in English [p, t, k] are said to be uttered with apparently greater force than the corresponding lax (or [−tense]) plosives [b, d, g]. The expectation for the experiments investigating this was that greater force would translate into greater muscular contraction. So in the case of the bilabials you would expect the lips to be closed with greater force for [p] than for [b]. Tatham and Morton (1969), among others, found that there was no significant difference between the two, and other researchers failed to find a consistent replicable difference either.

However, there *is* a difference in intraoral air pressure: [p] achieves a higher pressure than that achieved by [b] – of the order of 20 per cent greater. The greater pressure is easily explained by the fact that with [p] there is relatively low impedance of the transglottal airflow, whereas with [b] there is some impedance, allowing less pressure to build up in the oral cavity. It may well be that traditional phoneticians sensed this greater *air pressure* in the oral cavity, rather than greater *lip tension*, and that it was this that prompted the idea that [p] involved more force than [b]; similarly [t] vs. [d] and [k] vs. [g]. There are dozens of pressure sensors lining the oral cavity, and these are able to sense very small changes in air pressure, as well as contact pressure from the various articulators. Sensory feedback systems make this information available to the overall speech production system at both high (motor cortex) and low (coordinative structure) levels.

Non-synchronising parameters

Classical phonetic theory tended to focus on the whole segment as the preferred unit for describing speech as an articulatory or acoustic signal. We have seen that this idea runs into a number of difficulties, in particular the problem of segmenting running speech into such segments, and we have seen that in the 1960s Coarticulation Theory was devised to help explain the lack of segment boundaries in articulatory and acoustic data. The explanation rested on the idea that, because of aerodynamic or mechanical inertia in the speech production system, a blurring together of segments was bound to occur. Inertia is time-dependent, so it followed that coarticulation was time-dependent, with less blurring or overlap of segments occurring during slow speech than during fast speech.

But there were a number of problems with even this idea, including the following:

- There is the possibility that the different articulatory parameters involved in producing the sequence of segments behave differently because they have different inertial properties. Just considering weight, for example, the tongue is clearly heavier than the lips or the vocal cords – this will make a difference to any inertia due to time constraints.

- It may be the case that the musculature of different articulatory structures has different response times when it comes to interpreting motor commands, always assuming that the main motor commands themselves arrive simultaneously at the different groupings of muscles associated with the various articulatory parameters.

For example, in the English words *tip* /tɪp/, *tap* /tæp/ and *tarp* /tɑp/ (British) or /tɑp/ (US) we can track a number of constriction parameters, as shown in Figure 10.3.

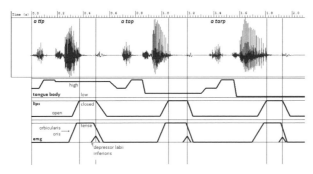

Figure 10.3 Waveform and stylised tongue body position, lip closure and electromyography (EMG) tracks for the words *tip*, *tap* and *tarp*. The EMG display shows the contraction of two muscles: m. orbicularis oris, which is partly responsible for lip closure, and m. depressor labii inferioris, which is partly responsible for lip opening. Notice that contraction to close the lips must begin significantly before closure to make sure it comes on time. Similarly the depressor muscle must kick in before opening to ensure correct timing. The lips, as we can see, are actively opened; they do not open because they are blown apart by the intraoral air pressure – this is true for all stops. With lingual stops, for example, the tongue is actively pulled away from the constriction at the right moment, necessitating firing the appropriate muscles before the required time. Notice, once again, how physical behaviour does not proceed from segment to segment in the way that abstract phonology does. Muscles, for example, must begin firing significantly before the event they are needed for.

Notice that parameters are often not synchronised in terms of their behaviour. The apparent boundaries between segments arise from the way we perceive speech; indicating a tendency in the assignment of perceived symbolic representations to disregard this asynchronicity in favour of sequences of isolated symbols.

PROSODY AND SUPRASEGMENTALS

Prosody is concerned with describing linguistic effects in speech which span beyond the basic segments (phonological units like phoneme and extrinsic allophone, or syllable); hence the alternative term *suprasegmentals*. Since the effects are longer than single segments or syllables they usually do not involve a characterisation of the segments themselves.

The unit within prosody is the SYLLABLE, and prosodic behaviour is usually modelled in terms of what happens to syllable strings. There are three prosodic features which form the focus of studies. They are cognitive objects and hence abstract, but as with abstract phonological segments, it makes sense to study their physical-world correlates in order to determine how speakers render them. An acoustic study also enables us to characterise what stimuli are available to listeners for decoding a speaker's prosodic intentions. Below is a table of prosodic features and their ACOUSTIC CORRELATES.

Prosodic features	Principal acoustic correlates	Secondary correlates
Intonation	Changing fundamental frequency as syllable strings unfold within phrases or sentences	Timing of consecutive syllables
Rhythm	Relative timing of syllable units within the phrase or sentence string	Acceleration and deceleration of delivery rate
Stress	Amplitude, fundamental frequency and duration of syllables relative to others in the immediate string	Cues like vowel reduction, elisions and deletions

The strings of syllables constitute the domains within which the description is relevant, and these strings are syntactically determined: phrases, sentences or even paragraphs. Because these syntactic units are also abstract we need to have acoustic markers to delimit them as domains: we usually identify periods of silence in the signal which loosely correlate with the equivalent markers in writing: punctuation marks like ' , ' , ' ; ' or ' . ', etc. There are really no hard and fast rules here because of individual styles and other factors like rate of utterance delivery, but researchers review the material before making measurements in order to determine by experience where the domain boundaries occur: this may have something to do with the duration of acoustic pauses, the syntactic or phonological structure of the utterance, or even the semantic or pragmatic structure of the utterance.

In the discussion so far on prosody there have been some anomalies which researchers find difficult to reconcile. So, for example, the usage of *syllable* is mixed: syllables are abstract phonological objects, yet studies often try to measure their physical acoustic properties, such as fundamental frequency, timing and amplitude. Vowel reduction is a phonological phenomenon; for example, an English word like *conduct* can be planned with stress on the first syllable, /'kɒndʌkt/, indicating the noun meaning *behaviour,* or on the second syllable, /kən'dʌkt/, indicating the verb meaning *direct* or *organise.* In the second case the now unstressed vowel /ɒ/ is also phonologically reduced to /ə/ – an extrinsic allophonic representation in the utterance plan. This means that somehow we have to have acoustic correlates of these phonological objects as well as the prosodic features. Remember: we are limited to measuring acoustic renderings of utterance plans, and we can *never* measure in the physical world what is in the plan itself or what has come before it. To repeat: we measure only *acoustic correlates* of abstract prosodic features, never the features themselves: intonation, rhythm and stress *do not exist* in the physical world and so cannot be measured.

INTONATION

Data

Figure 10.4 is a waveform and fundamental frequency tracing of the exemplar sentence *The boy stayed home; but didn't his dad go out to the pub?* We have marked rendered syllable nuclei on the waveform, together with a tentative reconstruction of boundaries between syllables. Remember, though, that marks of this kind on waveforms are not absolute; they are reminders of what underlies the rendering. We have used software to calculate and image the FUNDAMENTAL FREQUENCY of vocal cord vibration during the utterance and synchronise this in the display with the waveform. The waveform and fundamental frequency displays are accurate images of the sound wave. We have also shown a stylised abstract representation of the fundamental frequency as it might be for each of the syllables in the utterance: this is a series of horizontal lines, rather than the continuously variable tracing of the actual fundamental frequency. Speak the sentence for yourself to see whether your intonation pattern – the one you *intend* and *perceive* – matches the display.

Results

The detailed fundamental frequency is a physical measurement which we have shown in Hz on the scale. The abstract marking is notional, however:

FUNDAMENTAL FREQUENCY

Fundamental frequency is the repetition rate of the vibrating vocal cords. The measurement is usually taken on a period-by-period basis, by locating a zero crossing – where the waveform crosses the baseline – and measuring the time to the next similar zero crossing. This is the time for one period. The instantaneous frequency of this period is the reciprocal – a period of 10 ms equates to 100 Hz: frequency = 1,000/time (where time is measured in ms).

The fundamental frequency is rarely constant or completely monotone. There are subtle period-to-period changes, some of which the listener may be aware of, but many of which they will not notice. The changes noticed, as with almost all phonetic phenomena, are mostly the ones which have linguistic significance; those missed are the ones which are generally irrelevant to the linguistics of the utterance (see 'Perception as a Simple Generic Acoustic Detail Classifier', Chapter 8).

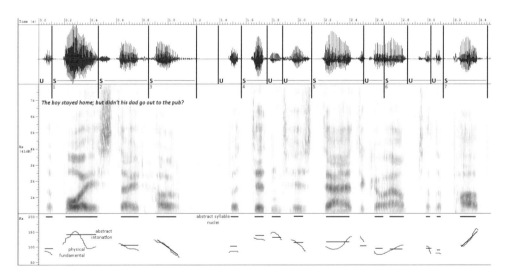

Figure 10.4 Waveform, spectrogram and fundamental frequency displays of *The boy stayed home, but didn't his dad go out to the pub?* Also included are markings indicating a stylised phonological intonation contour, which does not entirely match the f0 tracing. Above this we mark syllable nuclei – the rendering of the vowel nucleus of the various syllables. On the waveform we have indicated physical boundaries corresponding to rhythmic units, showing how these fit within the stressed/unstressed assignment of syllables. Be careful to distinguish between physical signals (waveform, rhythmic unit, spectrogram, fundamental frequency) and phonological abstract markers (stressed and unstressed syllables, intonation). At best there is a fair degree of correlation between physical and abstract objects, but at worst there can be wide discrepancy.

it shows mostly how the gross pattern rises and falls. Our *feelings* about the intonation may or may not match exactly these rises and falls. There is a great deal of variability across speakers. We are illustrating a principle here and the general method of using the waveform in experiments designed to cast light on utterance prosodics.

Discussion

Experiments in intonation have the usual hypotheses based on phonological observations. So, for example, phonology would predict that intonation falls at the end of declarative sentences or questions beginning with an interrogative like *What?* or *Why?* However, some speakers and some accents will raise the intonation towards the end of most questions. Indeed, in French, intonation is often used to carry the declarative/question contrast: *Jean, il est parti?* (rising intonation) vs. *Jean, il est parti.* (falling intonation). Figure 10.5 shows the tracings for these two utterances.

By and large, intonation patterns, both intended and perceived, follow the general direction of the fundamental frequency tracing, though not in detail. In languages like English which have patterns of stressed and unstressed syllables, perception seems to lock onto the stressed ones.

Rhythm and stress

Speech is rhythmic, meaning that there is regularity in the way units pattern in time as an utterance unfolds. As we have seen, the units of prosody are syllables, which can be stressed or unstressed (refer to Figure 10.4 above). Some researchers have argued for more than two levels of stress, but models of rhythm generally proceed with just two levels. Bear in mind that stress and rhythm are *perceived* features of speech, and, as before, investigations involving acoustic analysis are examining physical correlates of these features. So investigations of rhythm (Tatham and Morton 2002) seek to understand the patterning of STRESSED AND UNSTRESSED SYLLABLES within syntactic units like phrases or sentences.

In classical phonetics the unit of rhythm is the *foot*. Most writers speak of a foot as beginning with a stressed syllable and continuing until the next syllable – but not including it. Thus we might have the sequence:

$$U \mid S \mid S\ U \mid S \mid S\ U\ U \mid S \mid$$

where S means stressed syllable and U means unstressed syllable. The vertical lines mark the perceived rhythmic or foot boundaries. This would be an utterance consisting of five complete feet, with a *hanging* unstressed syllable at the beginning. All languages can be thought of as having a rhythm which is clearly linked to patterning of stressed items – thus rhythm and stress, two of the three prosodic phenomena, are closely

STRESSED AND UNSTRESSED SYLLABLES

A stressed syllable is one which bears phonological primary stress; that is, some kind of planned prominence which can also be perceived from the acoustic signal. The prominence distinguishes it from other, less prominent syllables. There is no fixed acoustic correlate of perceived prominence, but it is usually associated with enhanced amplitude, increased duration or abrupt change of fundamental frequency – or all three in any combination.

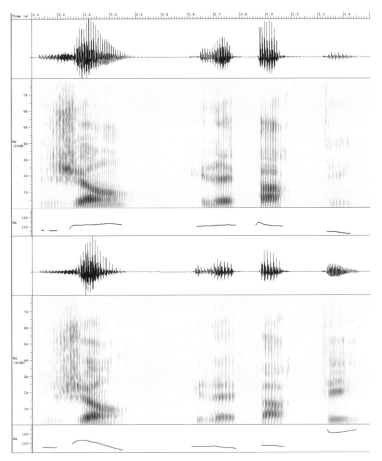

Figure 10.5 Waveforms, spectrograms and fundamental frequency tracings of French *Jean, il est parti.* (falling intonation) and *Jean, il est parti?* (rising intonation). Notice the f0 pattern, which correlates well with the expected intonation towards the end of the utterance. Looking at the spectrograms, you can see how the spacing of the vertical striations (corresponding to vocal cord vibrations) is different for the two utterances in the word *parti*: statement has high f0 followed by low f0, and question has low f0 followed by high f0. The closer the striations the higher the frequency of vibration.

linked. Even languages like French, which are often described as having no unstressed syllables, have a rhythm: each foot consists of just one syllable.

Isochrony

An observation often reported by phoneticians is that rhythm is *isochronic*. That is, all feet are equal in duration. It is easy, for example, to get a native speaker of English to tap along with their speech: they will invariably tap on the stressed syllables. They will also report that they feel the stressed syllables are equidistant in time. We can examine whether this idea holds up experimentally by measuring the *timing patterns* of feet. The term *foot*, however, is used in characterising what native speakers *feel* about the rhythm of their language. We need a physical unit which we can actually measure. We call this the *rhythmic unit* – it is the physical correlate of the foot.

RHYTHMIC UNIT

This is the physical unit of rhythm, corresponding to the perceived and more subjective foot. For the purposes of measurement, the rhythmic unit is usually taken to start with the beginning of the acoustic rendering of a stressed syllable (see Figure 10.4 above).

But, how do we actually delimit the RHYTHMIC UNIT? Is it the time from the start of a stressed syllable to the start of the next stressed syllable? The problem here is that *syllable* is an abstract phonological term, so we would be looking for some physical correlate of the start of the syllable. Or is it some other point? Some researchers have felt that a more appropriate point to measure from would be the *p*-centre – the perceptual centre – of the vowel nucleus in the syllable; that is, the physical point were the stress is felt to fall maximally (Harsin 1997). Experiments have been done to find the *p*-centre of vowels in syllables; they are not always the actual physical durational midpoint. Another point people have located for measuring from is the start of vocal cord vibration in the syllable. This could be used as the start of the vowel nucleus, or some other point could be used. For the moment we will use the start of the acoustic signal associated with a stressed syllable. In our own experiments we have used the definition of rhythmic unit which begins measurement from the start of a stressed syllable's acoustic correlate to the same point at the start of the next stressed syllable.

For languages like English, which has variable stressing of words, it is clear that a rhythmic unit could consist of just a single syllable with no further syllables before the next. But equally, a unit could consist of two syllables: S + U; or three: S + U + U; or even S + U + U + U. If rhythm is isochronic, each of these rhythmic units would have the same duration. It follows that sometimes we are fitting just a single syllable into a particular time span, but sometimes more. For example, take the phrases in the table below.

Phrase	Rhythmic unit	Unit's syllabic structure
the | cat . . .	cat	S
the | cat I | like . . .	cat I	S U
the | cat that I | like . . .	cat that I	S U U
the | cat that I would | like . . .	cat that I would	S U U U

There is certainly a subjective feeling in favour of the idea of isochrony here. In the last three phrases most people would opt for reporting or tapping (see above) in a way which indicates that they feel the time between *cat* and *like* is identical in all three.

With one or two exceptions (Tatham and Morton 2001), most researchers have abandoned matching the undoubted isochrony of abstract feet with the doubtful timing of physical rhythmic units. But then this situation is very little different from much of the argument in Chapters 7 and 8 on perception. There we spoke of the assignment of abstract labels to defective data, and we can do the same here. In this approach there is nothing unusual in assigning abstract isochrony to physical data which shows some regularity, but which is not precisely isochronic in terms of physical measurements.

In languages like French, or English in certain accents (though not British or American English), all syllables are felt to have stress. What this means is that in principle, according to the isochrony hypothesis, all syllables have equal timing as rhythmic units – since a rhythmic unit only ever consists of a single syllable. Some accents of English in the West Indies are like this. Conversely, some speakers of Canadian French have a stress pattern which is variable, like English. For example, although in metropolitan French *Canada* is pronounced /kanada/ with no particular stress pattern, or sometimes /kana'da/, some Canadian speakers will invariably say /'kanada/. Similarly, *Montréal* is pronounced /mõreal/ (metropolitan) and /'mãreæl/ (Canadian). English speakers often feel that metropolitan French is spoken quickly or in a staccato way – simply reflecting the feeling of regularity or isochrony of each sequential syllable.

MODELLING ASPIRATION

EVALUATION

Classical phonetics modelled aspiration as the occurrence of a third phase in initial voiceless stops or plosives. The first two phases are the stop and the release, and the third phase is aspiration, tacked on to the release; that is, the aspiration was seen as *part of the stop*.

In more recent THEORY we can model the aspiration as *part of the vowel*. So you should be asking two questions:

1. Doesn't this amount to the same thing?
2. What makes us think that it's better to render aspiration as part of the vowel rather than as part of the plosive?

> **REMINDER: THEORY**
>
> A theory is an abstract construct, the purpose of which is to
>
> 1. *observe* and bring together as much data as possible in the domain the theory is intended to cover – in our case, speech production and perception;
> 2. *describe* the assembled data in terms of any patterning which appears;
> 3. attempt to *explain* both the occurrence of the data and its apparent patterning.
>
> Thus, theories can be said to meet levels of *observational* or *descriptive adequacy*, and all aspire to meet the level of *explanatory adequacy*. Nascent theories would by definition fail to meet all three levels of adequacy.
>
> Up to the 1950s classical phonetics could be said to have met the criteria of descriptive adequacy, but our accumulation of data on the continuousness of the articulatory or acoustic signals could not be explained, causing the theory to fail and be replaced or augmented by Coarticulation Theory (see 'Coarticulation' in Chapter 3), which attempted both to *describe* segment conjoining and *explain* why it occurs. Eventually, in the 1970s Coarticulatory Theory itself began to fail, giving way to explanations of continuousness which were parametric and based on the idea of coproduction (see 'Action Theory' in Chapter 4).

Phonologically the difference between the words *pea* and *bee* lies with the initial segment – /p/ vs. /b/, with /p/ specified as [–voice] and /b/ as [+voice]. If we choose to focus on the featural makeup of the syllable we could say that in *pea* voicing begins where the vowel begins, and in *bee* where the consonant begins, and then spans the entire syllable. In either case, the vowel is specified as [+voice], as are all vowels in most accents of English. Look again at Figure 6.2 above, reading from right to left; that is, from the end of the vocal cord vibration back to the release. This duration is approximately the same for both words, though vibration does not occur all the way through in the case of *pea*. If we say that this delay in the onset of vibration after the release of the [p] in *pea* is the *insertion* of aspiration, we are now obliged to explain why the vowel has become shorter than it is in *bee*.

In this approach, we would need two rules:

1. Insert aspiration in syllable-initial rendering when the onset consists of a [–voice] stop.
2. Shorten the vowel if the onset is a [–voice] stop.

It's the vowel-shortening rule which is hard to explain. Much simpler, and, in the technical language of model building, much more *elegant*, is the model which accounts for the data in Figure 6.2 by pointing to the failure of vocal cord vibration at the start of the vowel – but without vowel shortening: it just doesn't have vibration for its full duration. The aerodynamic mechanism which *explains* what we see is described above, whereas the earlier model from classical phonetics offers no explanation: it just asserts its observations and describes much of their patterning.

FURTHER READING

Ball, M. and C. Code (1997), *Instrumental Clinical Phonetics*, London: Whurr.
Johnson, K. (2008), *Quantitative Methods in Linguistics*, Oxford: Wiley-Blackwell.
Popper, K. (1934, reprinted 2004), *The Logic of Scientific Discovery*, New York: Routledge.

CHAPTER 11 – EXPERIMENTAL WORK II – ACOUSTICS

INTRODUCTION

Acoustic signals can be uniquely described using three parameters: *frequency*, *amplitude* and *time*. All three are important in speech, and form the basis of measurement in acoustic studies (Fry 1958, 1979). Experiments using the acoustic signal fall roughly into two types:

1. those which simply investigate the acoustic nature of a particular phenomenon – we call this data-driven investigation;

2. those which are used to throw light on predictions made by hypotheses resulting from claims in the underlying phonology – hypothesis-driven investigation.

We give examples of the first investigatory type in Chapter 2, but here we are concerned with the second type: hypothesis-driven experiments. The field of experimental acoustic phonetics is vast, and we give examples. Readers wishing to investigate what acoustic experimental work in speech was like at its peak in the 1960s should consult the comprehensive collection of landmark studies in Ilse Lehiste's *Readings in Acoustic Phonetics* (1967).

INFORMATION FROM THE RAW WAVEFORM

The continuousness of speech

As speakers and listeners, we have a strong belief that speech consists of strings of abutted but discrete segments, usually of individual-sound size (see Chapter 7). This idea is strengthened by the fact that we can make most sounds – certainly the prolonged ones like vowels – individually and on demand. Classical phonetics is not entirely explicit about this, but certainly seems to imply that the model does not contradict the feelings of speakers and listeners.

From these observations we can formulate a hypothesis about the speech sound wave, and, by extension, the articulatory and aerodynamic processes underlying the sound wave. The hypothesis goes like this:

The waveform of a speaker's utterance will show the discrete sounds it seems to consist of.

As before, the hypothesis is couched in such a form that the strongest conclusion – that of rejection of the claim – provides us with the best insight. If, for example, we put the hypothesis round the other way, as *The waveform will show continuous signal with no breaks or boundaries*, then experimental results showing continuousness would have allowed just weak support of the hypothesis. To repeat: hypothesis rejection is always stronger than any tendency towards acceptance.

Data

The dataset for experiments to support or refute the hypothesis would consist of audio recordings of utterances, carefully imaged as detailed waveforms showing information covering a reasonable spectral bandwidth – say, ranging from 0 Hz to 8 kHz. Inspection of such displays should enable us to find individual segments, using what acoustic phoneticians have fairly exhaustively described as the properties of the sounds of speech. There are many such inventories in the literature, and most introductory textbooks have a section detailing the distinguishing properties of speech sounds (Johnson 2008). Features like formant distribution, vocal cord vibration, spectral details of frication, etc. are often invoked as able to specify various sounds uniquely. We saw in Chapter 8 that detail classifiers attempt to identify speech sounds using such features present in the sound wave.

We are not looking to discover how to distinguish between this or that sound, however; more to focus on the discreteness aspect of sounds. In other words we can use these descriptions in an attempt to locate segment *boundaries* in the waveforms.

Results – *The big black cat sat down*

The EXEMPLAR WAVEFORM of *The big black cat sat down* (see Figure 11.1 – we look at *How are you?* below) is a rather extreme example – there are plenty of what we call DISCONTINUITIES in the signal. The archetypal sound rendered with vocal cord vibration (or, at the phonological level, voicing) is a vowel – prolonged and resonant – and the archetypal sound rendered with no such vibration is a voiceless plosive – brief and lacking in the kind of sonorance we associate with vowel renderings. Plosive releases, with their very brief (perhaps just 3 ms) periods of wide spectral energy, are often easy to spot, and we have identified five such plosive bursts in this waveform: *The **b**ig **b**la**ck** **c**at sa**t** **d**own* [. . . b . . . gb . . . kk . . . t . . . td . . .]. Notice that for most accents of English spoken at normal speed without any particular emphasis, the initial plosive of the double or sequenced plosives has no release; it would sound strange and unnatural to

<aside>
DISCONTINUITIES

A discontinuity in the sound wave is a temporally abrupt change from one feature to another, as for example the brief burst of an initial plosive marking the end of the consonant rendering before the following vowel rendering starts. Another example of quite sudden changes, this time of spectral distribution, is the transition into and out of a nasal consonant. Such discontinuities are the exception rather than the rule in running speech (Figure 11.2).
</aside>

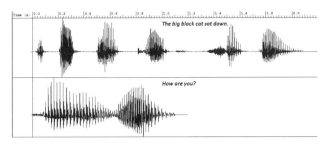

Figure 11.1 Waveforms of *The big black cat sat down* and *How are you*? Notice that in the top waveform there are clear breaks in the signal (corresponding to the stop phases of the plosives), but that in the bottom waveform there are no such clear boundaries – the continuousness of the signal with respect to the segments rendered is obvious.

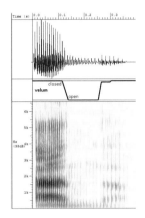

Figure 11.2 Waveform, velar opening tracing and spectrogram of the word *Anna*. The utterance plan calls for segments [–nasal] [+nasal] [–nasal], and you can see how these are rendered, especially at the 'boundaries' between the segments.

release both these stops. We can, of course, render the double release, but this is not usually called for in the utterance plan.

> **EXEMPLAR WAVEFORMS**
>
> An exemplar waveform – or indeed any exemplar object – is one chosen to be reliably typical of the data. *Every* waveform in the dataset will be *different* from this one, and we have to rely on *statistical tests* to link the various waveforms. In addition, statistics often enables us to take physical data and, by passing it through formal tests, reduce it – the process is called *data reduction* – to something more manageable. This avoids the need to deal with all of the data simultaneously – we can deal with just a derived *abstraction* of it. The statistical tests are carefully formulated to provide repeatable reduction of the data; that is, they do not produce random results. They provide us with insights into the *general* properties of the data relevant to our investigation.
>
> Take, for example, the use of averaging to reduce a dataset. Suppose we take three measurements: 6, 7 and 8. The average or arithmetic mean of these measurements is calculated by adding them together and dividing the result by the number of measurements: $(6 + 7 + 8) / 3 = 7$. The mean, 7, is not the same as the number 7 in the dataset: it is an abstraction of *all* of the measurements, for the simple reason that it was arrived at by taking *all* the measurements into account, not just selecting one of them.
>
> To make the point clearer: consider the four measurements: 5, 6, 8, 9. If we take the arithmetic mean of these, $(5 + 6 + 8 + 9) / 4$, we also end up with 7. Here is it clear that 7 does not exist in the database: it is an *abstraction* of the data, and if it had been in the dataset it would be an exemplar number.

We could say the release marks the end of a stop, though since the release normally lasts some 3–4 ms we would have to say whether we are looking at the beginning, middle or end of the release phase. We have been saying in this book that plosives are two-phase consonants, and that they consist of a stop phase followed by a release phase. We therefore end the plosive rendering at the end of the release phase.

But we must be very careful here. In our definition we are invoking what the speaker intends the rendering to be rather than the *result* of that intention. We are defining our segments as extrinsic allophones – abstract objects used to build the SPEAKER'S PLAN. In our example, we could argue that the speaker does not intend release of the first plosive in the pairs above (Figure 11.1), just as a speaker of many accents of English would not intend to release the /t/ at the end of an isolated word *cat* /kæt˺/. The justification for this is that the omission of the release cannot be a phonetic coarticulatory failure of release, simply because any speaker of English can – and does on some occasions – release the first plosive in such pairs.

REMINDER: SPEAKER'S PLAN

Remember, our model (see Tatham and Morton 2006) makes a strict distinction between what speakers intend and what actually happens as a result of the rendering process. A dynamic phonology – one that includes *time* – works out an utterance plan, an exhaustive statement of what the speaker intends the rendering would ideally be. As such, within the rules of building such a plan, coarticulation phenomena which distort the ideal rendering process cannot figure. There are a number of theoretical principles as well as practical reasons for using the plan as a complete and final representation of a speaker's intentions for sentences (in the STATIC MODEL) or a particular sentence (in the DYNAMIC MODEL).

REMINDER: STATIC AND DYNAMIC MODELS

A static model is one which proceeds without the inclusion of time. An example in phonology would be a model whose purpose it is to describe the units and processes in a particular language without any reference to their time-governed use on any one particular occasion. The original formulation of transformational generative phonology was like this: how the phonology was actually used was omitted from the theory. A dynamic model, by contrast, would include all of a static model, but would, in addition, model the use of units and processes in an actual language situation by a particular speaker or group of speakers, with time as an important dimension. There are applications of linguistics, such as speech and language therapy, where a dynamic model might often be more appropriate (see Chapter 9).

One such important principle is that we must have a *fixed* representation that can be rendered *differently* on different occasions to reflect the rendering environment. Thus a speaker who is drunk may well intend a particular utterance, but the rendering process will be heavily constrained by the effects of alcohol; nevertheless the intention will be the *same* as when the speaker is not drunk. That sameness must have a formal place within the model. Another example: two different speakers can have identical utterance plans for a sentence, and there must be a way of showing this even if their individual renderings turn out to be different.

Do not confuse different accents with different renderings. Accents involve the use of differing inventories of phonological units and different rules for combining them. The identity of segments underlying the use of different accents lies at the deepest phonological, or phonemic level. The table below illustrates just one simple example.

Word	Underlying representation (accent-neutral)	Chosen accent	Derived plan (accent-sensitive)	Representation of the final rendering
cat	/kæt/	English Received Pronunciation	→ /kæt/	→ [kʰæt]
		US English	→ /kæt˺/	→ [kʰæt˺]
		Cockney English	→ /kæʔ/	→ [kʰæʔ]
		Estuary English	→ /kæt˺/	→ [kʰæt˺]

So we located five plosive release signals in the waveform (Figure 11.1 above). These releases can help us navigate around the waveform: they are clearly identifiable in a way that few other features associated with segment boundaries are. But even here, notice that we have three so-called double-stop releases. The reason for this is that often in English, when two plosives occur in sequence the first is not released, though the time spent on the combined stop is rarely exactly the expected sum of the two.

They are somehow telescoped together. We can also see clearly the two types of source sound: periodic and aperiodic, associated respectively with vowels and fricatives. Thus the frication associated with [s] is easy to spot, but looking carefully at the spectrogram we can see that, rather than an abrupt change from one to the other, the frication clearly overlaps the periodic sound in a kind of amplitude dovetailing. So here there is no clear boundary. Likewise there is no clear boundary between [l] and [æ] in *black*, or between [aʊ] and [n] in *down*.

Results – *How are you?*
In this waveform (Figure 11.1 above) there are no relatively abrupt plosive releases to help us locate boundaries. In this respect, the waveform appears completely continuous. Changes in its qualitative structure can be seen (meaning that we will hear changes in the waveform sounds as it unfolds), and these do indeed correspond to the rendering of underlying units in the plan, but the changes are gradual with no real possibility of locating boundaries within them.

Discussion – *How are you?*
Sometimes we can find DISCONTINUITIES IMAGED IN SPECTROGRAMS in the waveform which we can ascribe to boundaries as segments abut, but despite the efforts of researchers there is no reliable way of segmenting a running waveform according to its correlating underlying planned segments. Below we develop this idea further, indicating some of the devices which we use to identify zones in the waveform which we can associate with the plan. These zones usually have fuzzy boundaries, though.

In this section we have been using waveforms to investigate possible boundary discontinuities between segments. We have avoided using spectrograms because of the nature of the analysis required to produce them. The analysis tends to de-focus *time* in favour of a focus on *frequency*; the mathematics of the analysis is such that a compromise has to be reached between the two. Waveforms are used when we are investigating time, and spectrograms when we are investigating frequency phenomena like formants.

We chose here to focus on time so as to enable the clearest imaging of any temporal discontinuities which might indicate boundaries. Because of this, the obvious choice of display is the waveform, which faithfully reproduces temporal phenomena. A spectrogram would have made objects like plosive releases seem fuzzy and difficult to measure precisely along the time axis. Figure 11.3 is an example of waveform and synchronised spectrogram showing ... *black cat* ... from the utterance in Figure 11.1. Notice how temporally sharp the plosive releases are on the waveform compared with the spectrogram.

Vocal cord vibration in consonants

Classical phonetics (and phonology) uses the terms *voicing* and *voiced* to help differentiate between members of cognate pairs of consonants. The theory speaks of voicing as a feature differentiating two subsets of consonants: those which have voicing and those which do not. In most accents of English we have the principal consonants shown in the table below.

Place → ↓ Manner	Labial		Coronal			Dorsal		
	Bilabial	Labio-dental	Dental	Alveolar	Post-alveolar	Palatal	Velar	Laryngeal
Plosive	p | b			t | d			k | g	
Fricative		f | v	θ | ð	s | z	ʃ | ʒ			h |
Approximant				| ɹ				
Flap				| ɾ				
Lateral approximant				| l				
Nasal	| m			| n		| ɲ	| ŋ	

This is a stylised International Phonetic Alphabet (IPA)-style consonant chart using symbols in the traditional way to represent articulations *and* sounds. In many CELLS there are two symbols: the one to the left stands for the voiceless version, and the one to the right for the voiced version of each consonant with that particular place and manner of articulation. Some consonants only occur voiced: these are the ones with nothing to the left of the vertical line. One consonant has only a voiceless version: [h] cannot be voiced since the vocal cords cannot be both very tense (to produce frication) and yet sufficiently slack to allow simultaneous vibration, the constraint probably being one of physical impossibility. In other cases voiced and voiceless versions are technically possible, although English does not make use of the entire set of possibilities.

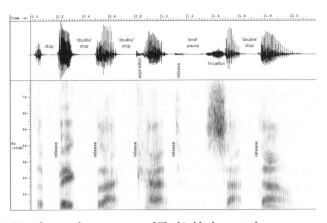

Figure 11.3 Waveform and spectrogram of *The big black cat sat down.*

CELLS

The chart used for consonants is a two-dimensional matrix of cells, though in a trivial way the placing of two symbols in some cells is an attempt at a third dimension, *voicing*, to supplement the other two dimensions, namely *places* and *manners* of articulation. Placing the symbols in the cells in a chart of this kind reveals obvious gaps, leading to two interesting questions:

- Why are there blank cells in the matrix?
- Why do some cells have only one symbol?

Classical phonetics does not address these questions in depth, but we could guess that some gaps represent physical impossibilities – for example, we cannot have a voiced laryngeal fricative. Others represent the language's preferences – for example, we could have voiceless nasals in English, but we just do not. Many languages, of course, do have some of the missing articulations: French has dental plosives [t̪|d̪], Spanish has bilabial fricatives [ɸ|β] and a voiced alveolar trill [r], and so on.

One very important constraint on cells produces a variable situation. Consider this proposition:

A language can have the dental plosive pair [t̪|d̪] or the alveolar plosive pair [t|d] *but not both*. For example: French and Spanish have the dentals, whereas English and German have the alveolars.

This is a very common constraint (see also 'Categorical Perception Theory' in Chapter 8). The reason is that although dental and alveolar plosives *are* acoustically different, the difference is so small that they cannot with any reliability be used in the same language for differentiating words. So in English or French, for example, we could not have the words *tap* [tʰæp_Eng]/ [tap_Fr]and *tap* [tʰæp_Eng]/[tap_Fr] meaning two different things in the *same* language. Particularly in rapid or quiet speech, listeners would not be able to tell the difference between the two words, all things being equal.

- A principle: languages do not use sounds so close in articulation or acoustics as to be difficult to replicate by the speaker and/or difficult to reliably discriminate by the listener.

This constraint holds right across the matrix, though we do not know of any systematic studies yet into exactly what is confusing and by how much, and what is not. The evidence we have to go on is simply the observation that patterning of sounds in languages does not usually involve violating this *perceptual discrimination constraint*, as we might call it. The constraint is important in determining the *precision* (see 'Production for Perception' in Chapter 7) with which segments are, uttered – the *closer* segments are either in articulation or acoustically, the more precision is required in their articulation to make sure they are not confused by the listener: imprecise articulation leads to confusion in these circumstances and is generally avoided.

The difficulty with the term *voicing* in classical phonetics or phonology is that correlation with vocal cord vibration is notional rather than actual. We prefer to confine the use of *voicing* and *voiced* to phonological descriptions which are essentially aoristic – that is, they characterise segments without referring to time: they form part of what is essentially a *static* model. So we can speak in phonology of a segment which is [+voice] to distinguish it from a segment which is [−voice]. This means that the distinction is being made in a cognitive appraisal of the two segments.

Having seen that the voicing concept is basically abstract and phonological – even in classical phonetics, a theory characterising what phoneticians *feel* to be the case – we are now in a position to formulate hypotheses which can lead to experiments casting light on the correlation between voicing and vocal cord vibration. So:

> *Hypothesis*: Consonantal segments which are phonologically [+voice] are rendered physically with vocal cord vibration.

We have to modify this a little because, although the concept of time is relatively meaningless at the cognitive phonological level, it cannot be ignored at the physical level. The best we can do is assume that a phonological segment, when rendered, has vocal cord vibration throughout; so:

> *Hypothesis*: Consonantal segments which are phonologically [+voice] are rendered physically with vocal cord vibration *throughout their* DURATION.

Prediction

Since /p/ and /t/ are voiceless, and /b/ and /ɛ/ are voiced, the hypothesis would predict that the word *pet*, which is represented in the utterance plan as /pɛt/, would be rendered phonetically as [pɛt] (using IPA symbols to represent the sound wave), or as

$$* - - - - - - \,|\, vvvvv - - - - \,|\, *$$

using a STYLISED WAVEFORM REPRESENTATION of the vocal cord vibration parameter.

> **DURATION**
>
> Duration is a physical concept often taken to correlate with the abstract concept *length*. Because they are physical, durations are measured in clock time using the normal units of seconds (s) and milliseconds (ms) in speech studies. In phonology, when referring to abstract length, segments may be *long* or *short*, and we speak of this segment being longer or shorter than that segment: clock time is never referred to in phonology.

> **STYLISED WAVEFORM REPRESENTATION**
>
> We use here a stylised representation of vocal cord vibration to show what happens as time unfolds. Each character represents around 10 ms of waveform, with ' – ' meaning *no* vocal cord vibration and 'v' meaning *some* vocal cord vibration. Stylising the representation enables us to present a generalised picture, rather than the single-utterance images of waveforms which constitute real data together with all the variability that this implies. The vertical lines represent the plosive bursts, and an asterisk is used to represent a word or syllable boundary.

The word *bet*, represented in the utterance plan as / bɛt /, would be rendered phonetically as [bɛt] (symbolically), or as

$$* vvvvvv \,|\, vvvvv - - - - \,|\, *$$

as a stylised vocal cord waveform representation.

Data

Using other stops as an example so that we can illustrate the generality of the phenomenon, take the phonological consonantal pair /t/ and /d/ in English. /t/ is [−voice] and /d/ is [+voice]. The hypothesis would prompt investigation of whether /t/ is rendered with no vocal cord vibration and

228

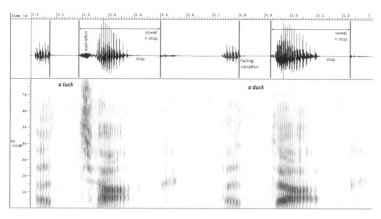

Figure 11.4 Waveforms and spectrograms of *a tuck* and *a duck*.

/d/ by contrast with vocal cord vibration. Both plosives are rendered as bi-phasal; that is, they consist of a stop phase followed by a release phase. Figure 11.4 shows exemplar waveform renderings of the pair using the carrier words *tuck* and *duck*, each preceded by the indefinite article, as in *a tuck* /ə tʌk/ and *a duck* /ə dʌk/.

Using our stylised vocal cord waveform representation, these look like

$$\star vvv\star\ -\ -\ -\ -\ -\ -\ |\ -\ -\ vvvv\ -\ -\ -\ -\ -\ |\ \star \text{ for } a \text{ tuck,}$$

and

$$\star vvv\star v\ -\ -\ -\ -\ -\ |\ vvvvvv\ -\ -\ -\ -\ -\ |\ \star \text{ for } a \text{ duck.}$$

The indefinite article was inserted here for two reasons: to establish a simple rhythmic pattern, helping to normalise the rate at which the words were spoken, and to help identify the start of the stop phase of the initial consonant. This phase is taken to begin at the moment of complete closure, shown by a sharp fall-off in the amplitude of the acoustic signal falling on the microphone.

Results

In these waveforms, vocal cord vibration occurs in the vowel renderings [ə] and [ʌ]. We have marked in Figure 11.4 the moments at which the stop takes full effect – the moment of closure when the tongue tip or blade touches the alveolar ridge, and the moment of release. In both cases it is clear that during the stop phase of [t] there is no vocal cord vibration, and that during the stop phase of [d] there is only a relatively *brief* period of vocal cord vibration right at the beginning. Also, in both examples there is no vocal cord vibration during the brief release phases.

Discussion

The two words are perceived to be different; so either the difference is a perceptual illusion (which is a serious possibility) or the perception of difference is not where our hypothesis predicted it would be. Classical phonetics has the two words as identical, except for the [+voice] feature – absent during /t/ and present during /d/. We find that in the rendering, [t] and [d] are almost identical from the point of view of vocal cord vibration, but the words *are* different in the way the following vowel is rendered. The vocal cord vibration which classical phonetics would predict to run throughout the vowels (since vowels in English are phonologically [+voice]) is delayed *significantly* following [t], and delayed just *slightly* following [d]. It is easy to hear the delay following [t], though much less easy to hear the slight delay following [d]. The conclusion is that these two words differ *not* in how the initial phonological segment is rendered but in how the *following vowel* is rendered. That one of the words begins with a phonological /t/ is probably cued to the listener by the delay in vocal cord vibration onset for the vowel; the near lack of this delay cues /d/ to the listener for the other word. We use the term FEATURE TRANSFER for this phenomenon; here the distinguishing feature is transferred from its phonological location in the initial consonant to the rendering of the next segment.

Vowel length and final consonant devoicing

Phonologically, and in classical phonetics, vowels are classified as either long or short. Remember this is notional abstract time rather than clock time. The main non-diphthongal vowels in British English are shown in the matrix below.

Long vowels	bead /bid/						bard /bɑd/	board /bɒd/			boot /but/
Short vowels		bid /bɪd/	bed /bɛd/	bad /bæd/	bird /bɜd/	bud /bʌd/			bod /bɒd/	hood /hʊd/	

In rendering these vowels the physical durations vary quite widely, with some short vowels being typically of less duration than others, and similarly for the long vowels. In this chapter what interests us is the notion in both classical phonetics and modern phonology that a given vowel is lengthened in certain circumstances – typically when followed by a consonant which is [+voice]. So, turning this into an experimental study, we would need a hypothesis like this:

> Vowels are rendered with greater duration when they are phonologically lengthened.

REMINDER: FEATURE TRANSFER

Feature transfer refers to the transfer of a distinguishing feature from one segment to an adjacent segment, such that phonetically the distinction (say, between two syllables) is now conveyed *unexpectedly* by a different segment. In the example in the text, *tuck* is phonologically distinguished from *duck* by the voicing feature on the initial consonantal segment, but is *phonetically* distinguished by the vocal cord vibration feature on the second vocalic segment.

The hypothesis is like this because we cannot measure length – so we cannot measure lengthening: these are abstract concepts, and are not open to direct physical investigation. But what we *can* do is measure durations, since part of the classical phonetics claim is that duration is a physical correlate of abstract length. We can usually, if we concentrate, perceive the lengthening the phoneticians are referring to, though untrained listeners are normally not really aware of it. The general claim is that if we can perceive it we can measure it in the physical signal, provided the claimed correlation holds true.

Thus if we compare two words like *pot* and *pod,* we would expect the vowel rendering to have greater duration in *pot* than in *pod* because of the vowel-lengthening rule in English:

> Vowels lengthen before consonants which are [+voice].

There is, however, another phonological rule in English which devoices word-final voiced consonants:

> Final [+voice] consonants change to [−voice] in word-final position.

The two rules are ordered, with vowel lengthening coming first. If they were round the other way, then vowels would not lengthen, because final consonants would always be devoiced.

Prediction

If phonological voicing is rendered phonetically as vocal cord vibration, and if lengthening of the vowel is rendered as increased duration, then we would expect the following:

pot: /pɒt/ → [pɒt] (symbolic representation)

-------|--vvvv-----| (stylised waveform representation)

pod: /pɒd/ → [pɒd] or

-------|--vvvvvv-----|

The stylised vocal cord waveform shows increased duration associated with the vowel and no vocal cord vibration associated with the [−voice] rendering of the final / d /.

Data

Using *a pot* and *a pod* with the indefinite article prefixed as before, exemplar waveforms are shown in Figure 11.5.

Using our stylised vocal cord waveform representation, these look like:

vvv------|--vvvv-----|* for *a pot,*

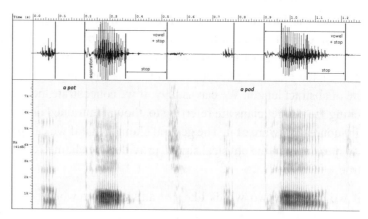

Figure 11.5 Waveforms and spectrograms of *a pot* and *a pod*.

and:

$$\text{*vvv*------|--vvvvvv---|* for } a\ pod.$$

Results

For both words the initial part of the vowel [ɒ] loses its vocal cord vibration, as expected from what we have seen earlier of the aerodynamic effects following plosive release. We also note that the vocal cord vibration continues for longer in *pod* than in *pot*, and that the stop phase for [d] has lost any vocal cord vibration that might have been expected for a [+voice] plosive.

These results appear to support the hypotheses that increased vowel length before a phonologically [+voice] turns up as increased duration of vocal cord vibration in the phonetic rendering, and that the loss of phonological voice in the final [+voice] plosive is shown by the lack of vocal cord vibration throughout.

But let us look more closely at the timing relationship between [ɒ] and [d]. Notice that

- the times between the start of the vowel (or the release of initial plosive) and the releases of [t] and [d] are quite similar;

- although the vocal cord vibration duration is greater in *pod*, the duration of the stop phase of [d] seems shorter than that for [t] – an *unexpected* result.

Discussion – a choice of model

If we look back at our previous experiment we see that we had

$$\text{*vvv*v-----|vvvvvv-----|* for } a\ duck.$$

Notice that there is a brief period of vocal cord vibration at the beginning of the stop phase of the [d]. This is in fact the residual of an attempt to produce vocal cord vibration throughout the stop phase. The speaker had *intended* vocal cord vibration, and had produced an utterance plan showing the stop phase as [+voice] to be rendered as vocal cord vibration. The vibration did not occur because the oral stop (the tongue blade against the alveolar ridge) had interrupted airflow out of the mouth, resulting in a heighted intraoral air pressure which had destroyed the balance between supra- and subglottal air pressures needed for spontaneous vocal cord vibration. In other words, we see no vocal cord vibration on the graph and hear no vocal cord vibration except for a very brief moment, but the speaker had wanted something else – that there *should* be vibration. Such coarticulatory effects happen all the time in speech: *what we want is not necessarily what we get.* This is normally unimportant because the listener's perceptual system is remarkably good at REPAIRING DAMAGED WAVEFORMS to meet the speaker's expectations.

> **REPAIRING *DAMAGED WAVEFORMS***
>
> A waveform can be regarded as damaged if it is not exactly as required by the speaker's utterance plan. The many coarticulatory processes that result from the mechanical design of the vocal tract, its control system and the resultant aerodynamics, all tend to produce damaged waveforms. The human perceptual system incorporates a mechanism for detecting and then repairing most of the damage back to what seems to have been intended. This remarkable property of perception is so efficient that listeners are usually quite unaware of its operation. Pronounce out loud for yourself the two words *pot* and *pod* used in our example experiment, or get someone else to say them to you. Before you read this chapter, would you not have been sure that the difference between the two words rests on the final sound? But the two final sounds are virtually identical (look at the waveforms above), so how could they be cueing the difference? We *hear* the difference in the vowel's duration, but we *perceive* the difference not on the vowel but on the following consonant, in which we actually hear *no* difference! In general we are aware not of what we hear, but of what we perceive – these are regularly not the same thing (see Chapters 7 and 8).

Turning back to *a pot* and *a pod*, we have a choice of model for the data in this experiment:

> *Model 1:* All the vocal cord vibration we see is associated with rendering the vowel /ɒ/, and we assert that the vowel's phonological *lengthening* has been rendered by increased *duration*.

However, to explain the data we now have to introduce a further rule:

> If the vowel is lengthened, the lengthening consonant following it must be shortened.

This shortening appears to be compensatory; that is, the overall length of the word is kept roughly the same. The rule tries to explain why we did not get the result predicted above – a word with greater overall duration.

> *Model 2:* The vowel length has not changed at all. What looks like *vowel* vocal cord vibration is in fact the start of the intended [+voice] *consonant*, in which the vocal cord vibration has failed because of the

coarticulatory aerodynamic effect explained earlier – the supra- vs. subglottal air pressure balance.

The first model rests on the idea that both vowel lengthening and final consonant devoicing are intended by the speaker and are therefore properly phonological rules. The second model puts forward the claim that vowel lengthening does not happen at all, and that final consonant devoicing is in fact final consonant failure of vocal cord vibration due to *unintended* physical artefacts. These two models could not be more different – but *both claim to explain the observed data,* and indeed they do. But they cannot both be good models because they seriously contradict each other. We need a method of choosing between the two.

In this case we will get nowhere by staying within the linguistics/ phonetics domain – a single discipline. We must do what *all* scientists must do to explain phenomena: we must step outside the discipline to seek an unbiased explanation. We ask the theories of mechanics and aerodynamics (nothing whatsoever to do with phonetics, and therefore impartial) about possible coarticulatory effects. The answer is that there are indeed such effects and that they cannot be denied – they cannot *not* happen.

If coarticulation is inevitable, then the effects we have just observed cannot have been intended simply as part of the language. They are a by-product of rendering and will occur in any language so long as human speaking continues to be done in the way we normally do it. If we say they were intended as part of the language, we are denying two external arbitrating disciplines – and this would be violating an important principle of scientific investigation.

The upshot: model 2 above does the better job at accounting for the data. The earlier rules of voice lengthening and devoicing are inappropriately placed in the phonology, and are better figuring in the phonetics as aerodynamic coarticulatory rules. There are many such inappropriate rules in the early modern phonology of the 1970s and 1980s, most of them persisting from yet earlier views within classical phonetic theory. To be fair, the experimental techniques we have available today were not available to phoneticians of the classical era: they had to rely on what they felt they heard and the explanations which seemed to them to be most appropriate. It is in the nature of scientific theory that changes in techniques for observing data will inevitably result in revisions to the theory (**EVALUATION – PHONOLOGICAL RULE OR PHONETIC RULE?**).

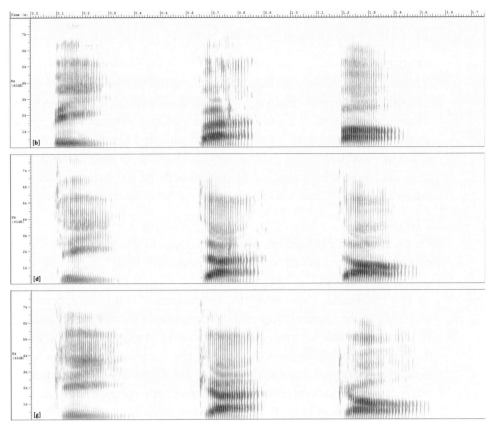

Figure 11.6 Spectrograms of the sequences [bi], [bæ], [bɑ], [di], [dæ], [dɑ] [gi], [gæ], [gɑ].

INFORMATION FROM SPECTROGRAMS

Loci, formant bending and Target Theory

Researchers in the 1950s noticed that formant bending is patterned (see 'Formant Transitions' in Chapter 3). Their data involved spectrographic analysis of plosive+vowel utterances over a range of combinations of different plosives with different vowels.

Data

Figure 11.6 shows six spectrograms imaged from nine examples of plosive+vowel utterances spoken by the same speaker on the same occasion.

Notice the centre frequencies of the first three formants on each of the spectrograms. Renderings of [+voice] initial plosives have been used because it is possible to image strong formants from almost the moment of release of the plosive. Similar formants are visible right through the vocal cord failure phase and onward, following the release of [−voice] plosives, though this is much weaker and difficult to image. We speak of *formant bending*, the term used to label that part of a formant which does not show the stable frequency associated with the vowel.

Results

It is easy to see the formant bending, but what researchers noticed was the patterning: the formant frequency changes seem to diverge from particular frequency areas around the plosive release phase in patterns which appear unique for each of the three different consonants. In English, there are three different vocal tract *constriction points* (in classical phonetics terminology these are *places of articulation*) associated with the plosives: lips, alveolar ridge and velum. This, it was hypothesised, was what determines the bending.

Discussion

Observations of this kind need more explanation. We have measured the data and described the patterning: this means two levels of our adequacy criteria for a theory (TUTORIAL – TRANSLATION THEORIES, Chapter 3). The *explanation* (from acoustics, not phonetics) is that the constriction itself sets up the spectral properties of the remaining vocal tract resonator, and that any further resonance after the moment of release will reflect how those spectral properties are changing as the vocal tract properties move towards the targets for the next segment. The model is one of sequenced, but *blending*, targets or articulatory specifications corresponding to each segment in the phonological sequence. This is precisely the basis of what was about to be called Coarticulation Theory. The original experiments on formant bending in the early 1950s could be said to have triggered the thinking which resulted in the formal presentation of Coarticulation Theory in the middle 1960s.

Formant bending reflects the blending process from one well-defined target to the next. The researchers noted that timing of the sequences is reflected in the formant bending – the slower the sequence, the less *steep* the formant bending appears to be in the spectrogram image (less steep means less frequency change per unit time). By the same argument, rapid speech will show steeper formant bending, or more rapid movement from target to target (see TUTORIAL – TARGET THEORY, Chapter 2) (**EVALUATION – THE ORIGINAL HASKINS LABS EXPERIMENTS**).

Intervocalic consonants and coarticulation

In the mid-1960s there was considerable interest in trying to explain the fact that individual segments do not appear sharply defined in waveforms or articulation. In fact, boundaries between segments are rarely seen in audio displays. Theorists used Coarticulation Theory to explain that segments blended together or overlapped because of mechanical or aerodynamic inertia in the speech production system. A basic premise here was that speakers *intend* speech to be segmented, but that in the production processes the segmentation is lost.

Most experiments of the period – for example, those by Öhman investigating coarticulation in vowel+consonant+vowel sequences – concentrated on plosives, but here we want to familiarise readers with liquids and semi-vowels and how these look when imaged using spectrograms.

Data and Results
We begin with simple data involving sequences in which the liquid or semi-vowel is rendered between two vowels. Examine in Figure 11.7 the exemplar spectrograms of the rendered sequences using British English: [ɑrɑ], [ɑlɑ], [ɑjɑ], [ɑwɑ], [ɛrɛ], [ɛlɛ], [ɛjɛ], [ɛwɛ].

Note especially the movement of the second formant as time unfolds. It is not possible to segment the utterances, since vocal cord vibration is continuous throughout and there are no complete constrictions to provide us with any abrupt acoustic markers like plosive bursts. Notice the dip in F1 during both [l] and [r], and movements of the other formants, enabling unique identification of both. The behaviour is similar whether the vowel context is /ɑ . . . ɑ/ or /ɛ . . . ɛ/.

This data is interesting because it shows the *linkage* nature of /l/ and /r/. These two consonants often show some unexpected behaviour. Take, for example, the way a normally planned /l/ often gets rendered in the English Cockney accent at the end of a syllable – either at the very end or immediately preceding a final consonant. So we have words like *wall* and *milk* producing the exemplar spectrograms shown in Figure 11.8.

Classical phoneticians refer to these sounds as vocalised /l/, and sometimes use the /ʊ/ symbol usually reserved for the vowel in a word like *put* /pʊt/. They would argue that the sound at the end of *wall* /wɒʊ/ or before the [k] in *milk* /mɪʊk/ is not a true vowel, because, phonologically, syllables are usually allowed only one vowel: the nucleus. Vocalisation of /l/ is not at all uncommon, in fact. Take the French word *cheval*, probably intended in Old French to be pronounced as /tʃə'val/, with a plural *chevals* /tʃə'vals/. The modern spelling for the plural *chevaux* betrays the vocalisation of the /l/ to /ʊ/ at some stage, giving us a diphthong /aʊ/ – subsequently to become the modern pronunciation /ʃə'vo/.

Discussion
Liquids like /r/ and /l/ and semi-vowels like /j/ and /w/ are sometimes thought of as playing a facilitating role in linking other sounds – particularly

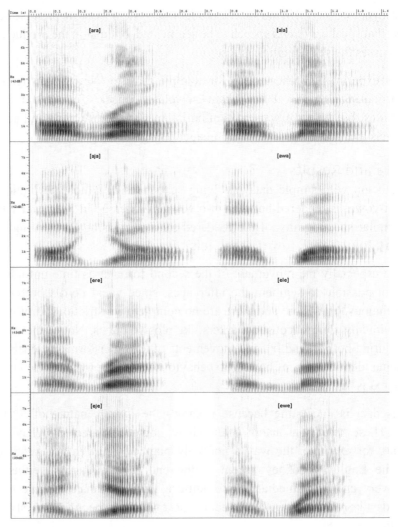

Figure 11.7 Spectrograms of the sequences [ɑrɑ], [ɑlɑ], [ɑjɑ], [ɑwɑ], [ɛrɛ], [ɛlɛ], [ɛjɛ], [ɛwɛ]. Notice the way in which the first three formants show differential bending.

vowels. Interestingly the formants (particularly the second formant) appear to move in opposite directions for members of the pairs. Whilst being informal, since we cannot deal with historical phonetics or phonology here, the kind of historical change that can occur with /l/ also occurs with /r/. In many dialects, especially General American, for example, what was historically a separate /r/ in a word like *cart* loses its separate identity to transfer an r-feature to the previous vowel: /kɑ̈t/. We speak of a *rhoticised* vowel.

Liquids and semi-vowels often behave differently in different languages. Take the final /r/, for example, in a word like *faire* in modern metropolitan French. Among some younger groups in the big cities like Paris we find

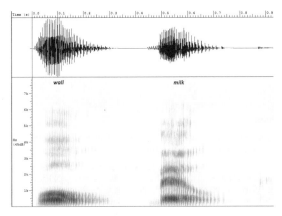

Figure 11.8 Waveforms and spectrograms of wall /wɒʊ/, and milk /mɪʊk/. In each case the vocalisation of /l/ is deliberate and forms part of the utterance plan: it is not a coarticulatory phenomenon because it is optional.

this word often pronounced as /fɜə/ – not unlike the pronunciation of the English word *fair* in Southern British English. The /r/ itself has been deleted, but not before the preceding vowel has been lengthened and diphthongised.

Notice the use of the / . . . / and [. . .] brackets above. /l/, /r/, /w/ and /j/, even if regarded as facilitating, have phonemic status in English – they can be permuted to identify different words. Processes like the vocalisation of /l/ and the addition of an r-feature to a vowel are phonological and decided by the speaker within the language community. These processes have phonological status, and are not coarticulatory – though coarticulatory tendencies may *explain* them. The point is that they are optional: the Cockney speaker can say /wɒʊ/ or /wɒlʲ/ for *wall* – there is choice. Whether or not choice is available is an acid test for coarticulation: if the process is optional and choice-based it is phonological; if it is not it is phonetic and coarticulatory.

Running speech and segments

Looking for acoustic phenomena corresponding to segmental phonological objects or properties in running speech is particularly difficult, as we have discovered several times in this book. Apart from obvious difficulties like hesitations and other phenomena prevalent in the real world of speech, there are serious problems simply identifying segments. All books on acoustic phonetics speak of the difficulties of finding segment boundaries.

But this is really no surprise. If our model of speech production is based on segments – like classical phonetics and subsequently Coarticulation Theory – then we are bound to be disappointed when there are no, or very few, segments to be found. It is not just that boundaries *were* there, but have become obscured by coarticulatory blending or blurring processes; if this were the case, we would be able to REVERSE ENGINEER the data to discover the segments.

REVERSE ENGINEERING

Reverse engineering is a process whereby underlying data is recovered from the surface by systematically negating the rules or processes which derived the surface in the first place, provided these are known.

In early straightforward *phonology*, for example, we could reverse engineer US English [ðə ˈmæn z ə ˈraiɾə] to the underlying segment sequence /ðə ˈmæn z ə ˈraitə/ – with attention drawn to the /t/ which becomes /ɾ/ – though it's in the nature of classical phonetics that there might be arguments about details of the transcriptions here. Reverse engineering applies the phonological rule that /t/→/ɾ/ following a stressed vowel and preceding /ə/ *backwards*. The phrase is, of course *The man's a writer*. The representation of the acoustic signal [ðə ˈmæn z ə ˈraiːɾə] will get reverse engineered to /ðə ˈmæn z ə ˈraidə/, and therefore to *The man's a rider*, because of the apparently greater vowel duration in *rider*, and the phonological rule which says that vowels lengthen before voiced consonants (but see the experiment above).

In *acoustics* we can reverse engineer some coarticulatory rules. So, for example, we know that there is an aerodynamic rule which causes a period of vocal cord vibration at the start of vowels following voiceless plosives to fail in most accents of English. An acoustic sequence which we might represent as [kʰəˈtʰæstʰrəfi], with aspiration preceding the full [ə], [æ] and [r], is easily recovered to /kəˈtæstrəfi/ (extrinsic allophones) and thence to /kæˈtæstrɒfi/ (phonemes) – *catastrophe*. Note that vocal cord vibration fails following [p, t, k], and to a certain extent [s, ʃ] in English not just before vowels but before the voiced facilitator consonants [l, r, w, j], as in *play* [pʰlei], *try* [tʰrai], *swing* [sʰwɪŋ] or *cue* [kʰju].

Recovery from representations of acoustic signals to representations of utterance plans is relatively easy since in linguistics we are used to deriving representations *from* representations – the data is already segmented in the representation. The difficult part is obtaining a *segmented* representation of the acoustic signal to begin with. The difference is that the waveform is not a *representation* of the signal – it *is* the signal, or at least an image of it. In Chapters 7 and 8 we speak of this recovery as the *assignment* of a representation to the waveform.

An exhaustive treatment of techniques for assigning a symbolic representation to an acoustic waveform is impossible here: it would take far too much space. The problem is that much of what phoneticians and phonologists do is craft rather than science, though this is simply because the rules for conversion between levels of representation still remain inexplicit to a certain extent. Remember, what we are trying to do is *label a waveform*. This means *assign a symbolic representation to the waveform*. Inevitably corners will be cut and assumptions made. In the hands of a competent and consistent labeller who has particular objectives in mind the process has proved very productive in linguistics. Speech technology engineers have also developed a number of different techniques for AUTOMATICALLY LABELLING WAVEFORMS.

AUTOMATICALLY LABELLING WAVEFORMS

In phonetics and phonology, waveform segmenting and labelling have always been performed by human transcribers using recognised alphabetic representations like the IPA. But a similar process is required in the speech technology called automatic speech recognition. Here segment (perhaps allophones, perhaps syllables, perhaps words) labels have to be assigned to stretches of waveform as part of the speech recognition process. Because we have not yet fully modelled explicitly the relationship between waveforms and their representations, there are often a great many errors in the process. See Chapter 9 for a fuller explanation of the problems of using speech technology to mimic or simulate the human processes of speech production and perception.

PHONOLOGICAL RULE OR PHONETIC RULE?

Phonological rules are usually constructed to explain regular patterns in speech which are not simply a property of phonetic rendering itself but which are there as an intended part of the language's use of available sounds. Phonological rules reflect a mental processing which expresses how we want our language to sound. For this reason, in actual speech production we say that this processing takes place to formulate an utterance plan *before* actual rendering takes place. Before means *logically* before – the plan must exist *before* it can be carried out or rendered.

The trouble is that the execution or rendering of the plan, because it takes place in the physical world, is far from perfect, with the result that, however clear our intentions as to how things should sound, they never quite turn out this way. Things go wrong – articulations and therefore waveforms get damaged – they are, in a sense, *degraded* versions of our intentions. The whole of Coarticulation Theory was designed to explain just how things go wrong in phonetic rendering.

Phonologists at the peak of generative phonology in the 1970s, following the phonology of the earlier classical phonetics, felt that in examining the data provided by articulatory and acoustic studies they could uncover a speaker's phonological intention. However, it often turns out to be difficult to decide whether an effect observed at the acoustic surface – like the apparent vowel lengthening we have been discussing – is the result of cognitive phonological *intention* or physical phonetic *accident*.

What researchers in phonetics do is consult the appropriate discipline outside linguistics or phonetics. Many coarticulatory phenomena can be explained, for example, by mechanics, and would therefore be accidental within the context of speech production theory. And for this reason many phonetic rules are inevitable – they are *not* the product of phonological processes but that of processes outside our domain.

So examples of phonetic processes might be:

- aspiration or VOT in English;
- loss of vocal cord vibration for final voiced consonants;
- vowel lengthening inasmuch as it exists at all;
- nasalisation in English;

and so on.

Examples of phonological or phonologically modified phonetic processes (see 'Articulatory Phonology', Chapter 3, and 'Cognitive Phonetics', Chapter 4) might be:

- lack of VOT in French – any aerodynamic coarticulatory tendency is to be overcome by improved precision of articulation;

- devoicing of final voiced consonants in German and Russian – this is true devoicing, with the utterance plan (unlike English) specifying rendering *without* voicing;
- place assimilation in words like *input* in English (the /n/ is rendered as a *bilabial* nasal [m] – this is *not* coarticulation because [n] and [m] do not involve the same articulators, a *sine qua non* of coarticulation);

and so on.

EVALUATION

THE ORIGINAL HASKINS LABS EXPERIMENTS

The group of researchers at the Haskins Laboratories (now in New Haven in the USA) became interested in something very important: how were these sequences *perceived*? They hypothesised that the perception of speech (segments or parts of segments) is *cued*; that is, there are properties of the signal which trigger us to assign to it *particular* labels. Using an early form of speech synthesis that they had devised, they proceeded to investigate this hypothesis. For this particular experiment, the synthesiser produced only formants, not plosive bursts.

Precisely copying the formant bending observed in spectrograms of human speech into the synthesiser produced a series of stimuli for testing on listeners – stimuli which included only the formants, no burst signal. The results were striking: listeners were almost always able to tell the researchers not just what the vowels were, but also what the *consonants* were – even to the extent that often the fact that the consonants were *missing* was not even noticed. Conclusion: listeners can use formant bending to assign plosive labels where there are no cues from the plosives themselves. And they can do this because of the unique patterning of the formant bending, identifying it with *particular* plosives.

- Be careful: listeners *can* use formant bending. This does not mean that they *do* use formant bending, or if they do, that they do it all the time. The experiment cannot rule out other, perhaps unknown, means at the disposal of listeners for recognising segments. Perceptual experiments need very careful design, and the data needs examining from different perspectives to be sure of exactly how people do their perceiving.

This series of experiments was a breakthrough in our understanding of speech production and perception: not only is speech coarticulated in a patterned way, but the perception of speech can proceed on several, sometimes not obvious, *cues* for *categorising* the data into a sequence of symbolic labels which reflect the speaker's original intentions rather than the detail of the acoustic signal. This point is often lost in detail classifier theory (see Chapter 8).

FURTHER READING

Fry, D. (1979), *The Physics of Speech*, Cambridge: Cambridge University Press.

Lehiste, I. (1967), *Readings in Acoustic Phonetics*, Cambridge, MA: MIT Press.

Conclusion

Modern studies of speech production and perception have grown out of earlier classical phonetics, a theory which peaked in activity in the first half of the twentieth century. At that time, researchers' goal was to describe spoken language using a universal symbol set that could be applied to all languages. This was to enable not only the study of a single language but also the comparison of different languages. Early applications permitted treatment of accent within a language and language teaching. The symbolic transcription system began to lend itself to noting and comparing the sounds produced in disorders of speech. In today's terms, the symbols represented the perceived meaningful sounds of a language and some of their possible variants.

Classical phonetics included a substudy called phonology. In this, the way in which the sounds of a language functioned within that language was examined and codified to a certain extent. A major change occurred around the middle of the twentieth century: phonetics and phonology became distinguishable as individual disciplines, each having its own structure, domain (scope of relevance) and metatheory (underlying theoretical principles). Phonetics described what phonologists thought of as the heard result of a predominantly automatic physical response as speakers rendered the cognitively organised sound patterns of the language. This idea, originating perhaps in the classic *The Sound Pattern of English* (Chomsky and Halle 1968), was quickly and successfully challenged by Action Theory (Fowler *et al.* 1980) and Cognitive Phonetic Theory (Tatham 1986b, 1990).

Today phonetics appears in three major areas:

- essentially as *an arts-based approach* to speech, used in language departments of higher education institutions. The purpose is to enumerate the different sounds of languages and to train pronunciation. This approach is sometimes backed up by simple illustrative experiments performed in a phonetics laboratory. The aim is to verify the physical existence of correlates of the perceived sounds.

- as *phonetics for phonology*. Rather emphasising the division into two subdisciplines along the lines of the mid-twentieth-century researchers, phonetics is providing some explanations for constraints on phonological claims – as seen for example in Optimality Theory (Prince and Smolensky 2004) and the work of Hayes (Hayes *et al.* 2004).

- as *speech production and perception modelling.* This work focuses on basic research into what human beings do during verbal communication. Most research is now being carried out by researchers trained in the fields of psychology, cognitive neuroscience and computer science. Increasingly research is conducted by teams, since it is rare to find a single individual with a working insightful understanding of such a range of ideas.

A major application area contributing to and profiting from speech production and perception model building is the field of communication disorders – using techniques and methods derived from biology and cognitive psychology. Here there is a productive movement away from earlier surface descriptions towards a search for underlying systems disorders.

In this book we have addressed some of the subject areas and their underlying methodologies which have contributed to speech production and perception modelling. We have tried to encourage students and researchers to read widely, and to illustrate for themselves some of the ways of thinking in our basic discipline of speech production and perception studies which may be productive in their own chosen fields.

References

Abercrombie, D. (1967), *Elements of General Phonetics*, Edinburgh: Edinburgh University Press.

Ball, M. and C. Code (1997), *Instrumental Clinical Phonetics*, London: Whurr.

Ball, M., M. Perkins, N. Muller, and S. Howard (eds) (2008), *The Handbook of Clinical Linguistics*, Oxford: Blackwell.

Ball, M., N. Muller, and B. Rutter (2009), *Phonology for Communication Disorders*, New York: Psychology Press.

Bell-Berti, F., R. Karakow, C. Gelfer, and S. Boyce (1995), 'Anticipatory and carryover implications for models of speech production', in F. Bell-Berti and L. Raphael (eds), *Producing Speech: Contemporary Issues*, New York: American Institute of Physics, 77–97.

Brady, M. and L. Armstrong (2009), 'Disordered Communicative Interaction: Current and Future Approaches to Analysis and Treatment', special issue of *Aphasiology*.

Bregman, A. (1994), *Auditory Scene Analysis: The Perceptual Organization of Sound*, Cambridge, MA: MIT Press.

Browman, K. and L. Goldstein (1986), 'Toward an articulatory phonology', in C. Ewan and J. Anderson (eds), *Phonology Yearbook 3*, Cambridge: Cambridge University Press, 219–53.

Carmichael, L. (2003), 'Intonation: categories and continua', in *Proceedings of the 19th Northwest Linguistics Conference*, Victoria, BC (compact disk).

Chomsky, N. (1957), *Syntactic Structures*, The Hague: Mouton.

Chomsky, N. (1965), *Aspects of the Theory of Syntax*, Cambridge, MA: MIT Press.

Chomsky, N. and M. Halle (1968), *The Sound Pattern of English*, New York: Harper and Row.

Clark, J., C. Yallop, and J. Fletcher (2007), *An Introduction to Phonetics and Phonology*, 3rd edn, Malden, MA and Oxford: Blackwell.

Cooper, F. (1966), 'Describing the speech process in motor command terms', *Status Reports on Speech Research SR 515*, New Haven: Haskins Laboratories.

Corr, P. (2006), *Understanding Biological Psychology*, Oxford: Blackwell.

Cruttenden, A. (2008), *Gimson's Pronunciation of English*, Oxford: Oxford University Press.

REFERENCES

Damasio, A. (1999), *The Feeling of What Happens: Body and Emotion in the Making of Consciousness*, New York: Harcourt Brace.

Damasio, A. (2003), *Looking for Spinoza*, Orlando: Harcourt.

Daniloff, R. and R. Hammarberg (1973), 'On defining co-articulation', *Journal of Phonetics* 1: 239–48.

Daniloff, R., G. Shuckers, and L. Feth (1980), *The Physiology of Speech and Hearing: An Introduction*, Englewood Cliffs, NJ: Prentice Hall.

Easton, T. (1972),'On the normal use of reflexes', *American Scientist* 60: 591–9.

Evans, V. (2009), *How Words Mean: Lexical Concepts, Cognitive Models, and Meaning Construction*, Oxford: Oxford University Press.

Evans, V., B. Bergen, and J. Zinken (eds) (2007), *The Cognitive Linguistics Reader*, London: Equinox.

Eysenck, M. (2009), *Foundations of Psychology*, Hove: Psychology Press.

Eysenck, M. and M. Keane (2005), *Cognitive Psychology: A Student's Handbook*, Hove: Psychology Press.

Fant, G. (1960), *Acoustic Theory of Speech Production*, The Hague: Mouton.

Fant, G. (1973), *Speech Sounds and Features*, Cambridge, MA: MIT Press.

Fillmore, C. J. (1976), 'Frame semantics and the nature of language', in *Annals of the New York Academy of Sciences: Conference on the Origin and Development of Language and Speech*, 280: 20–32.

Finkbeiner, M., R. Gollan, and A. Caramazza (2006), 'Lexical access in bilingual speakers: What's the (hard) problem?', *Bilingualism: Language and Cognition* 9 (2): 153–66.

Firth, J. (1957), *Papers in Linguistics 1934–1951*, Oxford: Oxford University Press.

Fowler, C. (1977), 'Timing control in speech production', PhD thesis, Indiana University Linguistics Club.

Fowler, C. (1980), 'Coarticulation and theories of extrinsic timing', *Journal of Phonetics* 8: 113–35.

Fowler, C. (1986), 'An event approach to the study of speech perception from a direct-realist perspective', *Journal of Phonetics* 14: 3–28.

Fowler, C. and E. Saltzman (1993), 'Coordination and coarticulation in speech production', *Language and Speech* 36(2, 3): 171–95.

Fowler, C., P. Rubin, R. Remez, and M. Turvey (1980), 'Implications for speech production of a general theory of action', in B. Butterworth (ed.), *Language Production. Vol. 1: Speech and Talk*, New York: Academic Press, 373–420.

Frith, C. (2007), *Making up the Mind*, Oxford: Blackwell.

Fry, D. (1958), 'Experiments in the perception of stress', *Language and Speech* 1: 126–52.

Fry, D. (1979), *The Physics of Speech*, Cambridge: Cambridge University Press.

REFERENCES

Garnham, A. (2001), *Mental Models and the Interpretation of Anaphora*, Hove: Psychology Press.

Gazzaniga, M. (2008, reprinted 2009), *Human: The Science Behind What Makes Us Unique*, London: Harper Perennial.

Gazzaniga, M. (2009), *The Cognitive Neurosciences*, 4th edn, Cambridge, MA: MIT Press.

Gibson, J. (1950), *The Perception of the Visual World*, Boston: Houghton Mifflin.

Givon, T. (2005), *Context as Other Minds*, Amsterdam: John Benjamins.

Goldsmith, J. (1990), *Autosegmental and Metrical Phonology: An Introduction*, Oxford: Blackwell.

Greenberg, J. (2005), *Universals of Language*, The Hague: Mouton de Gruyter.

Guendouzi, J., F. Loncke, and M. Williams (eds) (2010), *The Handbook of Psycholinguistic and Cognitive Processes*, London and New York: Psychology Press.

Gussenhoven, C. and H. Jacobs (1998), *Understanding Phonology*, London: Arnold.

Haggard, P., Y. Rossetti, and M. Kawato (eds) (2008), *Sensorimotor Foundations of Higher Cognition (Attention and Performance)*, Oxford: Oxford University Press.

Halle, M. (1959), *The Sound Pattern of Russian: A Linguistic and Acoustical Investigation*, 's-Gravenhage: Mouton.

Halle, M. and G. Clements (1983), *Problem Book in Phonology*, Cambridge, MA: MIT Press.

Hammarberg, R. (1976), 'The metaphysics of coarticulation', *Journal of Phonetics* 4: 353–63.

Hardcastle, W. and N. Hewlett (1999), *Coarticulation: Theory, Data and Techniques*, Cambridge: Cambridge University Press.

Harré, R. (2002), *Cognitive Science: A Philosophical Introduction*, London: Sage.

Harrington, J. and S. Cassidy (1999), *Techniques in Speech Acoustics*, Dordrecht: Kluwer.

Harsin, C. (1997), 'Perceptual-center modelling is affected by including acoustic rate-of-change modulations', *Perception Psychophysics* 59 (2): 243–51.

Hartsuiker R., R. Bastiaanse, A. Postma, and F. Wijnen (eds) (2005), *Phonological Encoding and Monitoring in Normal and Pathological Speech*, New York: Psychology Press.

Hayes, B. (2008), *Introductory Phonology*, Oxford: Wiley-Blackwell.

Hayes, B., R. Kirchner, and D. Steriade (eds) (2004), *Phonetically Based Phonology*, Cambridge: Cambridge University Press.

Hewlett, N. and J. Beck (2006), *An Introduction to the Science of Phonetics*, Mahwah, NJ: Lawrence Erlbaum Associates.

Hickok, G. and D. Poeppel (2007), 'The cortical organization of speech perception', *Nature Reviews: Neuroscience* 8: 393–402.

Holle, H., C. Gunter, and D. Koester (2010), 'The time course of lexical access in morphologically complex words: neuroreport', 21 (5): 319–23.

Holmes, J. and W. Holmes (2001), *Speech Synthesis and Recognition*, Wokingham: Van Nostrand Reinhold.

Jackendoff, R. (2002), *Foundations of Language: Brain, Meaning, Grammar, Evolution*, Oxford: Oxford University Press.

Jakobson, R., G. Fant, and M. Halle (1952, reprinted 1963*)*, *Preliminaries to Speech Analysis, Technical Report B. Acoustic Laboratory MIT*, Cambridge, MA: MIT Press.

Johnson, K. (2003), *Acoustic and Auditory Phonetics*, Oxford: Blackwell.

Johnson, K. (2008), *Quantitative Methods in Linguistics*, Oxford: Wiley-Blackwell.

Jones, D. (1918), *An Outline of English Phonetics*, 9th edn 1962, Cambridge: Heffers.

Keating, P. (1990), 'The window model of coarticulation: articulatory evidence', in J. Kingston and M. Beckman (eds), *Papers in Laboratory Phonology I*, Cambridge: Cambridge University Press, 451–70.

Keller, E. (ed.) (1994), *Fundamentals of Speech Synthesis and Speech Recognition*, Chichester: John Wiley.

Kent, R. (2006), 'Hearing and believing: some limits to the auditory-perceptual assessment of speech and voice disorders', *American Journal of Speech–Language Pathology* 5: 7–23.

Kent, R. D. (ed.) (2004), *The MIT Encyclopedia of Communication Disorders*, Cambridge, MA: MIT Press.

King, D. W. and D. Drumright (2009), *Anatomy and Physiology for Speech, Language and Hearing*, Florence, KY: Delmar Cengage Learning.

Kugler, N. P., J. A. S. Kelso, and M. T. Turvey (1980), 'On the concept of coordinative structures as dissipative structures: I. Theoretical lines of convergence', in G. E. Stelmach and J. Requin (eds), in *Tutorials in Motor Behavior*, Amsterdam: North-Holland, 3–48.

Ladefoged, P. (1965), *The Nature of General Phonetic Theories*, Georgetown University Monographs on Languages and Linguistics 18, Washington, DC: Georgetown University.

Ladefoged, P. (1967), *Linguistic Phonetics*, Working Papers in Phonetics 6, Los Angeles: University of California at Los Angeles.

Ladefoged, P. (1971), *Preliminaries to Linguistic Phonetics*, Chicago: University of Chicago Press.

Ladefoged, P. (1989), *Representing Phonetic Structure*, UCLA Working Papers in Phonetics 73, Los Angeles: University of California Press.

REFERENCES

Ladefoged, P. (2003), *Vowels and Consonants*, 3rd edn 2006, Oxford: Blackwell.

Ladefoged, P. (2006), *A Course in Phonetics*, 5th edn, Boston: Thompson, Wadsworth.

Lakoff, G. (1987), *Women, Fire, and Dangerous Things: What Categories Reveal about the Mind*, Chicago: University of Chicago Press.

Lakoff, G. and M. Johnson (1999), *Philosophy in the Flesh: The Embodied Mind and its Challenge to Western Thought*, New York: Basic Books.

Lashley, K. (1951), 'The problem of serial order in behavior', in I. Jeffress (ed.), *Cerebral Mechanisms in Behavior*, New York: John Wiley, 506–28.

LeDoux, J. (1996), *The Emotional Brain*, New York: Simon and Schuster.

Lehiste, I. (1967), *Readings in Acoustic Phonetics*, Cambridge, MA: MIT Press.

Levinson, S. (2005), *Mathematical Models for Speech Technology*, Chichester: John Wiley.

Liberman, A. and I. Mattingly (1985), 'The motor theory of speech perception revised', *Cognition* 21: 1–36.

Liberman, A., K. Harris, H. Hoffman, and B. Griffith (1957), 'The discrimination of speech sounds with and across phoneme boundaries', *Journal of Experimental Psychology* 54: 358–68.

Liberman, A., F. Cooper, D. Shankweiler, and M. Studdert-Kennedy (1967), 'Perception of the speech code', *Psychological Review* 4 (6): 431–61.

Lindblom, B. (1990), 'Explaining phonetic variation: a sketch of the H and H Theory', in W. Hardcastle and A. Marchal (eds), *Speech Production and Speech Modelling*, Dordrecht: Kluwer, 403–39.

Locke, J. (1690), *An Essay Concerning Human Understanding*, 2004 edn, Harmondsworth: Penguin.

Lubker, J. and P. Parris (1970), 'Simultaneous measurements of intraoral air pressure, force of labial contact, and labial electromyographic activity during production of stop consonant cognates /p/ and /b/', *Journal of the Acoustical Society of America* 47: 625–33.

MacNeilage, P. (1970), 'Motor control of serial ordering of speech', *Psychological Review* 77: 182–96.

MacNeilage, P. and J. DeClerk (1969), 'On the motor control of coarticulation on CVC monosyllables', *Journal of the Acoustical Society of America* 45: 1217–33.

Mather, G. (2006), *Foundations of Perception*, Hove: Psychology Press.

Matthews, P. (2003), *Linguistics: A Very Short Introduction*, Oxford: Oxford University Press.

Mattys, S., J. Brooks, and M. Cooke (2009), 'Recognizing speech under a processing load: dissociating energetic from informational factors', *Cognitive Psychology* 59: 203–43.

REFERENCES

Miller, G. (1967), *The Psychology of Communication*, New York: Basic Books.

Minifie, F. D., T. J. Hixon, and F. Williams (1973), *Normal Aspects of Speech, Hearing and Language*, Englewood Cliffs, NJ: Prentice Hall.

Morton, K. (1986), 'Cognitive phonetics: some of the evidence', in R. Channon and L. Shockey (eds), *In Honor of Ilse Lehiste*, Dordrecht: Foris, 191–4.

Morton, K. and M. Tatham (1980), 'Production instructions', in *Occasional Papers* 23, Department of Language and Linguistics, University of Essex, 112–16.

Myers, E. and S. E. Blumstein (2008), 'The neural bases of the lexical effect: an fMRI investigation', *Cerebral Cortex* 18 (2): 278–88.

Nijland, L. (2009), 'Speech perception in children with speech output disorders', *Clinical Linguistics and Phonetics* 23 (3): 222–39.

Nooteboom, S. (1983), 'Is speech production controlled by speech perception?', in M. van den Broecke, V. van Heuven, and W. Zonneveld (eds), *Sudies for Antonie Cohen: Sound Structures*, Dordrecht: Foris, 183–94.

Öhman, S. (1966), 'Coarticulation in VCV utterances: spectrographic measurements', *Journal of the Acoustical Society of America* 39: 151–68.

Öhman, S. (1967), 'Numerical model of coarticulation', *Journal of the Acoustical Society of America* 41: 310–20.

Okada, K. and G. Hickok (2006), 'Left posterior auditory-related cortices participate both in speech perception and speech production: neural overlap revealed by fMRI', *Brain and Language* 98 (1): 112–17.

Ortony, A., G. Clore, and A. Collins (1988), *The Cognitive Structure of Emotions*, Cambridge: Cambridge University Press.

Panksepp, J. (1998, reprinted 2005), *Affective Neuroscience: The Foundations of Human and Animal Emotions*, Oxford: Oxford University Press.

Panksepp, J. (2000), 'Emotions as natural kinds within the mammalian brain', in M. Lewis and J. Haviland-Jones (eds), *Handbook of Emotions*, New York: Guildford Press, 137–56.

Poeppel, D., W. Idsardi, and V. van Wassenhove (2008), 'Speech perception at the interface of neurobiology and linguistincs', *Philosophical Transactions of the Royal Society B* 263: 1071–86.

Popper, K. (1934, reprinted 2004), *The Logic of Scientific Discovery*, New York: Routledge.

Posner, M. (2005), 'Timing the brain: mental chronometry as a tool in neuroscience', *Public Library of Science* 3 (2): 2004–6.

Prince, A. and P. Smolensky (2004), *Optimality Theory: Constraint Interaction in Generative Grammar*, Malden, MA: Blackwell.

Raichle, M. (2003), 'Functional brain imaging and human brain function', *Journal of Neuroscience* 23 (10): 3959–62.

Raphael, L., G. Borden, and K. Harris (1980), *Speech Science Primer: Physiology, Acoustics, and Perception of Speech*, 5th edn 2007, Baltimore: Lippincott Williams and Wilkins.

Repp, B. (1984), 'Categorical perception: issues, methods and findings', in N. Lass (ed.), *Speech and Language 10: Advances in Basic Research and Practice*, Orlando: Academic Press, 244–355.

Rosner, B. and J. Pickering (1994), *Vowel Perception and Production*, Oxford: Oxford University Press.

Saltzman, E. and K. Munhall (1989), 'A dynamic approach to gestural patterning in speech production', *Ecological Psychology* 1: 333–82.

Scherer, K. (2001), 'The nature and study of appraisal: a review of the issues', in K. Scherer, A. Store, and T. Johnstone (eds), *Appraisal Processes in Emotion*, Oxford: Oxford University Press, 369–91.

Skinner, B. F. (1957), *Verbal Behavior*, Acton, MA: Copley.

Stevens, K. and M. Halle (1967), 'Remarks on analysis by synthesis and distinctive features', in W. Wathen-Dunn (ed.), *Models for the Perception of Speech and Visual Form*, Cambridge, MA: MIT Press, 88–102.

Sweet, H. (1877), *Handbook of Phonetics*, Oxford: Clarendon Press.

Tatham, M. (1969), 'Classifying allophones', *Language and Speech* 14: 140–5.

Tatham, M. (1986a), 'Toward a cognitive phonetics', *Journal of Phonetics* 12: 37–47.

Tatham, M. (1986b), 'Cognitive phonetics: some of the theory', in R. Channon and L. Shockey (eds), *In Honor of Ilse Lehiste*, Dordrecht: Foris, 271–6.

Tatham, M. (1990), 'Cognitive phonetics', in W. Ainsworth (ed.), *Advances in Speech, Hearing and Language Processing 1*, London: JAI Press, 193–218.

Tatham, M. (1995), 'The supervision of speech production', in C. Sorin, J. Mariana, H. Meloni, and J. Schoentgen (eds), *Levels in Speech Communication: Relations and Interactions*, Amsterdam: Elsevier, 115–25.

Tatham, M. and K. Morton (1969), 'Some electromyographic data toward a model of speech production', *Language and Speech* 12 (1): 39–53.

Tatham, M. and K. Morton (1972), 'Electromyographic and intraoral air pressure studies of bilabial stops', in *Occasional Papers* 12, Department of Language and Linguistics, Colchester: University of Essex, 15–31.

Tatham, M. and Morton, K. (1980), 'Precision', in *Occasional Papers* 23, Department of Language and Linguistics, University of Essex, 104–11.

Tatham, M. and K. Morton (2001), 'Intrinsic and adjusted unit length in English rhythm', in *Proceedings of the Institute of Acoustics-WISP 2001*, St Albans: Institute of Acoustics, 189–200.

Tatham, M. and K. Morton (2002), 'Computational modelling of speech production: English rhythm', in A. Braun and H. Masthoff (eds), *Phonetics and its Applications: Festschrift for Jens-Peter Köster on the Occasion of this 60th Birthday*, Stuttgart: Franz Steiner, 283–405.

Tatham, M. and K. Morton (2004), *Expression in Speech: Analysis and Synthesis*, 2nd edn 2006, Oxford: Oxford University Press.

Tatham, M. and K. Morton (2005), *Developments in Speech Synthesis*, Chichester: John Wiley.

Tatham, M. and K. Morton (2006), *Speech Production and Perception*, Basingstoke: Palgrave Macmillan.

Tatham, M. and K. Morton (2010), 'Two theories of speech production and perception', in J. Guendouzi, F. Loncke, and M. Williams (eds), *The Handbook of Psycholinguistic and Cognitive Processes: Perspectives in Communication Disorders*, New York and London: Psychology Press, 291–311.

Toates, F. (2001), *Biological Psychology: An Integrative Approach*, Harlow: Pearson.

Trubetskoy, N. (1939), *Grundzüge der Phonologie* (TCLP VII): Prague. Trans. from 3rd edn, Göttingen: Ruprecht, by C. Baltaxe (1971), as *Principles of Phonology*, Los Angeles: University of California Press.

Uttal, W. (2001), *The New Phrenology: The Limits of Localizing Cognitive Processes in the Brain*, Cambridge, MA: MIT Press.

Varley, R. (2010), 'Apraxia of speech: from psycholinguistic theory to conceptualization and management of an impairment', in J. Guendouzi, F. Loncke, and M. Williams (eds), *The Handbook of Psycholinguistic and Cognitive Processes: Perspectives in Communication Disorders*, New York and London: Psychology Press, 535–49.

Varley, R., S. Whiteside, F. Windsor, and H. Fisher (2004), 'Moving up from the segment: a comment on Aichert and Ziegler's syllable frequency and syllable structure in apraxia of speech', *Brain and Language* 88: 148–59.

Wells, J. (1982), *Accents of English*, Cambridge: Cambridge University Press.

Ziegler, W. (2010), 'From phonology to articulation; a neurophonetic view', in J. Guendouzi, F. Loncke, and M. Williams (eds), *The Handbook of Psycholinguistic and Cognitive Processes: Perspectives in Communication Disorders*, New York and London: Psychology Press, 327–43.

Definitions Index

Explanations Index

Author and Subject Index